D0458777

PRAISE FOR *CHURCHILL'S TRIAL*

"In a scholarly, timely, and highly erudite way, Larry Arnn puts the case for Winston Churchill continuing to be seen as a statesman from whom the modern world can learn important lessons. In an age when social and political morality seems all too often to be in a state of flux, *Churchill's Trial* reminds us of the enduring power of the concepts of courage, duty, and honor."

—Andrew Roberts, *New York Times* bestselling author of *Napoleon: A Life* and *The Storm of War*

"Larry Arnn has spent a lifetime studying the life and accomplishments of Winston Churchill. In his lively *Churchill's Trial*, Arnn artfully reminds us that Churchill was not just the greatest statesman and war leader of the twentieth century, but also a pragmatic and circumspect thinker whose wisdom resonates on every issue of our times."

—Victor Davis Hanson, senior fellow, The Hoover Institution, Stanford University

"In absorbing, gracefully written historical and biographical narration, Larry Arnn shows that Churchill, often perceived as inconsistent and opportunistic, was in fact philosophically rigorous and consistent at levels of organization higher and deeper than his detractors are capable of imagining. In *Churchill's Trial* Arnn has rendered great service not only to an incomparable statesman but to us, for the magnificent currents that carried Churchill through his trials are as admirable, useful, and powerful in our times as they were in his."

—Mark Helprin, *New York Times* bestselling author of *Winter's Tale* and *In Sunlight and in Shadow*

"*Churchill's Trial*, a masterpiece of political philosophy and practical statesmanship, is the one book on Winston Churchill that every undergraduate, every graduate student, every professional historian, and every member of the literate general public should read on this greatest statesman of the twentieth century. The book is beautifully written, divided into three parts–war, empire, peace–and thus covers the extraordinary life of Winston Churchill and the topics that define the era of his statesmanship."

—Lewis E. Lehrman, cofounder
of the Lincoln and Soldiers
Institute at Gettysburg College
and distinguished director
of the Abraham Lincoln
Association

"Yet another book on Churchill? *Yes*, and a very important one. Dr. Arnn has provided insights into Churchill's thinking and his doing. His thinking about modern war, the characteristics of leadership, the role of civil servants, the need for political compromise to achieve significant objectives, and so much more.

Churchill's Trial is an invaluable volume from an author who has committed much of his life to maintaining Churchill's reputation as the outstanding statesman of the twentieth century.

Read it and refer to it. It is full of insights that will remind you of his greatness, and the subtlety of his thought. Well done, Dr. Arnn!"

—Edwin J. Feulner, Ph.D.,
retired president of The
Heritage Foundation,
Washington, DC

CHURCHILL'S
TRIAL

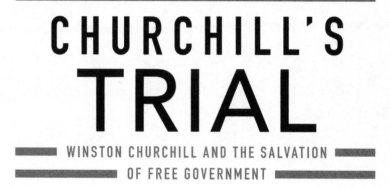

CHURCHILL'S TRIAL

WINSTON CHURCHILL AND THE SALVATION OF FREE GOVERNMENT

LARRY P. ARNN

NELSON
BOOKS

An Imprint of Thomas Nelson

Published in Nashville, Tennessee, by Nelson Books, an imprint of Thomas Nelson. Nelson Books and Thomas Nelson are registered trademarks of HarperCollins Christian Publishing, Inc.

Thomas Nelson, Inc., titles may be purchased in bulk for educational, business, fund-raising, or sales promotional use. For information, please e-mail SpecialMarkets@ThomasNelson.com.

Library of Congress Control Number: 2015943635

ISBN: 978-1-59555-530-4

Printed in the United States of America

15 16 17 18 19 RRD 6 5 4 3 2 1

To Sir Martin Gilbert, Master Teacher

CONTENTS

A Note on Style   xi

Preface: Why Churchill?   xiii

Introduction: Churchill's Trial   xvii

PART ONE: WAR
  1. The Fighter   3
  2. A More Terrible Kind of War   21
  3. The Statesman's Virtue   51
  4. The Strategist   69

PART TWO: EMPIRE
  5. Strategy and Empire   97

PART THREE: PEACE
  6. "Lo! A New England"   119
  7. "Some Form of Gestapo"   137
  8. Bureaucracy   163
  9. The Social Reformer   185

CONTENTS

10. The Constitutionalist   207

Conclusion: Churchill's Trial and Ours   245

Acknowledgments   257

Appendix I: Fifty Years Hence   261

Appendix II: What Good's a Constitution?   275

Appendix III: The Sinews of Peace   287

Notes   303

Bibliography   355

Suggested Further Reading   363

Index   365

A NOTE ON STYLE

I have used American spellings throughout the text, except in the case of proper nouns. Following the *Chicago Manual of Style* in use with my publisher, they and I have not capitalized many titles, offices, and official bodies that are commonly capitalized in other works.

PREFACE

Why Churchill?

The career of Winston Churchill presents a rare opportunity. From classic times people have thought that the virtue proper to the statesman is prudence, and prudence involves calculating and ordering many things that shift and change.[1] Every day we face obstacles and necessities, and we spend much of our time doing things that we must do, often things we would rather not do, again as often not doing things we wish to do. Yet we must try to do them in some way that is right, according to some standard of right that is both outside and above the details of our lives but also implicit in those details. For the statesman, these things are numerous and grave: numerous, because peoples and the matters that concern them are myriad; grave, because they involve justice and injustice, life and death. To cope with them is a special capacity and art. The ability to cope with them is constantly and urgently required, but those who can do it at a high level are uncommon. How do we acquire or even understand this art? Aristotle wrote that we can understand it best by studying those who have the reputation for it.[2]

The story of Churchill provides unsurpassed material for this kind of study. His career was very long: he was active in politics for more than fifty years. Those years spanned the most traumatic events so far in history: the greatest wars, the greatest depression, the greatest political transformations, the greatest social upheavals, the greatest advancements of technology and therefore of human power. Churchill wrote with ability and in quantity about his doings, and he lived in a time when information was beginning to be preserved in profuse detail. He left, therefore, one of the richest records of human undertaking.

This record is an opportunity and a problem. It is so large and is involved in so many contradictory necessities that it is difficult to discover the theme in it, if indeed that theme exists. One can find so many things in Churchill: bellicosity and balm, fixity and flexibility, contention and caution. He protected the free market, and he helped to found the welfare state. He thrived in war, and he feared it. He was the grandson of a duke, and he was a democrat. This is part of the reason Churchill has the reputation of opportunism. It is also why many think that his achievements during the greatest period in his life, World War II, called out an aspect of his character and ability suited for that unique circumstance, but not for most others in which he lived. In other circumstances, his life was, if not a "study in failure,"[3] at best a story of many failures that stemmed from his nature.

The claim that Churchill was simply an opportunist presents certain difficulties. Churchill was very careful to record the reasons for what he did and to preserve his papers. He often said that there would be a historical record, and he said as often that he would be the author of that record.[4] But this was at least partly a joke, because he knew very well that the views of his many opponents would also be preserved.

This effort of Churchill to write and preserve goes much beyond the normal, even for people in the public eye. He said and wrote that he was trying to impart something consistent. This book is an attempt to discover that something. If it is there, it may be of use to us today.

Churchill was a man of our time in at least two respects. In his lifetime, scientific weapons of the worst kind we know today were invented and came into use. In his lifetime, the comprehensive administrative state came into being in his country and most of the Western world. The world wars that Churchill helped to fight and lead are long past, but war is constant today, with potential destruction significantly worse than Churchill knew. World conflicts may become actual again. In Britain and the Western countries, generally, governments have grown beyond the size that Churchill saw and feared. These things grew up with Churchill, and they gave his career its shape and its great occasions. He had interesting things to say about these developments, and his actions in regard to them are among the most famous deeds of modern times.

There are practical reasons, then, to know the story of Churchill. There are lessons to be learned, both positive and negative, that can help us live our lives, cope with our problems, and serve the cause of our country as it appears today.

There are also reasons beyond the practical to study Churchill. The study of justice and injustice, of life and death, requires us to see things, if we can, that reach beyond our problems and lives. They require us to consider what our lives are for and how to face our deaths. Churchill faced his death repeatedly and bravely. He led many millions of people who did the same. Why did he and they do these things that we still remember and honor them for doing?

INTRODUCTION

Churchill's Trial

This book is about Winston Churchill and the trial that he faced throughout his career as a statesman. He thought this trial inherent in modern politics, having special features in Britain and the other liberal democracies in the twentieth century. He thought that war had always been a problem, but in modern times it was a different problem and worse. He thought that certain problems in peace, in domestic politics, had always been present, but in modern times these too were different and worse. He thought that the same factors made the problem of war and the problems of peace worse. He regarded these factors as unavoidable but necessary to mitigate and control. To him, the tools of mitigation were chiefly three: popular rule, statesmanship of a certain kind and quality, and constitutionalism of a certain kind and quality.

Winston Churchill was a democrat. Born the grandson of a duke at the end of the aristocratic age in his country, he, like his father, thought that the British people must be the ultimate repository of the fate of Britain and of their own well-being. He thought them the best single guardian of that fate.[1] He thought that they, like any rulers, were capable of falling short of that responsibility, in part because of the unprecedented dangers at home and abroad. Their control of the government must be arranged through an established and excellent constitution, which he believed they had, but which he also sought to improve. Also they needed statesmen of unusual capacity, at least from time to time, to lead and help them.

Churchill conceived statesmanship as an expression of rare and necessary human excellences. Like certain classic authors, he considered this combination of rarity and necessity one of the basic problems of politics. He believed that the most excellent levels of statesmanship depended upon natural gifts that could not be taught, but he thought they could be "armed."[2] He undertook this arming in many of his writings and speeches.

Churchill wrote as much as he acted, and he wrote about every action. His books number more than fifty. His speeches, written almost exclusively by him, take up more than eight thousand crowded pages in a series of books that only purports to be exhaustive. His articles are almost numberless, and his memos and letters stream out in eloquent profusion. The fifteen million words that he wrote have a dual character. They are like the actions he took in that they reflect ambition and practical purpose. They are meant to advance himself and his causes as much as any decision he made or any vote he cast, as much as any charge he launched or retreat he endured. At the same time they are explanations and reflections, commentaries on the way of politics, as politics reflects the way of life.

Churchill conceived constitutionalism as reaching its excellence in the British and the American Constitutions. The two constitutions are dissimilar in important ways, and Churchill had extensive things to say about their differences as well as their similarities. It was for him a subject of the first importance.

We should not take for granted that statesmen, even significant ones, are attached to constitutions, for statesmanship and constitutionalism are in some senses conflicting. Statesmanship is what individual men and women do at the head of the political community. The constitution is the form according to which they do what they do. Statesmanship in particular cases may pursue good objects or bad for good motives or bad, but it always begins with the wills or choices of the statesmen. This choice is always heavily influenced by the constantly shifting details and circumstances through which statesmen fight their way. Statesmanship is practiced right here, in the pressing and urgent now. Statesmen tend to be assertive people, or they never would get into places of authority.

On the other hand constitutions set limits as much as they grant authority; they establish boundaries on what both statesmen and citizens may do, even as they establish a domain where each may operate. The British and American Constitutions that Churchill admired were adopted a long time before his birth; they can take no account of the immediate circumstances in which he made his career. One can see why Churchill or any statesman would find constitutions inconvenient: they are fixed and hard to change; the law obstructs the will, and constitutions, the grandest of laws, obstruct the will most grandly.

For this reason many statesmen are torn between the pressures they face and the laws under which they operate. Some of them make a frank subordination of the latter to the former. Churchill rejected this in principle, however much he pushed to get his way and to get things done. He sought to reconcile the job he undertook as a member of Parliament and as a minister with the British Constitution, and in this he differed from many contemporary world statesmen. Churchill was especially concerned with the reputation of the British Constitution among the British people who lived under it, were sustained by it, and had the responsibility in their turn to sustain it.

This is all the more striking when we see that the trends around Churchill moved powerfully in the other direction. He had significant authority and influence through the greatest modern depression and the two greatest wars in history. We know from the classic authors that the meaning and purpose of peoples and nations are revealed when they are in motion, under stress.[3] We find out about them when they are called to some ordeal of conquest or survival, or both. We see what they value to the point of perishing; we see how they defend this most valuable thing; we see if they differ as to what this thing is or how to defend it, or both. We do not learn the whole story until they come to the testing point. Churchill and Britain stood at this point more than once during his life.

In regard to constitutionalism, Churchill stood against the main trends and also the tempests that raged through the twentieth century. Three of these trends are the terrain upon which he faced his trial: the rise of Nazism and of the Soviet Union, and the leftward turn in Western democracies.

THE RISE OF NAZISM

Forget for a moment that we know Hitler to be a monster.[4] Remember that he was for years one of the most exciting forces to arise in modern European history, and that he appeared to millions as a figure of hope. Following the First World War, his country was in the throes of steep decline, and he was returning it to order and health.

Germany was not at the time of Hitler such an old thing. It was a new thing comprising old things. Modern unified Germany was born in the Palace of Versailles in January 1871, only three years before Churchill's birth. One might say that Churchill and modern Germany grew up together. The wars of modern Germany were his wars, and the growth and influence of modern Germany a defining phenomenon of his time. Churchill's trial always involved Germany.

Before 1871 there was no Germany, only German states. The princes who led those German states gained access to the Palace of Versailles by joining together to conquer France in a war. They were maneuvered into that war, and the unity that followed it, chiefly by the statesman Otto von Bismarck. By this war and the other political and military struggles that preceded it, the German states were prepared to proclaim that Bismarck's master, the Prussian Kaiser Wilhelm I, was now Emperor Wilhelm I of the German Empire. This is a grand title, but it was less grand than the title "emperor of Germany"; the princes agreed that he was emperor over an empire, but not over Germany. More important, they agreed that he was sovereign over one nation, a nation born in war, its story to be dominated by war for three quarters of a century.

The greatest of Germany's wars and of all wars before Hitler was the Great War, the First World War. Germany joined Austria in launching this war in 1914. In July of that year the second German emperor, Kaiser Wilhelm II, agreed with his statesmen and generals that Germany should permit Austria-Hungary to attack Serbia. Serbia had provoked her mother (or perhaps stepmother) Austria by the murder on Serbian soil of the heir to the Austro-Hungarian throne, Archduke Franz Ferdinand. The Austrian Empire was then one of the longest surviving empires in history, but it had felt for ages many stresses of disunity; its many nations spoke many tongues and remembered many fathers. Among the worst of the disobedient children were the Serbs. Austria-Hungary saw in this assassination a grievous injury to be avenged and an opportunity to restore order.

To do this, Austria-Hungary needed help. The Serbs wrote with the same alphabet and worshiped in the same church as the Russians. The Russians had ambitions of their own in the Balkans and would not be happy to see their kindred harmed. Austria-Hungary looked to its own friend and sponsor. Where did Germany stand?

The Germans answered eventually that they were prepared to help. Never mind that these terrible steps to war began far to the south of Germany; it had been long planned that upon such an occasion Germany would provide help by attacking to the north, through little Belgium. Belgium had lived in fear of the growing power of modern Germany for decades. It took foolish comfort from an old treaty, which obliged Britain, Austria, Prussia, France, and Russia, to respect its neutrality.[5] This treaty meant nothing to Germany except opportunity, for Belgium was the highway along which Germany would travel to France. To support Austria-Hungary, Belgium, the Low Countries near it, and also France must be subjugated. Thus began the largest martial cataclysm to that time.

When Germany's statesmen and generals asked the permission of Kaiser Wilhelm II to launch this attack, his affirmative was the last important order he would ever give. Thenceforth war dictated and his generals gave the orders. The regime of the kaiser was not virulent or barbarous in the way of the Nazis. Still, Churchill referred to its actions as "scientific barbarism." For Churchill, the kaiser's regime fell on the wrong side of the great divide in government—the divide between nations where "peoples own Governments" and nations where "Governments own peoples."[6] He saw in the Germans after Bismarck a people dangerous because of their native talent and latent power, combined with an excessive willingness to give their rulers unchecked authority.[7]

By the end of the Great War, Germany was devastated. In 1918 its army went from powerful offensive to utter collapse, broken by the trenches upon which it had been breaking its enemies for more than three years and by the arrival of an American army of two million.[8] When it collapsed, it was still upon foreign soil. Though they suffered terribly, the German people had not felt the weight of the fighting as dreadfully as the nations in whose midst the war was prosecuted. This would make it possible eventually for Corporal Hitler to claim that Germany had been stabbed in the back by traitors at home, especially Jews.

The victors in the war, chiefly France, Great Britain, and the United States, also suffered grievously, especially the first two. By popular demand, they and their allies imposed a severe peace upon Germany. Also they imposed a new form of government, a republic, with no kaiser at its head. Wilhelm II lived out his days in the Netherlands, a small man in a world that he had made smaller for his country. The new republic, called Weimar, was left to gather up the rubble.

For a time the Weimar Republic did well, but even during the first decade of its existence there were stresses, and there were forces incubating and then growing in the bowels of the German state that were among the most vile. In the twenties came stampeding inflation. In 1929 the economy collapsed into depression. The extreme Left and the extreme Right worked their dark magic upon this field of disruption, and their strength grew. The most resolute of the extremes was the National Socialist German Workers' Party led by Adolf Hitler.

Hitler never won a majority in a national election until he had the nation in his grip and elections meant nothing. He did win several pluralities and built the largest and most influential party in the German state. His supporters saw him as the solution to the weakness of that state: he would restore discipline and order; he would recover the greatness of the nation; he would wring justice from its conquerors and undo the bitter peace of Versailles. For a time, Hitler did precisely those things. From the beginning he did many other things as well.

The specific character of the solution for his nation's problems personified by Adolf Hitler marked a trend in politics that spread to many parts of Europe, and significant people in many countries regarded it as a way forward for mankind. Its attitude to constitutionalism was unambiguous. One can see it in the way he took office.

Hitler was just short of his forty-fourth birthday when he became chancellor of Germany in January 1933. His rise had been astonishing. Into his twenties, he had been a street bum.[9] He distinguished himself in the Great War with the Iron Cross, but still he left military service only a noncommissioned officer. He was wounded at the end of the war, and the German army, his first happy home, collapsed while he was in the hospital.

Within sixteen years of his discharge from service he would sit in the office of the president of the German Republic, the venerated and venerable General Paul von Hindenburg, and bargain to become Germany's chief executive. These conversations must have been formidable to the former vagrant and corporal, seated before the supreme German soldier of his age, now the head of state.

Nonetheless, Hitler put forth hard conditions. He would not take the job unless Hindenburg would agree to support Hitler's appeal to the people for an Enabling Act. Under this act, Hitler and his cabinet would in essence be allowed to do whatever they pleased. Hitler was longing to rule, but he would not rule under a constitution. In acts of nerve and hubris, he refused office until this condition was met.[10]

Hitler justified his stand in the way it is always justified: exigency. There was a crisis, he said. The Great Depression was very deep, and Germany had sunk low in its defeat and subjugation in the Great War. He must have latitude to act. The only remedy to the emergency was not the law, but the will of a man and his few colleagues. It was time for an executive to execute.

By these arguments and by force, Hitler was able to establish a system that was the abnegation of constitutional rule. It featured no laws that all must obey, ruler as well as ruled. It featured no taking turns in ruling, at one point one person or group in authority, at another point another. Its form was the will of a man, a sole ruler who gave the law and changed it, who inflicted violence upon all who stood in his way. In Hitler's Germany, the alternative to constitutional rule was tyranny, and the alternative was adopted decisively.

This movement toward tyranny was not confined to Germany. There was also Italy, which became first an ally and then a servant of Germany. Little dictators in other European states joined or fell into the grip of German authority as well. Wherever the German influence was felt, leaders were ready to do the will of Hitler if they could get power. He helped them.

THE RISE OF THE SOVIET UNION

Nazism is understood to be a movement of the Right. There was also a growing tyranny in Europe, and eventually on other continents, of the Left. Churchill did not think this distinction between Left and Right so important: he said that the two tyrannies differ as the North Pole differs from the South.[11] They may be far apart, but they look the same, and they freeze their occupants with the same unforgiving frost. Both uphold a doctrine of history that reduces the human story to one of material evolution. Events control all, including human beings; events define rather than respond to human nature and all nature.

The supreme example of this tyranny of the Left was the Soviet Union, which the Bolshevik Communists established in Russia in 1918. The war that the kaiser's Germany waged against Russia aided these Bolsheviks. Indeed the Bolshevik leaders entered Russia, from which most of them had been exiled, with German assistance as a maneuver in war. Churchill wrote that the Germans "transported Lenin in a sealed truck like a plague bacillus from Switzerland into Russia."[12] Germany was in Churchill's opinion largely responsible for the Soviet tyranny that would prove a curse to freedom through so much of the twentieth century.

On the face of it, there are differences between the Nazi and the Soviet regimes. The Bolsheviks worshiped the class, not the hero; not the overman, but the party that embodies and enforces the will of history on behalf of the workers. But Communist practice did not follow Marxist/Communist dogma with precision. The Soviet Union found its own version of Hitler: its boss, Joseph Stalin. Stalin came to be called *khozyain,* meaning owner or boss, by his colleagues, despite the fact that he began as junior or no more than equal to them. Even before the death of Lenin in 1924, the Bolshevik Revolution had to choose between two things it valued. It emerged early in the revolution that the workers, the people the Bolsheviks claimed to represent, did not like the Bolsheviks or share their purposes. The Bolsheviks had either to amend their purposes or abandon the pretext of representation.[13] It was not hard for them to choose. "The Party," said Lenin's associate Karl Radek, speaking to the graduating class of the Soviet War College in 1921, "must impose our will to victory on our exhausted and dispirited followers."[14]

Lenin blessed this sentiment in practice when he undertook to destroy all opposition parties, including others on the Left or in coalition with the Bolsheviks. This meant that the rule of the party would not be the rule of the many, but of the few or of the one. Lenin hoped for the former. He sought to build a cohesive and cooperating group, and he left a *Testament*[15] that sought to arbitrate between his two most talented lieutenants in the Politburo, Stalin and Leon Trotsky. Lenin recommended that Stalin be removed from the general secretaryship of the party but remain one of the few in power. Trotsky, whose faults were also listed, would be among the moving spirits.

This *Testament* from the leader of the revolution was a

crisis for Stalin, one of many that he would survive. Over the next fourteen years, Stalin would overcome or destroy every one of his colleagues in the founding of the Bolshevik movement. Nothing displays his mastery so well as the comportment of his condemned colleagues, formerly his equals, at their show trials. All of them confessed to crimes, many of which they had not committed. When Nikolai Bukharin, the last and one of the most significant, confessed, he devoted two days of public testimony asserting that his confession and those of his predecessors were true, despite ubiquitous skepticism.[16]

Bukharin and the others knew that when their confessions were complete, they would be returned to prison to live a little better for a few days. Then a tread in the hall and a tap on the door would signal their walk down metal stairs to a dungeon corridor. The only condolence would be the tapping on cell doors by their fellow prisoners as they were led away. There would be no certain moment or particular spot for the bullet to come. At some point along the dark hallway, the guard would shoot them in the back of the head. It was death by anticlimax, with neither place nor time to commemorate the passing of a human soul; for it was not a soul destroyed, but an implement discarded.

Why would these old Bolsheviks confess to crimes they had not committed in deference to a man who had overcome them by maneuver and intrigue? The answer lies in their principles, which Arthur Koestler explains with grim beauty in *Darkness at Noon*.[17] The novel's main character is Rubashov, a hero of the revolution and a member of the original ruling elite. His time comes for arrest, interrogation, surrender, trial, and execution. But before he is taken he is sent abroad to discipline a minor agent of the party. Despite the agent's earnestness for the revolution, he has been critical of the party and has departed from its commands. Rubashov tells him,

> You and I can make a mistake. Not the Party. The Party, comrade, is more than you and I and a thousand others like you and I. The Party is the embodiment of the revolutionary idea in history. History knows no scruples and no hesitation. Inert and unerring, she flows towards her goal. At every bend in her course she leaves the mud which she carries and the corpses of the drowned. History knows her way. She makes no mistakes. He who has not absolute faith in History does not belong in the Party's ranks.[18]

The party was absolute, the voice of history itself. Its members, even its leading members, were nothing. This is the basis of the iron discipline its leaders enforced upon all and upon each other. This is the system under which Stalin grew and reached his maturity. In his mind he submitted himself to its iron rule; at the same time he used its principles to gain for himself a totalitarian mastery over his nation that the most absolute of the czars could not match. Millions starved by his order while entire railway trains were devoted to bringing him rare delicacies of food and drink. Stalin's sons and daughters and nieces and nephews sometimes saw the begging and starving masses from the luxury trains upon which they rode to holiday destinations. The family reported to him what they saw, and he dismissed the reports. But he also admitted the truth of what they said when he appointed Lavrentiy Beria, the harshest of the harsh, to bring what he called order to the nearby Caucasus.[19] And the death toll in the Soviet Union of

Stalin's "terror-famine" exceeded the death toll of all nations in the Great War.

Stalin's weapons were not limited to charm and ruthlessness; his greatest weapon was this logic of the party and of the infallibility of history. Following Lenin's example, his now-condemned successors committed atrocities in the name of these doctrines. Consequently, they could do nothing but obey the doctrines when their own time came to confess and die. Their honor, such as it was, demanded that they make the sacrifice they had extracted from millions of others.

THE LEFTWARD TURN IN WESTERN DEMOCRACIES

The rise of Nazism and of the Soviet Union were defining events for the world in which Winston Churchill lived and worked. They came with the promise of a new world to replace the strife and injustice of the old. Westerners of many political stripes looked to these new systems of governance as an authority and an example, some in fear, some in attraction. Some thought them good medicine for a world torn by war. Some thought them the gate to a new frontier and a better life. Some thought them fearsome, a menace that must be accommodated before it became overwhelming.[20] Churchill never believed the promises of communism or National Socialism. He did have good words for Mussolini for a time, but they were reserved and soon discarded.[21]

Thankfully, the politics of the Western democracies were not overcome by doctrines so extreme or violent as those that came to dominate Germany and Russia. Still, their own loyalty to their long-established constitutional forms was changing. In Britain the movement that led this change was socialism, embodied in the party that represented or claimed to represent the working class—the Labour Party, founded in 1900 and strong enough by 1924 to supplant the Liberal Party and form its first minority government. In the United States, the movement embraced not socialism but progress, another doctrine of history. This idea of progress affected both political parties profoundly—all three candidates for president in 1912: Woodrow Wilson, Theodore Roosevelt, and William Howard Taft, were confirmed Progressives—but it found its abiding home among the Democrats. Franklin Roosevelt, their greatest leader, articulated a new basis for understanding his country, the rights it was to protect, and the forms according to which it was to protect them.

Churchill regarded these movements in Britain and America with profound misgiving. Of the Labour Party, he warned that it would lead to the same kind of despotism that prevailed in Germany and in the Soviet Union. Of the Roosevelt administration—not, significantly, of Franklin Roosevelt directly—Churchill wrote that it featured "efforts to exalt the power of the central government and to limit the rights of individuals," and to "mobilize behind this reversal of the American tradition, at once the selfishness of the pensioners, or would-be pensioners, of Washington, and the patriotism of all who wish to see their country prosperous once more."[22] In other words, in the United States, too, there was a threat to freedom and to the Constitution that protected that freedom.

Nonetheless Churchill respected his wartime coalition partners from the Labour Party, and Franklin Roosevelt was his closest ally outside Britain. Together they helped to defeat Hitler's Germany and to preserve Britain through its finest hour.

Of Labour, Churchill said that the evil effects of the party's doctrines and policies were not what the party's members intended,
even if those effects were inevitable. Churchill said of Clement
Attlee, then Labour prime minister, that he was an "honorable
and gallant gentleman" and servant of the nation.[23]

In his eulogy of Roosevelt, Churchill called him "the greatest
American friend we have ever known, and the greatest champion
of freedom who has ever brought help and comfort from the new
world to the old."[24] Also he praised Roosevelt for his "love of his
own country, his respect for its Constitution."[25] We will see that
Churchill doubted the latter, at least for a time and at least in
regard to some actions of the Roosevelt administration.

This respect that Churchill paid to Labour and to Roosevelt
is part of the manner of constitutional rule as he practiced it.
This is not to say that Churchill was insincere. He was not a ran-
corous man, and he often held in personal esteem those against
whom he fought urgently in politics. More important, the good
words he said for Labour members and Labour ministers, and
for Franklin Roosevelt, were the respect he believed he owed to
people who had been elected under constitutional forms by the
citizens/subjects who have the rightful authority to elect.

These developments at home and abroad formed the strategic
landscape through which Churchill traveled. Abroad, a new and
powerful kind of tyranny arose, arming with modern science and
aiming to eliminate the private. At home, doctrines flourished
in Britain and America that, Churchill believed, threatened the
constitutional order of the liberal regime. We today may think of
Churchill triumphant, the winner of the greatest war, retiring in
glory and fame. He often thought of himself as fighting a battle
against formidable odds, caught in an ambiguous situation that

constrained his actions. If the constitutional process produces leaders and policies that will undo the Constitution, what is to be done? Churchill believed that powerful trends at home and abroad were running against him. His trial was to face them and prevent the evils he believed they portended. We shall examine how and why he did that.

PART ONE

WAR

1

THE FIGHTER

What does it take to lead a free nation in a vast and terrible war? One thing is fierceness.

Wars, wrote Lincoln, are not prosecuted with "elder-stalk squirts, charged with rose water."[1]

It has been proved, said Churchill, "not only that our men can die for King and country—everyone knew that—but that they can kill."[2]

"There are less than seventy million malignant Huns," Churchill said another time, "some of whom are curable and others killable."[3]

Churchill was a fighter. As a soldier in combat he had that deadly mixture of calm and aggression one can see in George Washington at Trenton, Princeton, or Monmouth. As a warlord he brought urgency and direction to everyone around him, even to the whole nation. He meant to win, and he found a way.

All of this was prefigured at the very outset of his career, when war was his calling and before he had any experience with politics. Consider his best adventure, which began on an armored train in South Africa on November 15, 1898.[4] The commanding officer was Captain J. A. L. Haldane, and he knew young Churchill from soldiering in India. He invited Churchill, at that moment a war correspondent, to go along for the ride.

Once the train was under way, the Boer enemy got between it and its way home, piled rocks on the track, and opened fire from a position that would drive the train toward the rocks. The locomotive, in the middle of the train, got up steam to run for it. Three of the cars up front hit the rocks with a terrible crash, derailed, and blocked the track. Going forward was impossible, and behind were the Boers, who opened fire from about one thousand yards with artillery and rifles. The assault was loud and the fire accurate: the Boers killed four men and wounded at least thirty others.

Churchill was fifteen days from his twenty-fifth birthday. He had been a commissioned officer for three years and ten months, and he was familiar with gunfire. He had been, with a few interruptions, a war correspondent for nearly as long as he had been a soldier. The prominence and makeup of his articles in the press had led to criticism—in one case in a letter he received from the Prince of Wales, another time in a letter published in the *Army and Navy Gazette* from "a General Officer." The latter charged that young Churchill was "careering over the world, elbowing out men frequently much abler and more experienced" than himself; furthermore, his articles criticized "general officers highly placed in authority" and influenced public opinion in ways that were out of proportion to Churchill's rank.[5]

These were fair points. Churchill was a young man in a hurry. Sometimes he would go to a scene of action even though the commander had forbidden him to be there. Later he would appeal to the same commander to give him material for a book about the adventure and be offended when he did not get it. When other young men waited outside the war office headquarters seeking an appointment, Churchill went to the place where the fighting was happening. He got himself into dangerous situations by these methods. His articles were popular, written without editing or prior comment from higher military authorities, and had considerable influence on the public impressions of the war. Beyond that, they made him a lot of money. Little wonder that colleagues might be cross.

But Churchill was undaunted by this "General Officer." He replied that it was unseemly for a ranking officer to "bandy words with a subaltern in the columns of public press" and argued that, "to make personal attacks on individuals, however insignificant they may be, in the publicity of print, and from out of the darkness of anonymity, is conduct equally unworthy of a brave soldier and an honorable man."[6] The young Churchill, like the older one, was not so easy to cow.

Churchill had resigned his commission in March 1899 in order to write his second book, *The River War*, and to run unsuccessfully for Parliament. He was given a lucrative contract to go to South Africa as a war correspondent to cover the Boer War. Criticism in the past notwithstanding, he applied for a commission upon his departure, just in case a good opportunity for soldiering should come up. The commission did not come through.

Never mind, however, his civilian status on the besieged armored train: Churchill volunteered in a heartbeat. "Knowing how thoroughly I could rely on him," Haldane put him to work.[7] Amidst heavy fire, with many wounded and several killed in the train, the locomotive itself damaged and threatening to explode,

Churchill began to walk about in plain sight, surveying the damage. Others, shielding themselves as they could, gaped in wonder.

Churchill formed a plan to use the engine to push the derailed cars off the track. It was delicate work, and he enlisted help. The wounded engineer of the train, a civilian, was about to abandon his post. To him Churchill said, "Buck up a bit, and I will stick to you."[8] Anyway, he continued, "no man was hit twice on the same day."[9] He added that the man would be decorated; later Churchill as home secretary would move the decoration personally. For more than an hour, he walked, looked, and labored, calm and calculating. The heat and smoke and noise were oppressive. Metal rained down. Men returned fire, bled, and died. Finally part of the train came free.

Brave men on a battlefield are often animated, obviously moving with and moved by the excitement of the fight. A few, George Washington for example, have a special kind of deliberateness. Young Churchill proved himself a member of that serene and lethal company on more than one occasion, but especially there beside the armored train.[10]

The engine got away with the wounded and Churchill on it. The rest of the force was left behind to be killed, wounded, or captured. Having reached safety, Churchill abandoned the train and went back on foot to help. On his way back, horsemen with rifles rode him down; he reached for his pistol, but he had laid it down while doing the work. He surrendered and was taken prisoner.

What did the people who saw Churchill's action at the armored train think? Haldane: "indomitable perseverance."[11] Captain Wylie: "as brave a man as could be found."[12] Thomas Walden, a former servant of Churchill's father who accompanied Churchill to South Africa, wrote, "Every officer in Estcourt thinks

Mr. [Churchill] and the engine driver will get the V.C. [Victoria Cross, the highest British military decoration for valor]."[13] Private Walls: "He walked about in it all as coolly as if nothing was going on. . . . His presence and way of going on were as good as 50 men would have been."[14] General Joubert, the Boer commander, urging the Boer government not to release Churchill from captivity: "[H]e must be guarded and watched as dangerous for our war; otherwise he can still do us a lot of harm."[15] Nevertheless, Churchill would make a daring escape to much fanfare.

What was Churchill thinking during the action? The record tells us four things.

First, Churchill was thinking about danger. Courage requires a sense of danger. On several occasions Churchill exposed himself to harm to gain the notice of others, and that was apparently part of his motive in this action of the armored train. To his mother he wrote, "Bullets . . . are not worth considering. Besides I am so conceited I do not believe the Gods would create so potent a being as myself for so prosaic an ending."[16] Earlier he had written: "Nothing in life is so exhilarating as to be shot at without result."[17] But the ambush produced a different mood: "I think more experience of war would make me religious," he wrote his American friend Bourke Cockran, an American congressman and mentor to Churchill, from the confines of the Boer prison. "The powerlessness of the atom is terribly brought home to me, and from the highest human court of appeals we feel a great desire to apply to yet a higher authority. Philosophy cannot convince the bullet."[18] Churchill was afraid. His fear reminded him of something outside the circumstances; something above them. He did what he did despite the fear, in mind of the thing above it.

Second, Churchill was thinking about politics. Speaking with Haldane soon after both of them were captured, Churchill thanked the officer for giving him the chance. He realized that Haldane would not get so much notoriety from the episode as would Churchill. Churchill had been able to act "in full view of the Durban Light Infantry and the railway personnel." This would open "the door for him to enter the House of Commons." He would, he committed, thank Haldane in the newspaper.[19] He took for granted that Haldane had wanted as much as he to get out there in the open and be shot at with people watching. Churchill was fighting his way into politics, which is full of sham heroism. War is a broad avenue into politics because it presents real tests of the moral virtues. The military demands a commitment of discipline and obedience; it disrupts the career and takes one from home for poor pay and bad conditions of work. Actual battle threatens death and wounds. To commit oneself to war is to demonstrate certain excellences that cannot be faked. To do this for the explicit reason of political ambition is a kind of ambition meant seriously.

Third, Churchill's mind following his capture and while planning his escape was on time. Upon capture, he began immediately a series of urgent appeals to the Boer government for his release, based on his being merely a war correspondent. In the letters he artfully downplayed his part in the action. Sweltering "in durance vile" was not part of his plan for himself.[20] One of his more revealing letters complained that he was almost twenty-five years old and was nearly out of time. He did not know that he would live to ninety, or that his greatest deeds would be done past age sixty-five.

Fourth, Churchill was thinking about victory. He wanted

to win. This had two aspects. One was grand and, above all, aggressive: by the time he reached his prison in Pretoria, the Boer capital, he had figured out the lay of the city and where the officers and the enlisted men were kept. Upon reaching the prison, he proposed to the British POW command that the officers overcome their guards and march to the nearby stadium. There they could liberate the British enlisted men, take the capital, seize the president, and end the war. The commanders refused despite much insisting, so Churchill confined himself to the more prosaic matter of his personal escape. He effected that soon enough, became a hero and, sure enough, a member of Parliament. He still regretted missing the chance to win the whole war with a single blow.

NAR: Photograph, Sab 1034

One of the best photographs of Winston Churchill was taken three days after his capture. It does not mean so much apart from knowing the events surrounding it. Yet in the context of those events, it reveals something about the man.

Notice that most of the men in the photo look bedraggled and down—as well they might, having fought a battle, watched their friends wounded and killed, suffered capture, stood and marched in the rain, traveled by train under guard, and arrived in the capital of the enemy to be displayed before the townspeople. Gathered around them are the burghers of Pretoria, gawking at the vanquished who have committed the indignity of surrender.

Two of the party seem different. One stands with his hands on his hips, his chin out. He is defiant. He looks a fighter. Likely the guards will watch him closely.

The other is aloof, off to the right, erect yet relaxed. He looks at the camera, and though we cannot know whether he saw the camera, he did know he was being observed by a throng. He looks unconcerned, not quite contemptuous. He seems at ease and untroubled. But you cannot quite mistake that he seems not only watched but also watching.

It is the contrast between the face and the posture and the actions he was taking throughout this time that makes one think. Churchill, the figure to the right, is embarked at that moment on planning and executing several contradictory courses of action. He will inspire an attack on the whole capital; he will argue that he is a noncombatant; he will write his friends of the valor of others while he calculates his election to Parliament as a hero; he will plan his escape; he will write for the press; and he will talk with his captors, befriend them, and find out information. All this is moving in his mind and very soon in his actions, and yet he shows neither distress nor impatience in his demeanor. As on the battlefield before exploding shells, so in the capital before his captors, he seems in the photograph we have of him indifferent.

One wonders, if a certain former German corporal had seen this photograph and known this story, would he have acted differently? The fatal decision of his life was to turn his back on this man and attack to the east. He exposed his entire nation to this calm captive, vigorous author, and proud warrior. Could he have foreseen in Churchill's letters and articles from South Africa the seed of an eloquence that could stir a nation to stand and fight? Could he have discerned in Churchill's negotiations with the Boers the portent of a skill that could finally outmaneuver the appeasers in 1940? Could he have foreseen in his capacity for self-effacement the stirrings of a capacity to stoop and to woo that would entice Franklin Roosevelt? Maybe not, for that takes study. In fact Hitler never did understand that he was fighting someone who could live amidst the fires of 1940 and sleep well every night, get up every morning ready to fight, and think it, even at the moment, the best time he ever had.

Clementine Churchill surely knew her husband when she wrote to a prime minister words worthy of a Spartan wife or mother: "[H]e has the supreme quality which I venture to say very few of your present or future Cabinet possess, the power, the imagination, the *deadliness* to fight Germany."[21]

FROM WARRIOR TO WARLORD

Churchill of course would go on to occupy higher stations, stations of command, where his deeds were not performed upon the battlefield. These higher stations demanded a different kind of courage and other virtues than those of personal valor.

The distinction did not come immediately or easily for him. Sir Edward Grey—foreign minister before and during the Great War and a senior and distinguished member of Parliament—described Churchill as a "hero" during that war. "I can't tell you how much I admire his courage & gallant spirit & genius for war," he said.[22] But Churchill realized his gallant spirit could lead him astray, as it did when, while serving as the first lord of the admiralty, he took direct and personal charge of the defense of Antwerp in 1914. The Germans were sweeping across Belgium on their way to France, and Antwerp, a fortified city, provided a chance to delay them and gain time. Churchill got to the scene of battle, and the next thing he was commanding troops. He did not save Antwerp, though his energy and judgments were much praised by those who saw them. King Albert of Belgium thought that the delay in the German advance was of "inestimable service" and that only Churchill had the "prevision of what the loss of Antwerp would entail."[23] Churchill nonetheless learned a lesson from the episode:

I ought . . . never to have gone to Antwerp. I ought to have remained in London and endeavored to force the Cabinet and Lord Kitchener to take more effective action than they did, while all the time I sat in my position of great authority with all the precautions which shield great authority from rough mischance. . . . Those who are charged with the direction of supreme affairs must sit on the mountain-tops of control; they must never descend into the valleys of direct physical and personal action.[24]

Churchill here was lecturing himself. He admired his ancestor, the first Duke of Marlborough, for his ability to command himself and his armies while near the front. He deplored the generals who commanded from far in the back, the battle unseen and unheard, and he compared them to managers of stock markets or stockyards.[25] During World War II his colleagues had to persuade the king to intervene to prevent him from going to the front. This suggests that although he learned the lesson in principle, it did not fully sink in. But he did obey the king.[26] As on a battlefield, so in a wartime cabinet there are excellences appropriate to the work. In both places they involve fighting spirit. Churchill was not only a warrior; he was growing into what Carlo D'Este calls him, a warlord.[27]

Shortly after the start of World War II, Churchill joined the Chamberlain government as first lord of the admiralty, his job at the opening of the Great War. While Churchill was still first lord, Chamberlain appointed him chairman of the Military Coordination Committee, a body that included the chiefs of the military services, with the power to summon the group as he felt necessary.[28] One can recognize the spirit of the swift and deadly, almost reckless, young officer in the mature man of state.

On March 14, 1940, Churchill described his thinking to Lord Halifax. The war cabinet had been discussing whether to seize Norwegian ports to gain a foothold in Norway and eventually access to the Baltic Sea. The decision had been taken to forgo the opportunity (this was later reversed, and the Norway invasion, partially under Churchill's control, would fail). Frustrated by the decision, Churchill wrote a revealing letter to Halifax. The war, he said, "is not less deadly because it is silent. The days are full of absorbing work: but they cost six millions each. Never was less result seen for money. There is no possibility of any positive project to gain the initiative, and acquire direction of events, getting through the critical and obstructive apparatus which covers up on every side."[29] As on the battlefield, so wartime cabinet combatants should seek to gain the initiative. They must not waste money or time or men in idleness. Churchill concluded by making a direct connection between the situation of the suffering citizens and those in the cabinet who lead them: "Considering the discomfort & sacrifice imposed upon the nation, public men charged with the conduct of the war sh'd live in a continual stress of soul. Faithful discharge of duty is no excuse for Ministers: we have to contrive & compel victory."[30]

This idea is manifest in Churchill's first speech as prime minister, likely the most famous of his life. It was a business speech, abrupt and startling. Churchill had over the weekend restructured the government extensively, and many people— all of them Conservative leaders, members of Churchill's own party—had lost their jobs or been demoted. Churchill apologized to these people for the "lack of ceremony" with which it was necessary to act. They were the first political casualties of the Churchill administration. The heart of the speech, little more than two hundred words, indicated that there would be many more casualties. He concluded with these famous words:

> We have before us an ordeal of the most grievous kind. We have before us many, many long months of struggle and of suffering. You ask, what is our policy? I can say: It is to wage war, by sea, land and air, with all our might and with all the strength that God can give us; to wage war against a monstrous tyranny, never surpassed in the dark, lamentable catalogue of human crime. That is our policy.
>
> You ask, what is our aim? I can answer in one word: It

is victory, victory at all costs, victory in spite of all terror, victory, however long and hard the road may be; for without victory, there is no survival. Let that be realized; no survival for the British Empire, no survival for all that the British Empire has stood for, no survival for the urge and impulse of the ages, that mankind will move forward towards its goal.[31]

Churchill nonetheless ended the speech in confidence: "I take up my task with buoyancy and hope." This sentiment would prove contagious, though not immediately so. Churchill recollected in his war memoirs that he was greeted "with some reserve" by his Conservative Party. They instead cheered for Chamberlain, though many recognized his ouster was right. Churchill was supported best by the Labour opposition benches, a remarkable fact given his relations with them over many years. Meanwhile, in the House of Lords the name of Chamberlain received "a full-throated cheer, whereas Winston's name was received in silence."[32] Churchill would need all the buoyancy he could muster; the British political system was about to be subjected to immense pressure.

THE WEAPONS OF A STATESMAN

As the breakup of France was being completed, the Italian government under Mussolini, not yet a combatant in the war, sent an offer to Britain and France to host and mediate a peace conference with Germany. This proposal was received by Lord Halifax, who was foreign minister and a member of the five-person war cabinet along with Churchill and Neville Chamberlain of the Conservative Party and Clement Attlee and Arthur Greenwood of Labour. Halifax favored taking up the proposal. On May

28, 1940, the war cabinet extensively discussed this proposal. Churchill believed that opening negotiations at a moment of weakness would place the British on a "slippery slope."[33] If the Germans should attempt an invasion and fail, Britain would be stronger and the situation would be "entirely different."[34]

Halifax argued that Britain might get the best terms now, before the French went out of the war and before British aircraft factories were bombed. Churchill replied that Hitler's terms would put Britain completely "at his mercy."[35] The ability to carry on the war would be diminished by the negotiations, and any peace at that time would deprive Britain of its ability to rearm. Chamberlain thought that Britain would lose nothing if it said it was prepared to "fight to the end to preserve our independence," but was "ready to consider decent terms if such were offered to us."[36]

Churchill had been in several discussions over the previous few days about this matter, and no agreement had been reached.[37] If he had announced that the matter was closed, the remedy open to Halifax or Chamberlain or any member of the war cabinet was resignation. Chamberlain and Halifax were popular in the dominant party in the House of Commons. Their resignations might result in the fall of the Churchill government. Churchill was not in a position simply to command.

A few days earlier, when Churchill had replaced Chamberlain as prime minister, he had said to Chamberlain that they were too busy to be moving house.[38] Churchill then resided in the quarters for the first lord of the admiralty, which were just across the Horse Guards Parade from Downing Street. This is the reason there are photographs of Churchill as prime minister walking across the Parade and to the back gate of Downing Street to arrive at his offices. It was a gracious offer, in keeping with Churchill's repeated kindnesses to Chamberlain until Chamberlain's death six months later.[39] One must think that this offer was inspired by something more than the inconvenience of moving house. Churchill liked the phrase "stoop to conquer," which he regarded as a virtue of the statesman. He attributed this quality, for example, to the first Duke of Marlborough.[40] Here he exercised it.

Unable simply to command, Churchill employed other devices. One was charm. Another was rhetoric.[41] At 6:00 P.M., immediately after the meeting of the war cabinet, a meeting of the full cabinet, numbering twenty-five, convened to discuss the offer of a peace conference. Martin Gilbert describes this meeting as "one of the most extraordinary scenes of the war."[42] Churchill gave the cabinet a report of the war, of the evacuation under way at Dunkirk, of the likelihood that Hitler would soon "take Paris and offer terms." He remarked that the Italians also would "threaten and offer terms." There was no doubt whatsoever, Churchill said, "that we must decline anything like this and fight on."[43] In other words, Churchill was repeating for the entire cabinet the arguments he had made immediately beforehand to the war cabinet.

Churchill spoke extensively without prepared remarks. Hugh Dalton, a Labour member and minister of economic warfare, made detailed notes on the speech in his diary. He wrote that Churchill was "quite magnificent. The man, and the only man we have, for this hour." He recorded Churchill's closing remarks:

> I have thought carefully in these last days whether it was part of my duty to consider entering into negotiations with "That Man" [Hitler]. But it was idle to think that, if we tried to make

peace now, we should get better terms than if we fought it out. The Germans would demand our fleet—that would be called "disarmament"—our naval bases, and much else. We should become a slave state, though a British government which would be Hitler's puppet would be set up—"under Mosley or some such person." And where should we be at the end of all that? On the other hand, we had immense reserves and advantages.

Churchill continued,

> And I am convinced . . . that every man of you would rise up and tear me down from my place if I were for one moment to contemplate parley or surrender. If this long island story of ours is to end at last, let it end only when each one of us lies choking in his own blood upon the ground.[44]

There were at this point, Dalton recorded, "loud cries of approval all round the table." Many went up to speak to Churchill.

Churchill reconvened the war cabinet at 7:00 P.M. He remarked to them that he "did not remember having ever before heard a gathering of persons occupying high places in political life express themselves so emphatically."[45] In *The Second World War*, Churchill wrote that the demonstration surprised him. "Quite a number seemed to jump up from the table and come running to my chair, shouting and patting me on the back." He added that, "had I at this juncture faltered at all in the leading of the nation I should have been hurled out of office. I was sure that every Minister was ready to be killed quite soon, and have all his family and positions destroyed, rather than give in. In this they represented the House of Commons and almost all the people. . . . There was a white glow, overpowering, sublime, which ran through our Island from end to end."[46]

After this cabinet meeting, the war cabinet met to reach a resolution. Neville Chamberlain, who had been dubious about Halifax's idea of mediation, volunteered that the prime minister of France, Paul Reynaud, should be persuaded that it was worth his while to go on fighting. It would even be premature to try to involve the United States at that point. It was time to make "a bold stand against Germany," which would command "admiration and respect" in the United States.[47]

Those were fateful meetings. We know from a Churchill friend and colleague that Churchill was "most anxious" during these times. A few days earlier he asked private secretary John Martin to find for him the text of the famous prayer recorded by author George Borrow from the siege of Gibraltar. The prayer reads: "Fear not the result, for either shall thy end be a majestic and an enviable one, or God shall perpetuate thy reign upon the waters."[48] Churchill was afraid, and he was praying for courage. Courage requires fear. Churchill had both.

This episode was not known to the public, but many other examples of Churchill's rhetoric were heard by the whole nation and were well known. Soon enough the bombing would begin. For more than a year Britain would face overwhelming odds without a significant ally. Few are alive today who heard Churchill on the radio during those months, but countless numbers in Britain remembered late into their age the phrases and even the arguments of his speeches. And there were those abroad, listening furtively to the proscribed BBC in occupied Europe, including a Belgian woman who, decades later, placed a hand on the arm of Churchill's daughter, Lady Soames, to confide what those speeches had meant to the conquered.[49]

"Fight on the beaches."[50]

"Never in the field of human conflict was so much owed by so many to so few."[51]

"If the British Empire and its Commonwealth last for a thousand years, men will still say, 'This was their finest hour.'"[52]

Churchill composed but did not deliver a speech to be given upon the landing of German troops on British soil. He had been advised that if the Germans made their way across the water, they could not be met on the beach because there was too much coastline to defend and the British forces would have to concentrate northward. This meant that much territory would be given up to the Germans. London, located in the southeast of the nation, would likely fall. Any landing would then be serious, without precedent for almost a thousand years, and the life of the nation would be at stake. Churchill intended to proclaim to the British people, "You can always take one with you."[53]

We may take this as the first lesson of strategy from Churchill: One must be ready to fight. He must have courage. And someone must have the tongue to remind people of this hard and necessary truth.

2

A MORE TERRIBLE KIND OF WAR

One can make a nice romance about Winston Churchill. It begins with Young Winston. He was dashing and brave. He was eloquent and prolific. He fought and he wrote his way into politics; he fought in order to write; he wrote about his fighting, and the books are good and catch attention. The enemy takes him prisoner, and he gets away. He enters Parliament.

The romance concludes with Old Winston, no longer a prodigy, much rejected, rising like a phoenix from political death to lead in a terrible war. The ardent spirit of his youth survived into age, and it was needed in 1940 when the nation entered the valley of death. He was made to operate in that valley, and he led the nation out of it. He was not a statesman but a warlord. Thank heaven we seldom need such people. Thank heaven Churchill was there when we did.

It is a good story, exotic and even beautiful. The trouble is, it does not quite work. One can begin to see why in the most unlikely of clues: in the curious way Churchill wrote about a certain battle at a remote place called Omdurman.

The Battle of Omdurman was part of the 1898 campaign for the Sudan. A British force made its way almost two thousand miles southward along the Nile River to retake the city of Khartoum from its ruler, Muhammad Ahmad, "the Mahdi of Allah." This Mahdi had taken the city from the British imperial hero, General Charles George Gordon, popularly known as "Chinese Gordon," who had led with distinction in China and other places. The Mahdi had beheaded the general in 1885 and decimated the British force sent by camel corps to the relief of the general and the city. Herbert Kitchener, later Lord Kitchener, led this new effort in 1898. He was a friend and comrade of many who were killed in 1885, and he had wept for their loss. Churchill would make much history with Kitchener.[1] At the time, Kitchener knew of Churchill and his reputation for forwardness. He refused permission for Churchill to join the expedition, despite entreaties from many senior people at home. Churchill persisted by many routes to press Kitchener and finally won a grudging assent.

This war in the Sudan was popular, and it ended in glory. Churchill fought well in it. The British won an overwhelming victory, as one-sided as any of the American tank or air battles in the recent Gulf Wars. Churchill's account of the war in one of his best books, *The River War*, is like most of his writing, meant to burnish his reputation and advance his political career. The British, at that time an imperial people, were indignant over the killing of Gordon and happy at his revenge. Churchill was all for the empire, all his life, and he had every reason to write proudly of this glorious episode.

Moreover the Mahdi's forces, known as dervishes, had established a regime that Churchill would describe as odious. Gathered from disparate Arab tribes in the 1870s under the banner of the Mahdi (the Messiah or Guiding One), these dervishes slowly transformed Sudan into the first modern Islamic state practicing sharia law.[2] In 1880 the Madiyyah (path of the Mahdi) erupted as an armed movement. That was how they came to decimate the forces sent to relieve General Gordon, to kill or capture his forces in the city, and to behead the general.

The Mahdi is not hard for us to understand today, for his progeny are with us. His great-grandson, Sadiq al-Mahdi, is among the current rulers of Sudan, and his brother-in-law Hassan al-Turabi helped to give none other than Osama bin Laden his education in jihadist doctrine and terror.[3] Today's northern Sudanese government operates under the principles of the Mahdi, including the despotism of clerics, oppression of women, hostility to other faiths, and propensity to violence that have been the hallmark of theocratic republics operating now in several places. Churchill went to the Sudan to fight the prototype of these regimes against which Britain, the United States, and other countries still wage war.

Nor is it any mystery what Churchill thought about this. In the first edition of *The River War*, he wrote this passage, omitted in later abbreviated editions:

How dreadful are the curses which Mohammedanism lays on its votaries! Besides the fanatical frenzy, which is as dangerous in a man as hydrophobia in a dog, there is this fearful fatalistic apathy. The effects are apparent in many countries. Improvident habits, slovenly systems of agriculture, sluggish methods of commerce, and insecurity of property exist wherever the followers of the Prophet rule or live. A degraded sensualism deprives this life of its grace and refinement; the next of its dignity and sanctity. The fact that in Mohammedan law every woman must *belong* to some man as his absolute property—either as a child, a wife, or a concubine—must delay the final extinction of slavery until the faith of Islam has ceased to be a great power among men. Individual Muslims may show splendid qualities . . . but the influence of the religion paralyses the social development of those who follow it. No stronger retrograde force exists in the world.[4]

Churchill obviously found the dervishes and their religion repugnant. He also feared this Mahdist movement. He wrote that it had "already spread throughout Central Africa, raising fearless warriors at every step." The Christian West would be vulnerable to this, "were it not that Christianity is sheltered in the strong arms of science." Otherwise, "the civilization of modern Europe might fall, as fell the civilization of ancient Rome."[5] The West's weakness may be repaired by the power of modern science, but that makes this kind of science an alternative to the virtues. Churchill believed, we shall see, that this fact constitutes another kind of vulnerability.

There are so many reasons for Churchill to glory in the triumph at Omdurman. Yet he wrote in sympathy with the dervish warriors, both their commanders and their soldiers. One reason is the dervish army's possession of the two virtues that tell in war: courage and generalship, the latter a form of prudence or practical judgment. It is the dervish generals who are called skillful, their plan of attack that "appears to have been complex and ingenious," and the dervish soldiers who are deemed "as brave men as ever walked the earth."[6] Churchill wrote of his conviction "that their claim beyond the grave in respect of a valiant death was not less good than that which any of our countrymen could make."[7]

Still the destruction of the dervish army was certain. Only one of the 14,000 dervish soldiers who charged came within 150 yards of the British line, according to Churchill. When that soldier was struck down, even he had not had a good look at the British. The dervishes suffered about 4,000 killed and wounded; the British, Egyptians, and Sudanese, 150.[8] Nor did it matter that the dervish commanders were skillful. Churchill described their charge:

[The infantry] fired steadily and stolidly, without hurry or excitement, for the enemy were far away and the officers careful. Besides, the soldiers were interested in the work and took great pains. But presently the mere physical act became tedious. The tiny figures seen over the slide of the back-sight seemed a little larger, but also fewer at each successive volley. The rifles grew hot—so hot that they had to be changed for those of the reserve companies. The Maxim guns exhausted all the water in their jackets, and several had to be refreshed from the water-bottles of the Cameron Highlanders before they could go on with their deadly work. The empty cartridge-cases, tinkling to the ground, formed small but growing heaps beside each man. And all the time out on the plain on the other side bullets were shearing through flesh, smashing and splintering bone; blood spouted from terrible wounds; valiant men were struggling on through a hell of whistling metal, exploding shells, and spurting dust—suffering, despairing, dying.[9]

This juxtaposition between the mechanized modern army and the valiant but impotent cavalry portends a generation of writing that Churchill will do about the character of modern war, the immense destructiveness it implies, and the moral problem it presents. He understood this moral problem beyond the common way most of us see it: a very large number of people can die. Churchill hated that aspect of it, but worse than this deadly arithmetic is the severance of the moral virtues, particularly courage, from the achievement of victory. Now it would be "a matter of machinery."[10] Worse also is the way modern organized societies, when impelled upon each other, could be required to devote their every resource, even "the last dying kick"[11] to war.

Churchill called the British advantage in the battle "unfair."[12] Lest one think this a small word, remember that "fairness" is a synonym for *justice*, chief among the public virtues, the central aim of statesmanship. The British with their modern weapons faced no serious challenge in this part of the battle. And Churchill, the young cavalry officer full of higher ambition, sympathized and invited his readers to sympathize with the dervishes; even, he implied, to think that right was in some sense on their side.

The battle was decided months earlier, not by an exercise of physical courage or skill on the battlefield, but by the repair and extension of a railway. Lord Kitchener had built this railway from a place where the Nile was deep, around stretches of shallow water hundreds of miles long, to another deep place in the river. His decision regarding this "involved the whole strategy of the war. No more important decision was ever taken by Sir Herbert Kitchener, whether in office or in action."[13] Experts told Kitchener that one part of the railway could not be built; he ordered it built anyway. Churchill praised Kitchener for this order more strongly than for anything else; it was an act of moral courage, and it was the heart of the matter. After it was accomplished, the British transported all the modern implements of war, including gunboats, over this railway to the scene of the battle. Once the railway was complete, the dervishes were doomed.

Churchill did not regret the victory, but he regarded the fate of the dervish army a "tragedy," "horrific," and "unfair." The generalship of Kitchener had its virtues, but excepting the exhibition of a certain element of moral courage, they were the virtues of the engineer more than of the general or the statesman.

A MORAL DECLINE

This initial dervish assault represented the "first phase" of the Battle of Omdurman. Such charges on foot and horseback across an open field against positions prepared with automatic weapons and artillery had occurred previously in the American Civil War. The Great War soon to break out would reveal the devastation of modern war in all its frightfulness, and the wounds it would inflict on Europe last to this day. Churchill did not like this kind of war, either at Omdurman or later.

Not all of the Battle of Omdurman was fought this way, however. Once the first phase was over, both armies began a sprint to occupy the nearby city of Omdurman, just north of Khartoum, which had been emptied of soldiers for the dervish assault.

Kitchener dispatched cavalry to reconnoiter the ground between the British fortifications and the city. They saw a dervish force described as "hundreds of tiny white figures heaped or scattered; dozens hopping, crawling, staggering away; a few horses standing stolidly among the corpses; a few unwounded men dragging off their comrades."[14] They reported this to the commander and received the order to advance, clear the left flank, and use every effort to prevent the enemy from reentering Omdurman. And so the Twenty-First Lancers, of which Churchill was a member, launched the last significant British cavalry charge. Here where the artillery and automatic weapons were absent, the Battle of Omdurman regressed to an older kind of warfare.

The desert often appears flat when actually it undulates. The Twenty-First Lancers charged a position they thought occupied by seven hundred dervish infantry; they found two thousand more in a depression, ranked twelve deep behind the visible front line. The lancers were at the gallop when they discovered the odds they faced. They cut their way through with heavy loss. "The other might have been a massacre," wrote Churchill, "but here the fight was fair, for we too fought with sword and spear. Indeed the advantage of ground and numbers lay with them."[15] Churchill was making a moral as well as a strategic point. The developments that have produced modern war have also helped to produce a moral revolution. Churchill saw this revolution, too, and he saw it early.

Even before he witnessed the Battle of Omdurman, Churchill was writing a novel—his only novel—which was published after the battle.

The novel, *Savrola,* is fiction near to autobiography. It is a story of revolution and romance. The hero, Savrola, is a man of the people, opposed to the despot Molara but also to radical forces identified with socialism.[16] The setting is a nation called Laurania, a naval power much like Great Britain. Molara is married to a beautiful woman, Lucile. Of course Savrola eventually gets the state and also the woman who once belonged to the despot.

There is a chapter in which Savrola and Lucile explore with each other grand themes of politics and civilization.[17] In one of these episodes of wooing, Savrola claims that civilizations eventually become corrupt, lose their virtue, and fall. But that will not happen to the current civilization, Savrola asserts:

> Ah, we have other weapons. When we have degenerated, as we must eventually degenerate, when we have lost our intrinsic superiority, and other races, according to the natural law, advance to take our place, we shall fall back upon these weapons. Our morals will be gone, but our Maxims will remain. The effete and trembling European will sweep from the earth by scientific machinery the valiant savages who assail him.[18]

Lucile asks, "Is that the triumph of moral superiority?" Savrola replies: "At first it would be, for the virtues of civilization are of a higher type than those of barbarism. Kindness is better than courage, and charity more than strength. But ultimately the dominant race will degenerate, and as there will be none to take its place, the degeneration must continue."[19]

In the passage quoted earlier about the curses of Islam, Churchill wrote that "Christianity is sheltered in the strong arms of science."[20] Here Savrola tells Lucile that "Maxims" will last longer than "morals." The Maxim is the first automatic machine gun, unveiled in 1884 by Sir Hiram Stevens Maxim. This gun and the power shift it represents constitute an alternative to moral force and are therefore potentially its enemy. The natural thing is that the best, the most civilized, should rule. They bring "kindness" as well as "strength." Science brings strength, surely, and strength is a kind of virtue and has a claim of its own to rule. But science does not necessarily bring either kindness or civilization.

When he began *Savrola*, Churchill had not yet seen the valiant dervishes, although he had seen the valiant tribesmen of Afghanistan. He thought the British civilization superior to those societies, both in principle and in actual condition at the time he was writing. The British soldiers on the Afghan frontier and at the Battle of Omdurman distinguished themselves for courage whenever they fought on equal terms. Yet if their civilization declined, as decline it must, it would not necessarily recede in power to give way to something healthier. In this sense "science" replaced civilization and its virtues.

Against this elevation of power over virtue, Churchill stressed the importance of "*the fighting man*,"[21] who embodied a restoration of the sovereignty of certain moral and intellectual forces: the moral virtue of courage and the intellectual virtue of prudence, especially in the form of generalship on the battlefield. It meant the restoration of the connection between might and right.

Right has never been simply sovereign over might, but it has been a component of it, and previously a larger component. Now what matters is invention and the proper organization of invention into practical power. We see in our day that the application of this growing power becomes easier and requires less in the way of organization. None of the countries from which the 9/11 terrorists hailed could produce a jetliner. But nineteen of their citizens, spending modest amounts and taking a few months of preparation, could destroy the two tallest buildings in the United States, damage the Pentagon, threaten the White House, and kill nearly three thousand people in a few hours' work.

THE CHALLENGE OF LIBERAL GOVERNMENT

Churchill considered these strategic questions in political as much as military terms, and his reactions were not governed chiefly by the question of the best way to fight. Kitchener had found that way at Omdurman. Churchill was happy at the victory but also appalled at the manner of it. He saw that this manner of fighting carried implications for war generally but also for liberal societies, their freedom, their limited governments, and their safety. Little wonder that Churchill soon left soldiering for politics, where his thoughts increasingly dwelt.

As was Churchill's mind, so his actions were operating in more than one realm and upon more than one level. To achieve this he had to move at speed. One can get a sense of the pace of Churchill's life by following him for the twenty-five months that passed between the Battle of Omdurman and the by-election (that is, an interim election) on October 1, 1900, when he was elected a member for Oldham, outside Manchester in the north of England. In September 1898 he left the Sudan by train and then boat for London, more than 3,000 miles as the crow flies. He was in London a few months before departing for duty in India, a distance of more than 4,000 miles. He returned to London to write and to run for office unsuccessfully. Then he was off on a 6,000-mile trip to South Africa as a journalist, a passenger on an armored train, a prisoner of war, and an escapee. Then back to London again. He made all these journeys without a plane. The last return trip to London took ten days, not the twelve hours it would take today. He arrived at the port of Southampton, on the southern coast of England, on July 20, 1900. He accepted the nomination of the Conservative committee of Oldham for Parliament on July 25. By that time he had three books in print and had published more than 125 articles in the press. He had observed a war in Cuba, fought in Afghanistan and the Sudan, and survived his adventure in South Africa.[22] On the day of his election he was two months short of his twenty-sixth birthday. Churchill had been busy.

In politics, Churchill remembered the things he had observed about war. He was elected a war hero, and so he had authority to speak on matters of war and empire. His Conservative party had been waging the wars in which he fought and about which he wrote. He had reason to support its war policy and all its other policies. And so he surprised everyone. In his maiden speech, he said, "[I]f I were a Boer fighting in the field—and if I were a Boer I hope I should be fighting in the field." Joseph Chamberlain muttered in response, "That's the way to throw away seats."[23]

Then Churchill proceeded to oppose a Conservative plan to double the number of corps in the British army. His reasons were far-reaching. They included the reasons that had inspired the curious way he wrote about the Battle of Omdurman. In a fine speech on May 13, 1901, Churchill imagined what war would be like when two armies of the quality of the British forces at Omdurman collided. He warned,

We must not regard war with a modern Power as a kind of game in which we may take a hand and with good luck and good management may play adroitly for an evening and come safe home with our winnings. It is not that, and I rejoice that it cannot be that. A European war cannot be anything but a cruel, heart-rending struggle, which, if we are ever to enjoy the bitter fruits of victory, must demand, perhaps for several years, the whole manhood of the nation, the entire suspension of peaceful industries, and the concentrating to one end of every vital energy in the community.[24]

It was not only science in the sense of technology—of machines and inventions—that made war more terrible. Developments in political thought, some of them happy developments, were also changing the nature of war. Modern regimes were more inclusive, and upon a larger scale, than any in the ancient or medieval world. Churchill continued:

In former days, when wars arose from individual causes, from the policy of a Minister or the passion of a King, when they were fought by small regular armies of professional soldiers, and when their course was retarded by the difficulties of communication and supply, and often suspended by the winter season, it was possible to limit the liabilities of the combatants. But now, when mighty populations are impelled on each other, each individual severally embittered and inflamed, when the resources of science and civilization sweep away everything that might mitigate their fury, a European war can only end in the ruin of the vanquished and the scarcely less fatal commercial dislocation and exhaustion of the conquerors. Democracy is more vindictive than Cabinets. The wars of peoples will be more terrible than those of kings.[25]

In a government owned by the people, great fierceness in war is possible. That is one reason why the Greeks could overcome the Persians despite much smaller numbers. In the age of democracy, Churchill thought, this effect is multiplied. Democracy will fight fiercer wars than have ever been known, and that was why Churchill observed that modern war cannot be regarded as a "kind of game in which we may take a hand and with good luck and good management may play adroitly for an evening and come safe home with our winnings." That was why he said that a larger army might make the British people "venturesome," for the British did not know as well as the continental powers the real cost of war. They might, with their larger army, develop "feelings of pride and power"; they might be susceptible to popular newspapers that "urge us into war." Better, Churchill said, for it not to seem so easy to the British to "intermeddle in the European game."[26] In light of the danger of modern war, the British themselves must practice a greater restraint. Given that they had not fully felt its cost, and given that they lived in a society in which they had political ownership, they might lack this restraint.

Later, we will see, Churchill comes to believe that democracy of the kind practiced in Great Britain and the United States becomes more a safeguard than a danger. That is in comparison to the modern forms of tyranny that will soon arise and become combatants in the greatest wars in history. Churchill believes that, in contrast to them, the democratic societies are much more given to peace. This makes them vulnerable to a different danger, not from excessive activity but from excessive passivity.

One can hear in these prophetic passages the echoes of Churchill's reaction to the Battle of Omdurman. This "great change" is a revolution in strategy, in morality, and in politics. It presents a fearsome outlook.

THE WORLD CRISIS

These predictions would come true soon enough. The catastrophic European war that Churchill feared broke out in August 1914, when Germany and Austria let loose their war machines upon Serbia to the south and upon Belgium and France and their allies to the north and west. Churchill entitled his five-volume memoir of this war *The World Crisis*. He wrote that this crisis brought together "all the horrors of all the ages." It differed from any ancient war in the "immense power of the combatants and their fearful agencies of destruction." It differed from modern wars in the "utter ruthlessness with which it was fought." Germany was first responsible for "having let Hell loose," and then she "kept well in the van of terror." But Germany was followed "step by step by the desperate and ultimately avenging nations she had assailed."[27] The trend therefore affected all nations, even if it was established and led by the dictatorships. He continued,

> The wounded died between the lines: the dead moldered into the soil. Merchant ships and neutral ships and hospital ships were sunk on the seas and all on board left to their fate, or killed as they swam. Every effort was made to starve whole

nations into submission without regard to age or sex. Cities and monuments were smashed by artillery.

Bombs from the air were cast down indiscriminately. Poison gas in many forms stifled or seared the soldiers. Liquid fire was projected upon their bodies. Men fell from the air in flames, or were smothered, often slowly, in the dark recesses of the sea. The fighting strength of armies was limited only by the manhood of their countries. Europe and large parts of Asia and Africa became one vast battlefield on which after years of struggle not armies but nations broke and ran.

When all was over, Torture and Cannibalism were the only two expedients that the civilized, scientific, Christian States had been able to deny themselves: and these were of doubtful utility.[28]

Churchill described a war almost as fierce as that waged by Alexander against the rebellious Thebes, when he defeated and then razed a city of fellow Greeks and sold its women and children into slavery. Alexander could not, with the best will in the world, do the same to all of Greece, let alone all of Europe. He did not resort to cannibalism; Churchill implied that the combatants in the Great War might have done so, had they seen a use in it.

These quotations are from the opening chapter of *The World Crisis*, the chapter entitled "The Vials of Wrath." These "vials," a reference to the plagues of John's Apocalypse, were filled to a level never seen with assets of immense power. The nations possessing this strength did not know they had it until the war called it forth. They had unprecedented "resources in force, in substance, in virtue." The cataclysm was prepared by a growth in their virtues along with other of "those elements and factors which go to make up the power of States."[29] They had perceived the growth in their virtues. They did not know the doom latent in their progress. It is not surprising to learn that Churchill maneuvered urgently in the years and the days before the Great War to avoid the conflict. Beginning with the Agadir Crisis in 1911, he proposed several kinds of agreements with Germany to prevent war and also alliances with France and Russia to preempt aggression.[30]

CIVILIZATION AGAINST ITSELF

Churchill did not think that this mighty strength made us kinder. He compared our modern practices to those of Queen Anne in the eighteenth century, who assured the subjects of France and Spain living on English soil that they would be well treated, so long as they "demean themselves dutifully towards us."[31] Nowadays, Churchill continued,

> . . . all enemy subjects, even those whose countries were only technically involved, even those who had lived all their lives in England, and the English women who had married them, would, as in every other state based on an educated democracy, be treated within twenty-four hours as malignant foes, flung into internment camps, and their private property stolen to assist the expenses of the war. In the twentieth century mankind has shaken itself free from all those illogical, old-world prejudices, and achieved the highest efficiency of brutal, ruthless war.[32]

In former times, this "archaic conduct" of good treatment of foreign nationals at home also prevailed on the battlefield. Both sides, especially the victors, "labored to rescue the wounded, instead of leaving them to perish inch by inch in agony in No Man's Land." The "great causes in dispute were stated with a robust vigor and precision which we have now lost," but "no hatred, apart from military antagonism, was countenanced among the troops."[33]

His comments did not mean that Churchill considered free and liberal societies more dangerous than or morally inferior to more despotic regimes. He often argued the contrary. In his only Fourth of July speech, given in the last year of the Great War to the Anglo-Saxon Fellowship in London, Churchill described the "scientific barbarism" of the Germans. The war, he continued, was a contest "between nations where peoples own Governments, and nations where the Governments own peoples."[34] That was one of Churchill's favorite expressions and a summary of what he meant by both constitutionalism and the foundation of civilization. It corresponds to the classic distinction between tyranny and just rule: in the former, government is carried on for the benefit of the rulers; in the latter, for those who are ruled or for the public interest.

The modern tendency toward despotic government was connected, Churchill thought, to an attitude toward science, from which came the power of modern weapons. The new attitude to science brought, Churchill feared, a corresponding change of moral outlook, an attitude that affected how the rights of people were understood and how their rightful ownership of their governments was protected. This tendency was worse in Germany, which was one reason the Germans must be fought. But at the outset of his career Churchill was afraid that this change in moral conviction would affect Britain. As we shall see later, he thought that the Socialist movement in Britain represented just such a shift.

SHALL WE ALL COMMIT SUICIDE?

Churchill stated the problems posed by modern war most fully in a 1924 essay entitled "Shall We All Commit Suicide?" He began, "The story of the human race is War. Except for brief and precarious interludes, there has never been peace in the world; and before history began, murderous strife was universal and unending." From his propensity to slaughter, man has been saved so far only by his incompetence: "The means of destruction at the disposal of man have not kept pace with his ferocity. Reciprocal extermination was impossible in the Stone Age. One cannot do much with a clumsy club."[35]

But then, Churchill continued, war becomes a collective enterprise. Roads are cut. Armies are organized. Improvements "in the apparatus of slaughter are devised." Animals are harnessed to the destruction. Yet still man is not able to do the worst because his governments are not "sufficiently secure." His armies are "liable to violent internal disagreements." It is difficult "to feed large numbers of men once they were concentrated, and consequently the efficiency of the efforts at destruction became fitful and was tremendously hampered by defective organization." This made "a balance on the credit side of life."[36]

Only in the twentieth century has man gained the competence to destroy himself. Now man is organized into great states and empires. Science and organization bring prosperity, a blessing to man, but the factors of production are also factors of destruction. And democratic institutions give "expression to the will-power of millions." Education, the press, and religion supply their encouragements. Above all, "Science unfolded her treasures and her secrets to the desperate demands of men, and placed in their hands agencies and apparatus almost decisive in their character."[37] Churchill summarized the point in one of the most dismal passages he ever wrote:

> Mankind has never been in this position before. Without having improved appreciably in virtue or enjoying wiser guidance, it has got into its hands for the first time the tools by which it can unfailingly accomplish its own extermination. That is the point in human destinies to which all the glories and toils of men have at last led them. They would do well to pause and ponder upon their new responsibilities. Death stands at attention, obedient, expectant, ready to serve, ready to shear away the peoples *en masse*; ready, if called on, to pulverize, without hope of repair, what is left of civilization. He awaits only the word of command. He awaits it from a frail, bewildered being, long his victim, now—for one occasion only—his Master.[38]

Progress, then, presents a logical problem. This is the lesson of Omdurman and later of the Great War. Men are still what they were: their virtue is not improved, and their guidance is not wiser. And yet they have accumulated such powers that a single use of them can pulverize civilization. This new power, afforded by scientific progress, draws upon the very virtues of men to make them more dangerous to themselves. The tools of science, of good organization, of the unprecedented ability to involve the opinions and interests of millions into the making of state policy, take man to a place he has never been before. And now these new capacities turn their attention upon man himself. This is the cause of the new peril of war, a cause that can overcome everything. Science has, Churchill wrote in 1931, "laid hold of us, conscripted us into its regiments and batteries, set us to work upon its highways and in its arsenals; rewarded us for our services, healed us when we were wounded, trained us when we were young, pensioned us when we were worn out. None of the generations of men before the last two or three were ever gripped for good or ill and handled like this."[39] In this essay, entitled "Fifty Years Hence," Churchill predicted many things that have come to be: the nuclear age, advances in microbiology, and telecommunications. These are all fact, and greater things still are coming to be.

Science is necessary, and also science is a master. As the human ability to make grows, the human ability to control the engines by which we make diminishes. The logical problem is relentless: we may stay as we are and lead shorter lives of pain and trouble, or we may use our capacity to make our lives easier and safer. If we do that we will gain power, and we can use that power against ourselves.

Churchill raised the hope that science itself will lead to the amelioration of these dangers but was quick to discard this hope: "[T]he hideousness of the Explosive era will continue; and to it will surely be added the gruesome complications of Poison and of Pestilence scientifically applied."[40] Mankind is progressing toward destruction. Only an improvement in certain virtues of man—especially the virtue of wisdom or of "wiser guidance"— stands in the way of his elimination.

CHURCHILL'S TRIAL

This perception of the terror of war deepens and extends throughout Churchill's life. It comes to its culmination with two changes that erupt into the world after the Great War and during World War II. The first is the emergence of totalitarian states, a new kind of politics that exacerbates to extremism certain tendencies that Churchill believed latent in modern society. They were latent even in the constitutional democracies, even in Britain, although those societies, including Britain, were blessed with powerful safeguards against their extremism.

The second is the invention of atomic weapons. Churchill had known for decades that they were possible.[41] He was heavily involved in the development of those weapons, and he did not regret the action. He was as much as anyone the inventor of the idea of nuclear deterrence, and he was determined that the few nations that possessed the bomb should keep it to themselves for purposes of deterrence.[42] Yet he regarded the development of these weapons as potentially calamitous for mankind.

Nuclear weapons were the subject of his last major speech in the House of Commons, which he gave on March 1, 1955, shortly after the announcement of the hydrogen bomb by the United States. The hydrogen bomb was much more powerful than the atomic weapons used against Japan, and Churchill thought the change in power important, a difference in degree that amounted to a difference in kind. It revolutionized "the entire foundation of human affairs" and placed mankind "in a situation both measureless and laden with doom."[43] He continued: "Major war of the future will differ, therefore, from anything we have known in the past in this one significant respect, that each side, at the outset, will suffer what it dreads the most, the loss of everything that it has ever known of."[44]

No advocate of the nuclear freeze or of unilateral nuclear disarmament ever spoke more dreadfully about the prospects of nuclear war. The terror presented by this kind of war amounts to a change in the moral situation of men.

Here then is the new situation: men can now build societies in which large populations can enjoy security, comfort, freedom, and plenty. The tools that enable them to build such societies, unknown in the ancient world, can also be used to destroy those societies. This changes the relationship between construction and destruction, between building and tearing down, between saving for the future and living for the present. It is in principle a demoralizing fact if by morals we mean the virtues that lead to peace, harmony, and plenty in a modern society.

MASS EFFECTS

War has become what Churchill called a "mass effect." He published one of his most important essays on the subject of mass effects in 1931.[45] Entitled "Mass Effects in Modern Life," it describes a general movement in modernity affecting politics at home and abroad, in policy both foreign and domestic. Just as in peace these mass effects complicate the problem of statesmanship, so in war they complicate the problem of generalship—and "the intense light of war illuminates as usual this topic more clearly than the comfortable humdrum glow of peace." The modern commander is now "entirely divorced" from the heroic aspect of war by the "physical conditions which have overwhelmed his art." Modern commanders do not sit on their horses on the battlefield and by their words and gestures direct and dominate the course of a supreme event. Instead they are more likely to be found "at their desks in their offices fifty or sixty miles from the front, anxiously listening to the trickle of the telephone for all the world as if they were speculators with large holdings when the market is disturbed."[46]

Churchill continued:

> Calm sits the General—he is a high-souled speculator. He is experienced in finance. He has survived many market crashes. His reserves are ample and mobile. . . . His commands are uttered with decision. Sell fifty thousand of this. Buy at the market a hundred thousand of that. . . . No, we are on the wrong track. It is not shares he is dealing in. It is the lives of scores of thousands of men. To look at him at work in his office you would never have believed that he was fighting a battle in command of armies ten times as large and a hundred times as powerful as any that Napoleon led. . . . It is hard to feel that he is the hero. No; he is not the hero. He is the manager of a stock-market, or a stock-yard.[47]

Such is the fate of the dervish soldiers, charging so bravely, but mowed down almost as cattle in the slaughter chute. Their individual characteristics counted for nothing. They were reduced to the level of beasts—or mere numbers on a tote board. As man becomes more powerful, men seem to become weaker and smaller. On the battlefield and off, they are more likely to be treated as commodities or as beasts for slaughter in the stockyard.

Churchill perceived these terrors from the evidence of relatively small battles on the imperial frontiers; they soon became apparent to everyone in the vast slaughter of the Great War. A powerful literary work gave evidence of the revulsion the war provoked. The German author Erich Maria Remarque published one of the poignant novels about the tragedy of war, *All Quiet on the Western Front*, in 1929. It describes the randomness of death in the trenches and the weariness and despair that came over those who fought there. It also describes the incredible endurance they achieved. The film version ends when the main character, a soldier at the front, is shot at the moment he is reaching up to touch a butterfly. The book and the film saddened millions in many countries and remain well known and available today. Both were banned in Nazi Germany.

The British play *Journey's End* ran for two years on the London stage and has been frequently revived there and in several countries. It, too, was made into a popular film and is the basis for scenes in several others. Churchill saw the play and described it as "brilliant" and "remarkable." He wrote the author, R. C. Sherriff, with questions about the plot and received an answer.[48]

At the conclusion of *Journey's End*, a leading character has been gravely wounded and borne on a stretcher to a trench dugout. He dies while another officer is fetching him a blanket to keep him warm. Then the officer is called away, and a shell explodes atop the dugout and obliterates the entire scene.

Churchill fought in such trenches in 1916, and he observed both the misery and the gallantry that were common. In *The World Crisis*, he wrote,

> But nothing daunted the valiant heart of man. Son of the Stone Age, vanquisher of nature with all her trials and monsters, he met the awful and self-inflicted agony with new reserves of fortitude. Freed in the main by his intelligence

from medieval fears, he marched to death with inherent dignity. His nervous system was found in the twentieth century capable of enduring physical and moral stresses before which the simpler natures of primeval times would have collapsed. Again and again to the hideous bombardment, again and again from the hospital to the front, again and again to the hungry submarines, he strode unflinching. And withal, as an individual, preserved through these torments the glories of a reasonable and compassionate mind.[49]

In the aftermath of the war, shattered peoples and their leaders sought to guarantee that they had fought "the war to end all wars."[50] The League of Nations and other efforts at collective security, which Churchill generally supported, provided hope that proved ill-founded. Churchill also favored the Pact of Locarno, signed in October 1925 by Germany, France, Belgium, the United Kingdom, and Italy. The treaties gave certain border guarantees on the western and eastern sides of defeated Germany, and it provided for the possibility of adjustments in the east by arbitration. Foreign ministers Sir Austen Chamberlain (Britain), Aristide Briand (France), and Gustav Stresemann (Germany), would win the Nobel Peace Prize for the treaty. All the signatories promised to defend one another from any breach of their borders. Churchill believed this pact could help secure the peace of Europe.

Also statesmen began to look for new ways to avoid war. If weapons are dangerous, they should be eliminated. If war is disastrous, it should be outlawed. Several countries, often led by the United States, sought means of accomplishing both. Germany was at least officially disarmed under the provisions of the Treaty of Versailles, and negotiations among the victorious countries sought to guarantee their disarmament too.

In 1928–29, sixty-two nations signed the General Treaty for Renunciation of War as an Instrument of National Policy. The treaty is known as the Kellogg-Briand Pact for the secretary of state of the United States, Frank B. Kellogg, and the foreign minister of France, Aristide Briand. It includes this passage: "The High Contracting Parties agree that the settlement or solution of all disputes or conflicts of whatever nature or of whatever origin they may be, which may arise among them, shall never be sought except by pacific means." The first signatories included Germany, already busy rearming itself even before the rise of Hitler and in violation of the Treaty of Versailles.[51]

In 1930 France, Italy, and the United States signed the Treaty for the Limitation and Reduction of Naval Armaments, known as the London Naval Treaty. Japan, busy building a fleet that would eventually reach across the Pacific to Pearl Harbor in 1941, also signed the treaty. This was one of a series of naval treaties that sought to limit the number, firepower, and size of surface and submarine combatants.

Churchill had profound reasons to support these or any efforts that could forestall the cataclysms he foresaw. He opposed them instead. He explained why in a speech in October 1928 by relating a "Disarmament Fable":

> Once upon a time all the animals in the Zoo decided that they would disarm, and they arranged to have a conference to arrange the matter. So the Rhinoceros said when he opened the proceedings that the use of teeth was barbarous and horrible and ought to be strictly prohibited by general

consent. Horns, which were mainly defensive weapons, would, of course, have to be allowed. . . . [T]he Lion and the Tiger took a different view. They defended teeth and even claws, which they described as honorable weapons of immemorial antiquity. . . . Then the Bear spoke. He proposed that both teeth and horns should be banned and never used again for fighting by any animal. It would be quite enough if animals were allowed to give each other a good hug when they quarreled. . . . The discussion got so hot and angry, and all those animals began thinking so much about horns and teeth and hugging when they argued about the peaceful intentions that had brought them together that they began to look at one another in a very nasty way. Luckily the keepers were able to calm them down and persuade them to go back quietly to their cages, and they began to feel quite friendly with one another again.[52]

In 1955, under the threat of nuclear weapons, Churchill made an argument about disarmament that was ultimately the same, but it proceeded in reverse order. "The best defense would of course be bona fide disarmament all around," he said. "This is in all our hearts. But sentiment must not cloud our vision." The Soviet Union would not be a ready or reliable disarmament partner, and "it is the communist dictatorship . . . and their proselytizing activities that we are bound to resist."[53] Apparently Churchill meant that we are "bound to resist" these things even at the most dire cost. They present questions about which there is no room for negotiation or compromise.

The terrible power of modern (especially nuclear) weapons makes for a change of emphasis, but for Churchill it does not call forth a change in principle. It is tempting, in the face of nuclear terror, to believe that the distinctions between good men and bad, between good regimes and bad—even between good and evil themselves—do not bear in the same way.

The trouble is, people and nations do not have "keepers" to maintain the peace. But they have natures, just as much as lions, tigers, and bears. It is in their nature to fight, and they cannot be prevented from fighting simply by extracting pledges, unless they have a moral intention to keep them, or by outlawing their weapons, unless they are not aggressive and can trust others also not to be.

This question of the kinds of regimes is more sharply defined in the nuclear age because the world is more sharply divided than ever. The world is made smaller by technology but not more congenial. Because of this, Churchill argued, we are living in some ways in the worst period in human history—a time when "the whole world is divided intellectually and to a large extent geographically between the creeds of Communist discipline and individual freedom." These antagonisms are "as deep as those of the Reformation," but "now they are spread over the whole world instead of only a small part of Europe." The geographical division is like that of the Mongol invasion in the thirteenth century, "only more ruthless and more thorough. We have force and science, hitherto the servants of man, now threatening to become his master."[54] This last is a close paraphrase of the paragraph about mankind's ability to destroy itself in "Shall We All Commit Suicide?" The problem of modern war is more intractable than the visionaries understand. The dilemma that Churchill described in "Shall We All Commit Suicide?" is still more difficult to escape. Men are not more virtuous, and their

49

leaders are not wiser than in former days. As the bear reverts to the nature of the bear, so the man to the man.

Worse, the nature of the man is different from the nature of the bear. It is both better and worse. The bear will hug his enemies, but he will not embark on an effort to conquer his nature, to control all his fellows, to remake and control all the world. The bear will not invent weapons for himself to augment his ability to hug, to augment his hugging to the place where it can destroy all the bears and everything else.

And in that fact is written, Churchill believed, a forecast of doom.

The solution Churchill found is not perfect, but it is found in the same nature that produced the danger in the first place. Perhaps man has made things that he cannot unmake. He must then try to manage them. That is the task of statesmanship.

3

THE STATESMAN'S VIRTUE

War being so terrible, it stands to reason that it takes special qualities to manage it. Churchill had a lot to say about the kind of person capable of this, the qualities he possesses, and the station that he occupies. In explaining this, he articulated a relationship between the general or military leader and the statesman or political leader. This amounts to an explanation of Churchill's understanding of himself.

If war is what the general does, politics is what the statesman does. They are very different. Politics is a form of community written in the rational and moral nature of man; appearances notwithstanding, it is essentially a form of cooperation, not strife, and the strife it produces is mitigated rather than exacerbated by its excellences. Armies and navies are needed to defend political communities, but the real work of politics begins where war ends—and ends where war begins.

Or is the relationship really so neat and tidy? For one thing, is war an activity only of strife? There is the fact that armies and navies must cooperate within themselves in order to fight. Moreover the societies they represent must stand behind them, must provide the matériel and the troops with which they fight. War actually calls forth the most intense forms of cooperation, the ones in which some people give, as Lincoln put it at Gettysburg, "the last full measure of devotion" so that others may live and live well. In this sense war is not only a cooperative and political event: it is the supreme event of that kind.

Moreover the purposes of war sometimes supplant those of politics. Sometimes the stakes of war involve the life of the state itself. For the state to continue, in the hope of recovering itself and its ultimate purposes, it might need to sacrifice very greatly in war. It might do things—even to its own citizens— that it otherwise exists *not* to do. Facing imminent defeat, it might make agreements with people who mean destruction to the whole purpose of the state. That was the choice of Marshal Philippe Pétain in 1940 when he gave to Hitler by agreement what Hitler had already seized by blitzkrieg: northern France, and soon enough the rest of France. In this agreement Pétain sacrificed his small remaining ability to defend the rest in exchange for a promise from a liar that the rest would be left French. Facing a similar though not quite identical choice, Churchill chose differently. "[N]ations which went down fighting rose again," he said, "but those which surrendered tamely were finished."[1]

It seems then that the relationship between politics and strategy is not neat or tidy, nor is their priority always the same. At moments of high urgency, they become intertwined, and then they produce terrible choices and subject those who make them to terrible doubts. Some rare people put themselves in places to make such choices and think they were made to do so. If they are correct, they are still rarer.

According to Churchill, superior commanders manage to make the gravest choices well because they combine the functions of statesman and general. For example, Churchill wrote that his ancestor Marlborough was a "statesman and warrior,"[2] and that King William III and Marlborough were "warrior-statesmen."[3] Superior to William, Marlborough possessed a "threefold combination of functions—military, political, and diplomatic." This combination would not be seen again until Napoleon, "the Emperor-statesman-captain."[4] It does not matter how much the nation needs this; it is rare. The battles of Napoleon and those of Marlborough were separated by a century and a half, and according to Churchill no one of this quality appeared in the interval between them.

FAILURES OF CHOICE AND CHANCE

Churchill believed it tragic when the purposes of politics must give way to the urgencies of war.[5] He regarded this as most tragic when it stemmed from a failure of human choice, when the tragedy might have been prevented by better choices. Statesmanship, when successful, vindicates human choice. Statesmanship, even more than generalship, raises and answers the question whether we can guide our futures through "reflection and choice," as opposed to "accident and force."[6] Churchill wrote that the catastrophes of modern war were commonly prepared and suffered in countries "ill-directed or mis-directed by their rulers."[7] Better rulers, Churchill implied, would prevent these catastrophes. We remember Themistocles, Scipio, Marlborough, and Wellington because they rose in the face of danger to prevent death or eclipse for their nation. These examples inspired Churchill. He saw them as proof that mankind can manage its affairs, at least when people of extraordinary ability are present.

Churchill found a curious proof of the existence and importance of this capacity for statesmanship in the existence of chance. In "Mass Effects in Modern Life" he wrote:

> Is history the chronicle of famous men and women, or only of their responses to the tides, tendencies and opportunities of their age? Do we owe the ideals and wisdom that make our world to the glorious few, or to the patient anonymous innumerable many? The question has only to be posed to be answered. We have but to let the mind's eye skim back over the story of nations, indeed to review the experience of our own small lives, to observe the decisive part which *accident and chance* play at every moment.[8]

It is a long leap from the "ideals and wisdom" of "famous men and women" to "accident and chance." In this sense chance is the opposite of human art. Accident is not intended, either by art or by nature. Works of art and the choices that produce them must be intended by definition. Accidents often interfere with our choices, in which cases chance overcomes choice. Far-seeing people are sometimes able to avoid misfortune, in which cases choice overcomes chance. Obviously choice and chance are competitors. How then can the existence of chance prove the sovereignty of art?

Chance was to Churchill also the friend of the statesman. One might say that the space occupied in causality by chance and the space occupied by art is a shared space. If chances can occur, then nature is not simply dominant, not simply the cause of everything. For Churchill the existence of chance helped to resolve the doubt that men can command their affairs toward just purposes.[9] It helped to overcome the evidence—for example, in the story of the Great War—that sometimes in the largest matters human beings cannot command their affairs. Churchill ranged himself "with those who view the past history of the world mainly as the tale of exceptional human beings." He cited as evidence of this something that we all observe in "the experience of our own small lives." In those lives "accident and chance play at every moment" a "decisive part." If this is true in the small things we see, "how much more potent must be the deflection which the Master Teachers—Thinkers, Discoverers, Commanders—have imparted at every stage."[10]

In the preface to his biography of John Churchill, the first Duke of Marlborough, Churchill described the duke as a man almost beyond chance. He "never fought a battle that he did not win, nor besieged a fortress he did not take. Amid all the chances and baffling accidents of war he produced victory with almost mechanical certainty." That was a different kind of mechanism than the sort Churchill deplored in *The River War*, and he wrote that it was unique: "Nothing like this can be seen in military annals." He "never rode off any field except as a victor."[11] Was that not the very idea of the statesman, the man who conquered chance? And what did such mighty personalities have to do with the little accidents that divert or dominate our personal lives?

But the lives of these powerful people show also the power of chance, for in their lives it is multiplied just so much as the power of their art is multiplied. Those who chose Sir Robert

Watson-Watt, the inventor of radar, for his post did not fully know what he would do with the job; as regards their choice, his achievement was partly a matter of chance. Einstein, growing up a Jew in a country that did not favor Jews, might, except for a bit of fortune here and there, have spent his life as a patent examiner. Hitler was gassed, alas not to death, in the Great War. Had he been killed, his story never would have developed into the monstrosity it became; instead his injury became an item on his résumé that helped his advancement. Many times Churchill might have been killed on battlefields, and he made much of the fact that an annoying invitation from a general caused him, during the Great War, to be away from his bunker when it was hit by a German shell.[12] Churchill was not annoyed any longer when he saw the damage done to his station when he returned.

The power of chance implies the power of art: if a deflected stone can hit a man and change the history of the world, then a man can stand on the mountain above the road and aim the stone to cause the same effect. The space occupied by chance is the same space, up on the mountain or anywhere else, occupied by human art and ingenuity. To eliminate the one is to eliminate the other.

In Churchill's view, the "mass effects" that were transforming both war and peace begin in an attempt to conquer the obstacles we face that are found in nature and in chance, but they end in overcoming man himself. This was evident to Churchill in the awesome scale of war, so large that the statesmen who attempted to manage it seemed like puny figures. Churchill asked, of those who governed during the Great War, "how far were they to blame?" Were there among them men of "real eminence and responsibility whose devil heart conceived and willed this awful thing?" He continued,

> One rises from the study of the causes of the Great War with a prevailing sense of the defective control of individuals upon world fortunes. It has been well said, "there is always more error than design in human affairs." The limited minds even of the ablest men, their disputed authority, the climate of opinion in which they dwell, their transient and partial contributions to the mighty problem, that problem itself so far beyond their compass, so vast in scale and detail, so changing in its aspect—all this must surely be considered before the complete condemnation of the vanquished or the complete acquittal of the victors can be pronounced. Events also got on to certain lines, and no one could get them off again.[13]

Churchill's life may be seen as an attempt to supply through statesmanship a vindication of human choice. He described in many places the qualities such a statesmanship would exhibit. They begin oddly enough in the smallest place, in a certain ability to perceive details.

THE MEASURE OF A STATESMAN

In *Marlborough*, Churchill described the War of the Spanish Succession in which Marlborough commanded, but also he described the structure *of war itself.* In a chapter entitled "The Structure of the War," Churchill explains "not one but many operations of war." How does the general choose among his options? "Circumstances alone"—which are many in number and constantly moving—"decide whether a correct conventional maneuver is right or wrong."[14] How many are the enemy? What is his location? In which direction is he going? How does the ground lay? Is it raining, or will it?

One can apply the same reasoning to statesmanship. The right thing to do depends on the circumstances. Politicians are usually rated by their fidelity to principle. One politician believes in limited government, private property, and such old things; he is admired on the Right. Another favors government action, to keep up and to make "progress"; he is admired on the Left. Does that tell either of them how to vote on a given bill? What if, by passing a certain bill that appeals to the Left, the party of the Right can gain votes to dominate yet larger questions? The one on the Right might support the bill for that reason, and the one on the Left oppose it. Compromise is everywhere, even among the principled—or rather, *only* among the principled, for the unprincipled compromise nothing as they blow with the wind. Especially to the principled, the details and the circumstances matter. It is very different to *contemplate* the good than it is to *do* the good. As Churchill wrote, "A man's Life must be nailed to a cross either of Thought or Action."[15]

Churchill wrote that this doing of the good on the battlefield cannot be "calculated on paper alone, and never copied from examples of the past." The solution must be "evolved from the eye and brain and soul of a single man." This man was making calculations constantly, making errors often, but achieving an "ultimate practical accuracy." It is easy to describe after the fact what might have been done. "Any intelligent scribe" can do it. To him the "campaigns of the greatest commanders often seem so

simple that one wonders why the other fellow did not do so well."
Churchill continued,

> The great captains of history, as has been said, seem to move
> their armies about "as easily as they ride their horses from
> place to place." Nothing but genius, the daemon in man,
> can answer the riddles of war, and genius, though it may be
> armed, cannot be acquired, either by reading or experience.
> In default of genius nations have to make war as best they
> can, and since that quality is much rarer than the largest and
> purest diamonds, most wars are mainly tales of muddle. But
> when from time to time it flashes upon the scene, order and
> design with a sense almost of infallibility draw out from haz-
> ard and confusion.[16]

The superior general differs from the "intelligent scribe" in
his ability to bring these shifting details into order and comprehension. Without this capacity wars are mainly tales of muddle,
chaos, confusion, or all of them. One can see a certain parallel with one of the arguments upon which Plato's ideal republic
fails. The cities will be miserable until philosophers are kings,
but these philosophers will not serve willingly, and we who
would benefit from their rule cannot force them because we
lack the knowledge of who and what they are.[17] Churchill was
not talking about philosophers, at least not exactly and not yet.
He was talking only about the immediate and shifting details in
which the right choice was to be found—variables that presented
challenges few could meet.

Yet for Churchill these challenges were not the only difficulty. Something more was required to cope with events and

steer them to some chosen outcome. Churchill indicated what that was in another essay, one of his most charming and also instructive on many levels.

A SINGLE UNITY OF CONCEPTION

Churchill knew a lot about painting, and he could write and speak about it and about himself without obvious boasting, a gift for which the readers and audiences of modern politicians may pine. In a 1925 essay entitled "Painting as a Pastime," Churchill depreciated his ability to paint—never mind that his paintings are competent enough. It is a fact that some famous painters gave him instruction. By the time he was finished, his paintings, including many that he had painted prior to 1925, were exhibited at the Royal Academy of the Arts on no fewer than thirteen occasions, the last a one-man exhibition devoted to his works. Yet Churchill wrote that "there is no subject on which I feel more humble" and "at the same time more natural."[18]

"Just to paint is great fun," one paragraph begins. "The colors are lovely to look at and delicious to squeeze out." But this paragraph is not about the fun of painting or the deliciousness of squeezing out the colors; rather Churchill violated his habit of announcing his paragraphs with clear topic sentences. From the fun of painting, the paragraph proceeds to launch a battle. Churchill wrote that as one "slowly begins to escape from the difficulties of choosing the right colors . . . wider considerations come into view." Churchill "slowly" began to escape from the difficulties of painting. Though not obvious, this is a claim to competence. Having begun to escape those difficulties, Churchill could understand painting more fully. For him painting a picture is "like fighting a battle; and trying to paint a picture is, I suppose, like trying to fight a battle." It is, he wrote, "more exciting than fighting it successfully."[19] Did Churchill mean that?

It appears that Churchill had something serious to say in this funny essay, but he did not want the essay to seem serious. Otherwise he might be vaunting his experience fighting and his experience painting, which would not work so well for any of his purposes.

Churchill fought battles successfully, and he painted many pictures. One wonders whether he was more excited as he painted than he was in the heat of battle. He continued, "But the principle [of painting and fighting a battle] is the same." How so? "It is the same kind of problem as unfolding a long, sustained, interlocked argument." It seems then that painting a picture is not only like fighting a battle but also like making an argument. Moreover "it is a proposition which, whether of few or numberless parts, is commanded by a single unity of conception." Painting and arguing and fighting have to do with more than details, although details are essential to the problem presented by each. The details have no order without "a single unity of conception." Painting a great picture requires an "all-embracing view which presents the beginning and the end, the whole and each part, as one instantaneous impression retentively and untiringly held in the mind."[20]

Churchill used the paintings of the masterful J. M. W. Turner as an example.[21] He painted canvases "yards wide and tall." They were done in one piece and represented one single moment of time. The details were innumerable, and the canvases were huge. Yet each detail, "however distant, however subordinate, is set forth naturally and in its true proportion and relation, without effort, without failure." That, Churchill wrote, was "an intellectual manifestation the equal in quality and intensity of the finest achievements of warlike action, of forensic argument, or of scientific or philosophical adjudication."[22] The statesman, like the painter and the general, must achieve a "unity of conception" and an "all-embracing view."

At the same time Churchill pointed in his writing to the sovereignty of circumstances, to the weight of necessity, that shape the choices of statesmen. In his 1927 essay "Consistency in Politics," he defends the changing of policy whenever new facts arise, including facts arising from failure of previous policy. He also defends changes "of mood or heart" that come over nearly everyone in the course of their lives: "the normal progression is from Left to Right." We will show evidence that Churchill became more conservative, in some respects, as he aged. The differences have to do chiefly with constitutional practice, and they are differences of emphasis and degree. In "Consistency" Churchill also says there are limits to these changes of mood and heart. Dealing differently with the same facts and the same principles at different stages of life leads to "self-stultification." The statesman who is led to "divorce himself from a great body of doctrine to which he formerly sincerely adhered" is "unlucky."[23]

Under these notions, it is hard to see what change might not be justified by the demands of circumstances. Nonetheless Churchill pointed to something beyond circumstances that must affect what the statesman does. In a beautiful statement in 1941 he explained why it was necessary to send relief to Greece as the Nazis invaded. Never mind that Britain was besieged. Churchill said,

By solemn guarantee given before the war, Great Britain had promised them her help. They declared they would fight for their native soil even if neither of their neighbors made common cause with them, and even if we left them to their fate. But we could not do that. There are rules against that kind of thing; and to break those rules would be fatal to the honor of the British Empire, without which we could neither hope nor deserve to win this hard war.[24]

Where might we find these "rules" that command people to risk their lives and the life of their nation? Apparently, they can be known. Apparently, they are beyond the power of circumstances, and in some cases they too must decide "alone."

In the Marlborough biography, Churchill wrote about events that happened two hundred years before his lifetime. He directed us to the details, to their commanding nature, to the necessity they represented. When we are studying history or evaluating the actions of others, especially in politics, these details are distant from us. We know our own circumstances very well. We act in accord with them. We forget that others, including powerful statesmen, must do the same. For this reason we lose proportion. Great achievements diminish in our eyes; we fall into the easy and satisfying habit of thinking we could do better. We expect utopian solutions.

When he spoke about the relief of Greece, Churchill was acting as a statesman in desperate circumstances. The life of the nation was threatened. Death, wounds, and servitude awaited the population, man, woman, and child, and they knew it. London was in flames. Churchill called on them never to surrender. Circumstances were urgent. If the circumstances were to decide "alone," what could they possibly decide? The British could not save the Greeks; they would fall anyway. The British forces were needed desperately at home. So why send them? Because there were ultimate principles beyond any circumstances that must not be violated. Those things were more precious than victory, more precious than life itself. Would those things demand that everything be sent to the Greeks, not just a force, but also the whole force? Apparently not. But something sufficient must be done to satisfy honor and keep faith, or the very deserving of victory would be sacrificed.

In his speculative writings, then, Churchill pointed in some cases to the most immediate practical necessities. Yet in pursuing the most urgent tasks, he pointed in some cases to the heavens. When did he do which? That, too, seemed to depend upon the circumstances, and it seemed, as if by order of heaven, to be right that it be so.

In "Painting" Churchill gives an example from his own life how the useless activities of the higher arts, including painting, can provide a satisfying end even to the statesman. After he lost his place in the Cabinet and his ability to help direct the war, Churchill was left "gasping." He "knew everything and could do nothing." Of course he did not know or claim to know "everything"; he knew everything about the war and the choices required. This is practical knowledge, and the purpose of such knowledge is not knowing, but doing. The result of prudential reasoning is a choice, and the result of a choice is an action. The kind of knowledge Churchill possessed had become useless, and he was "like a sea-beast fished up from the depths, or a diver too suddenly hoisted." His veins "threatened to burst." He was at "leisure," against his will.[25]

Then Churchill found utility in a useless kind of knowledge: "And then it was that the Muse of Painting came to my rescue— out of charity and out of chivalry, because after all she had nothing to do with me—and said, 'Are these toys any good to you? They amuse some people.'"[26] In fact such useless things as painting provide an ultimate solace, and an ultimate purpose, for human beings. Churchill criticizes the Nazis on many grounds, high among them that "Venerable pastors, upright magistrates, world-famous scientists and philosophers, capable statesmen, independent-minded, manly citizens, frail, poor old women of unfashionable opinions, are invaded, bullied, and brutalized."[27] Notice how the list alternates between people of practical effect and people of useless or relatively useless activity. The Nazis oppress them all. It is obvious why they would oppress the useful arts: capable statesmen and independent-minded citizens are formidable; they can overturn regimes and resist despots. But useless things are powerful too, and the Nazis know this at least by instinct. The Nazis are "afraid of words and thoughts: words spoken abroad, thoughts stirring at home—all the more powerful because forbidden."[28]

Indeed useless things are the most powerful things. In "Fifty Years Hence" Churchill imagined a world in which people were manufactured to specific tasks, their "mental development" interfered with to confine them to those tasks. He imagined also that people had so much power that they could live as long as they wanted, go where they pleased in interplanetary space, and enjoy pleasures "incomparably wider" than we enjoy. They had "mastered nature." Then Churchill asks: ". . . what was the good of all that to them? What did they know more than we know about the answers to the simple questions which man has asked since the earliest dawn of reason—'Why are we here? What is the purpose of life?'" Churchill continues: "No material progress, even though it takes shapes we cannot now conceive, or however it may expand the faculties of man, can bring comfort to his soul."[29]

We may think it a gloomy fact that we cannot settle the questions that beckon us to the highest places. Churchill does not. Rather it is "more wonderful than any[thing] that Science can reveal," and it "gives the best hope that all will be well." Even when we deal with forces that are "terrific" and "devastating," our "hearts will ache" and our "lives will be barren" without "a vision above material things." No powerful Science, and no Nazi, can erase that fact or satisfy that need.[30] Resistance to despotism is therefore written in the nature of man.

Painting places the painter in contact with something above any human authority. The painter, Churchill wrote, must be an attentive observer of "Nature." His "reserves" consist in proportion and relation. In other words, he must see things as they relate to one another in magnitude, significance, and causality.[31] Seeing in this way is not just seeing the details but seeing the order in the details. These are shifting constantly, as the sea battles and the ships in stormy seas that Turner painted are scenes of constant motion. Turner's paintings took hours and days and weeks to complete, yet the scenes that he painted lasted only minutes. He transformed the actual event into something two-dimensional and static, and yet he captured the whole and its dynamism. Somehow that was the same feat that the general and the statesman achieved in their minds as they surveyed the unfolding events around them.

Like the details, the conception of the work must be true.

For the painter, nature appears on the canvas with "startling obedience," but only when the painter studies it attentively and faithfully. He must not commit the error of the French painters, who painted their seas with up-and-down strokes and their tree trunks with side to side. They were guilty of "falling in love with one's theories, and making sacrifices of truth to them in order to demonstrate fidelity and admiration."[32] The painter's art—and also that of the general, the philosopher, and the statesman—does not consist in admiration for or faith in theories. That art is rather a service to the truth as it is to be observed in nature, in the natures of things and in the nature of things. This nature is more than and different from the details of which it is composed. The nature of the thing seems to bring in *qualitative* factors, factors that are apparent only in the details, but factors that are not the same as the details. Thought and action are different, and they demand different sacrifices and capacities.

Action, then, depends for its direction and purpose on thought, specifically upon thinking about things that are useless. And yet these useless things do not live in a dimension by themselves. The urgent actions of the here and now may depend upon them, but also they depend upon those actions. They represent the pinnacle of civilization, but civilization does not begin with them nor stand upon them. They are not, for Churchill, the foundation.

Churchill was the longest serving chancellor of the University of Bristol. In 1938 he spoke at the University to its graduates, about to enter a world of strife. He entitled his short speech "Civilization." He said:

There are few words which are used more loosely than the word "Civilization." What does it mean? It means a society based upon the opinions of civilians. It means that violence, the rule of warriors and despotic chiefs, the conditions of camps and warfare, of riot and tyranny, give place to parliaments where laws are made, and independent courts of justice in which over long periods these laws are maintained.[33]

Hitler, whose power loomed over the ceremony at Bristol, dressed in military uniforms and spoke in military language as a matter of course in his civic offices. Churchill here manifests the opposite spirit. For him the world of action can never bring the ultimate satisfaction available from an appreciation of the purest beauty. At the same time our appreciation of that beauty in friendship, and our transmission of that beauty to those who follow us, depends upon the conduct of politics and the outcome of war. "A society based upon the opinion of civilians" is a society in which the strong, in their uniforms and bearing their weapons, obey and protect the weak, who practice the arts of peace. This is the heart of the rule of law, and from it grows, Churchill says, "freedom, comfort and culture."[34]

For Churchill, practice makes no sense apart from the principles of right, and they have no protection except in the rule of law. The statesman is the guardian of things that supply the end of all action. Those principles cannot protect themselves against the likes of Hitler, unless someone as strong and fierce as he fights on their behalf. The statesman lives and judges amidst the details of action. He serves a master beyond all particulars.

4

THE STRATEGIST

Once we understand how dangerous Churchill believed war to be, we have to adjust our thinking about him and about war. The famous and defiant Churchill was a real man. The one whose spirit rose at the prospect of battle or of managing a war was a real man. The one who maneuvered around the armored train, the one who kept his equanimity and even his sense of humor in the trenches was a real man. The one who refused Mussolini his peace conference, the one who invited his cabinet colleagues to face death by choking upon their own blood, was a real man. But the other Churchill, the one who was afraid of war and cautious in approaching it, was equally real. The two men came together in the subject of strategy, which requires the alternation of pugnacity and reserve, of advance and retreat, of thought and action. It was for Churchill the discipline that brought statesmanship and generalship, politics and war together. *Strategy* comes from the Greek word for "army" and remotely from the word meaning "area" or "field." An army is big enough to occupy a field, and the movement or control of such armies is the discipline common to the general. Strategy concerns big things and the big people who do them, especially in war.

Strategy is required of the general and necessary on the battlefield. In the Great War, wrote Churchill, the British and French military authorities led their people into a "tale of the torture, mutilation or extinction of millions of men, and of the sacrifice of all that was best and noblest in an entire generation." They engaged in the "brutal expedients" of the war of exhaustion and the frontal attack. They were prepared to sacrifice even two or three of their own to kill one German, and they made "grim calculations" that the "Allies would still have a balance of a few millions to spare."[1]

This, Churchill argued, was a failure of the military art. Generals are supposed to add something to war to bring it to the right conclusion and to mitigate its effects. "Battles are won by slaughter and maneuver. The greater the general, the more he contributes in maneuver, the less he demands in slaughter." The battles that are "masterpieces of the military art, from which have been derived the foundation of states and the fame of commanders, have been battles of maneuver." These often employ "some novel expedient or device, some queer, swift, unexpected thrust or stratagem." Often the victor suffers few casualties, and this is the "contribution" of the general. He brings not only "massive common sense and reasoning power, not only imagination, but also an element of legerdemain, an original and sinister touch, which leaves the enemy puzzled as well as beaten."[2]

These comments presage Churchill's description of the genius of Marlborough. Such genius is rare, but also it is necessary, more necessary in modern times than in the time of

Marlborough. In modern times the state can and will support the kind of war that was waged in the Great War, the kind of war that can consume the stored wealth of generations.

The general worthy of the title, the true *strategist*, does not do this. Others are powerfully tempted to the costly form of war because maneuvers are dangerous for the army that moves as much as for the army that is moved against. The frontal assault, though bloody, brings its own comfort to the commander, at least while the battle is under way. It provides the commander information about the location of the enemy, and confusion is reduced. It is a logical or geometric fact that to seek the flank of the enemy is to expose one's flank. To set one's army in motion is to abandon its defenses. These considerations encourage the general to safety: the battlefield is a dangerous place, and the image of the enemy, breaking through the lines to rout and ruin, rises like a specter in the mind of any general. To think amidst this pressure is a rare gift. To think amidst battle with the right mixture of aggression and caution, with the flair of deception and innovation, is almost unknown. Yet "the foundation of states" as well as the "fame of commanders" depend upon it.

Marlborough was to Churchill both a statesman and a warrior in part because he conducted war in ways that were compatible with the aims of politics.[3] At Malplaquet, Marlborough defeated Marshal Villars in one of the bloodiest battles of the eighteenth century. Churchill writes that Marlborough was "unmanned" and physically ill at the carnage. The battle was a victory, and yet he bemoaned it. Churchill praised those sentiments of distress in Marlborough. War has not imparted upon him a "detachment from human suffering," and in this regard he was superior to Napoleon or Cromwell.[4]

These sentiments also reflected a reality of the strategic situation. The fact that the carnage was so great on both sides and the fact that the French left the battlefield defeated but proud and intact deprived the battle of much of its force. "No one doubted that [the victory] had cost more than it was worth, and that it cast a lurid reproach upon the failure to make peace in spring, when all was so near."[5] It is not enough to win. One must win in the right way in order to serve the purposes of peace, which are the purposes of politics.

Churchill often used the term *strategy* as a synonym for *politics*. He also used it as a synonym for *economy* in several senses and thereby showed the profound connection among three distinct things. The right kind of war fighting protects the needs of politics in part because it is economical. Wars fought strategically are cheaper, in both men and matériel. They happen faster, and so they economize the time spent in conflict. They demand less from the liberal society, which depends upon a vibrant and large private life not consumed by public needs. Therefore they preserve an economy in which individuals may flourish and care for themselves, their families, their communities, and their nation. In protecting the ground of economic strength, they protect the foundation of free politics and also the ability to fight wars with strength.

STATESMEN AND GENERALS

Several times this book cites quotations from a chapter in Churchill's *The World Crisis* entitled "The Deadlock in the West." There Churchill began his defense of the Dardanelles campaign. He was critical of both the generals and the statesmen who conducted the Great War, and in this criticism he revealed his understanding of the connection that binds or ought to bind generals and statesmen. He wrote, "There are many kinds of maneuvers in war, some only of which take place upon the battlefield." There are maneuvers "in time, in diplomacy, in mechanics, in psychology; all of which are removed from the battlefield, but react often decisively upon it." Their object is to "find easier ways, other than sheer slaughter, of achieving the main purpose." Then Churchill famously added, "[T]he distinction between politics and strategy diminishes as the point of view is raised. At the summit true politics and strategy are one."[6]

In the chapter "The Deadlock in the West," Churchill said that he felt entitled to make his case about the Dardanelles because he had made the same case before the event, and he had made it in writing.[7] Choices are made in time—in distinct circumstances—and so Churchill sought to ground his history in the conditions in which his statesmanship operated.

The Dardanelles was a turning point for Churchill and, Churchill believed, for human history. After the first battles of the Great War, the front stabilized: running from the North Sea down through Belgium, into France, and turning somewhat east as it reached the latitude of Paris. The forces engaged were simply huge, and they occupied the whole territory from the coast in the north to the mountains in the south and the east. Barbed wire, machine guns, and artillery made frontal assaults costly as no war had been previously.

Churchill and others at the Admiralty began to look for a way around. This required some kind of flanking of Western Europe itself. There were only two options, north or south. One plan developed to seize an island off the coast of Germany in the north. Another plan developed to go around Europe to the south and then to the Eastern Mediterranean. There lay the straits of the Dardanelles. These straits connected the Mediterranean with the Black Sea. They divided Europe from Asia. They offered a way to join the Western front of the war to the Eastern.

At first Churchill favored the northern option. Upon deliberation, and with the support of several significant military leaders, the Dardanelles was adopted instead. Churchill supported this. There were plans for naval and for military operations. Sometimes these were planned to happen together. In this event, a naval assault was tried first, failed, and then a land invasion of the Gallipoli Peninsula along the Dardanelles was attempted.

Churchill, not the earliest friend of the campaign, was willing however to be its most persistent one. In the face of setbacks, he pressed on for greater efforts. This left him holding the blame. Deservedly or not, he suffered from the disaster in every way except in the learning he gained. The Dardanelles campaign succeeded only in producing a second scene of the very trench warfare it was designed to flank, a scene farther away and more difficult to supply. Casualties were high. The government was forced into a coalition with the opposition. Churchill lost his position and carried a reputation for recklessness for decades. "What about the Dardanelles?" was the cry against him. It was a debacle for the nation and for him.

Churchill learned something from his bitter experience with the Dardanelles, something oblique to the question whether the campaign was a good idea. He consistently defended the attack, which was an expression of his deepest thoughts about modern war and strategy. Churchill did, however, admit an error and drew a lesson from it: he should have withdrawn his naval assault when Lord Kitchener offered but then delayed reinforcements. He wrote, "I became accountable for an operation the vital control of which had passed to other hands. The fortunes of the great enterprise which I had set on foot were henceforward to be decided by other people. But I was to bear the whole burden in the event of miscarriage."[8] Some enjoyed the authority, and others bore the responsibility, and this did not prove beneficial to either party or to the war.

Years later Churchill gave evidence that he had learned this lesson. When he delivered his May 13, 1940, "Blood, Toil, Tears and Sweat" speech, he had been busy reconstituting the government. Soon enough key appeasers Samuel Hoare and Viscount Halifax would be sent out of the country to hold ambassadorships, the former to Spain and the latter to the United States. Churchill placed himself in the center of war strategy and war making. He was to serve not only as prime minister but also as minister of defence. Later his government would be challenged with a motion of no confidence as opponents demanded he give up some of his offices. Churchill's answer? He was the servant of the House of Commons and would submit his resignation upon a moment's notice. But, no, they could not take *one* of his jobs. They must take them *all* if they were to have any.[9] Churchill would not give up unity of command. He noted elsewhere that the American Constitution admirably provides for the unity of the executive; the British not necessarily so well.[10] In his second premiership, when times were not so urgent, Churchill began the administration as both prime minister and minister of defence, but he soon surrendered the latter to General Harold Alexander.

Unity of command was essential, Churchill believed, because war was an encompassing undertaking—especially in modern times when it absorbed the entire resources of states and spanned the globe. More starkly than ever before, modern war presented the issue of human choice. At the critical moment of the Great War, the Allies made mistakes, and "the opportunity was lost of confining the conflagration within limits which though enormous were not uncontrolled." At that key moment, the "terrific affair" might have been "grasped in human hands and brought to rest in righteous and fruitful victory before the world was exhausted, before the nations were broken, before the empires were shattered to pieces, before Europe was ruined."[11] Alas, they made the wrong choices.

For Churchill, war was emphatically a business for statesmen, however much battles and merely military strategy were the work of generals. Churchill protested before and during the Dardanelles campaign that it was the business of the cabinet and the generals to give the soldiers not a cause but a plan.[12] The business of statesmanship was choosing. If choice in the grand sense, in the sense of human control of its own affairs, is to be vindicated, then statesmen must choose at the moment when choices are possible, in the present when the future "though imminent is obscure."[13] And they must choose well.

Such a moment came in 1915, before the wastage of the trenches, when a way around could still be sought. "Deadlock in the West" presents the moment clearly: armies of unprecedented size were placed in trenches that stretched across whole nations and could not be flanked. They sat behind barbed wire and machine guns. The Germans took whole countries and much of France at the outset of the war, when maneuver was still possible. The French and their allies had to find a way to dislodge them. They could not permit the Germans to sit forever where they were.

The deadlock was a problem for statesmen because it was at the summit a political and not a military problem. The whole resources of the state must be wagered on some strategy: to remain on the defensive (and thereby permit the Germans to continue to abide in Allied territory), to go at the entrenched German army, or to go around it. The second would be costly as no war had been. The last would open whole new theaters of war and involve new nations in the conflict. "The maneuver which brings an ally into the field is as serviceable as that which wins a great battle," Churchill wrote. "The maneuver which gains an important strategic point may be less valuable than that which placates or overawes a dangerous neutral."[14] Fighting the war in the proper way upon the battlefield was the business of generals, although statesmen were ultimately responsible for it. Therefore statesmen had or ought to have the authority to appoint and remove generals and to supervise their work. Setting up the war, dealing with allies and enemies and neutrals, deciding what cost to pay, was decisively the business of statesmen.

We have many examples from Churchill of such strategic thinking. In the Great War he proposed two different ways around the trenches, one to the north and one to the south. He proposed a way through the trenches without the extreme cost in life: the tank, which he helped to invent while he was first lord of the admiralty.[15] Later he would propose several strategies for confronting Hitler: forming alliances with Russia and the United States, supporting Czechoslovakia, and above all building military aircraft at a rapid pace. After World War II, he proposed a strategy to confront but not to fight, Churchill prayed, the powerful Soviet Union.

Churchill made the last proposal in one of his best and most significant speeches, which he gave in 1946, after he had become a national and world hero. The speech provides an example of strategy applied to the modern world, where weapons are devastating and the globe is small.

THE SINEWS OF PEACE

Churchill gave his famous "Iron Curtain" speech (or "The Sinews of Peace," as he called it) on March 5, 1946. By that year he had carried Britain through the war against all odds, and his efforts were appreciated around the world. Despite the victory over Hitler, in some ways the world was in a worse situation in 1946 than before the war. The Soviet Union had risen as a terrifying power. Churchill's wartime ally Franklin Roosevelt was dead, and his successor, Harry Truman, was not well known to Churchill. The atomic bomb had been invented and used, and it presented a danger different in degree—and, Churchill argued, in kind—to any that the world had known. Churchill and his Conservative Party had been soundly defeated in the 1945 election, and socialism was the doctrine and practice of Britain. Britain was financially weaker after the war, having spent its capital as well as its blood in the battle. Economically and politically, it was a divided and disrupted land.

The invitation to give this speech presented Churchill a significant opportunity even in his significant life. None other than President Truman introduced him, and he was speaking in the president's home state at Westminster College in the town of Fulton, Missouri. Truman had added a postscript to the letter inviting Churchill to speak, which means that the invitation both did and did not come from the president of the United States. That ambiguity would prove useful.

Churchill arrived at the White House on March 4 to travel to Fulton on the train with President Truman. On the previous day, the Soviet Union had announced that it would not leave northern Persia at the agreed-upon time, and it was putting pressure on the Turks to install a government more friendly to it. Truman informed Churchill that he was sending the body of the recently deceased Turkish ambassador back to Turkey aboard the USS *Missouri*, accompanied by a powerful flotilla to make a demonstration of strength in the area.[16] A few days before Churchill's arrival, Truman had received the famous Long Telegram from George Kennan that helped to inspire the policy of containment.[17] Tension was growing with the Soviet Union, and Truman was beginning to react in ways that would be fully revealed later with the Marshall Plan, the Truman doctrine (giving economic and military support to Greece and Turkey to keep them from falling into the Soviet sphere), and the Berlin airlift.

Churchill had already written to Truman in June 1945 of his "profound misgivings" that the US Army was retreating westward to the American line of occupation. That would bring "Soviet power into the heart of Western Europe and the descent of an Iron Curtain between us and everything to the Eastward."[18] Notice Churchill's use of the term *Iron Curtain*, which he would make famous at Fulton. Truman was well aware of Churchill's thinking when the invitation to speak at Fulton was issued.

Here then is a situation like the one that prevailed in the years preceding the two world wars. Great powers faced each other in heavily armed hostility. Churchill had tried to prevent both those wars. Because of the reknown he had won in the second war, because of the strength of the United States, and because of the insight of Harry Truman, he got at Fulton a superior opportunity to try again.

Churchill reported that Truman read the speech on the train on the way to Fulton and called it "admirable," saying that it "would do nothing but good, though it would make a stir."[19] Later when the wave of protests against the speech in British and especially American newspapers rose, Truman held to the line that Churchill was speaking only for himself and he had not known in advance what Churchill was going to say.[20] Churchill did not regard the loss of the 1945 election as a blessing, but there in Fulton it was useful to both Truman and Churchill.

After a little joke about being familiar with Westminster, Churchill began his speech with the disclaimer that he was speaking as a private citizen. He had "no official mission or status of any kind," and he spoke "only for [himself]. There is nothing here but what you see."[21] Of course, what the people saw, literally, was one of the most famous statesmen and the chief executive of the strongest nation on earth, together on a podium.

The speech is structured as a movement from the general to the specific, from the universal to the particular. Its complexity arises partly from the fact that the specific things Churchill said enriched but also altered and qualified the general and universal things he said.

The United States, Churchill said, stood "at the pinnacle of world power." That gave it "an awe-inspiring accountability." It must form an "overall strategic concept," a phrase, Churchill said, of which American generals were fond. The overall strategic concept must be "nothing less than the safety and welfare, the freedom and progress, of all the homes and families of all the men and women in all the lands." These myriad homes and families must be shielded from the two "giant marauders, war and tyranny." This must be accomplished through a "world organization," the newly created United Nations. This United Nations must have real power, "courts and magistrates" and also "sheriffs and constables," meaning an international armed force provided by the "Powers and States" that were members. These would act under the orders of this United Nations, with the reservation that they may not be required to attack their home country.[22]

Here is the first lesson from Churchill after the two great wars: one must think and speak universally. War and tyranny have spread to every land and injured every home in every land; these lands and homes must be protected.

These universal ambitions were not without precedent in Churchill's thinking. He had strongly supported the failed League of Nations, though he regarded its structure as "airy and unsubstantial."[23] The United Nations must be "a reality and not a sham," he said at Fulton; "a force for action, and not merely a frothing of words"; "a true temple of peace in which the shields of many nations can some day be hung up." Notice the words "some day."

The United Nations must not be "merely a cockpit in a Tower of Babel," an interesting mixed metaphor.[24] A cockpit is only by extension the command center of a ship or aircraft; in its root it is a place where roosters fight. The Tower of Babel was the place where God deprived people of the ability to speak to one another and thereby separated them into different countries. He did this to discipline their hubris, and once he did, the people were set at odds. Apparently fighting and the inability to converse are related. Those who cannot talk to each other are likely to fight like roosters.

Reason and force are the two alternative sources of political authority. The United Nations must be able to exercise force, but its authority cannot be complete until something more than force upholds it. Until this condition can be met, Churchill said, we cannot "cast away the solid assurances of national armaments."[25] Somehow the United Nations must command a legitimacy like that held in, say, the United States and Great Britain. Until that day, it is apparently not able to be the chief protector of the homes and families in all the lands against war and tyranny. Churchill did not say precisely how that was to be accomplished, but suggestions were to come.

Each of the two marauders, war and tyranny, was given a section in the Fulton speech. The section on war made plain that the solution lay chiefly in the United Nations. On the other hand, nations must keep their weapons until the United Nations met all the conditions, until it was not a "cockpit in a Tower of Babel." In particular, one weapon, the overwhelmingly important weapon, must be held by the three nations that had it then, and only by them: "It would nevertheless be wrong and imprudent to entrust the secret knowledge or experience of the atomic bomb, which the United States, Great Britain, and Canada now share, to the world organization, while it is still in its infancy. It would be criminal madness to cast it adrift in the still agitated and un-united world."

The United Nations must be armed, but not with the ultimate weapon. The nations that hold that weapon now can be trusted with it: "No one in any country has slept less well in their beds because this knowledge and the method and the raw materials to apply it, are at present largely retained in American hands. I do not believe we should all have slept so soundly . . . if some Communist or neo-Fascist State monopolized for the time being these dread agencies."[26]

Up to this point, Churchill had focused on nations and their common interest, on all nations working together for safety from the two marauders. But here Churchill raised for the first time the distinction among kinds of nations. There would be a United Nations, but the nations it included were of different kinds and not ready, therefore, to unite toward a common end. It would be "criminal madness" to arm such a group with the ultimate weapon.

This is the second lesson from Churchill after the two great wars: the free nations must lead, and they must protect themselves first.

One must ask, if the United Nations cannot be trusted with the atomic bomb, why should it be trusted with any kind of force? The answer from Churchill was that mankind possessed the means of its own destruction. The quarrels among men and nations twice blew up the world. It was time to try something as big as the problem. But how to try it?

That question brought up the second of the two great marauders, tyranny. "The liberties enjoyed by individual citizens throughout the British Empire are not valid in a considerable number of countries, some of which are very powerful," Churchill said. Those states had "police governments." They exercised their power without restraint under "dictators or by compact oligarchies operating through a privileged party and a political police."[27] The existence of these tyrannies was the prime threat, as Hitler was the prime threat before his defeat. What was to be done about that?

Churchill recommended one kind of restraint and another kind of assertion. The restraint was both military and diplomatic: ". . . it is not our duty at this time when difficulties are so numerous to interfere forcibly in the internal affairs of countries which we have not conquered in war." The force that tyrants used against their own people would not necessarily be met with force from outside. The relief of the oppressed people must wait, even if their relief was part of the "overall strategic concept."[28] Churchill's strategy concerned priorities—just as generals must prioritize when they fight.

Because Churchill was famous for war, we forget the many times he exercised or counseled restraint. The boldness of the Dardanelles campaign was matched by a sense of restraint in his opposition to attacking from the trenches across no-man's-land. In 1919 Churchill wanted to restore the Turkish Empire in the Middle East, under "strict form of international control," rather than gain British possessions there.[29] In 1921 as colonial secretary he wrote, "everything else that happens in the Middle East is secondary to the reduction in expense."[30] Before both world wars, when the dangers were first coming into view, Churchill showed reluctance to make alliances or give guarantees to France.[31] In 1925 he would undertake no obligations of "an unlimited character"; instead he would proceed "'in stages, by means of regional agreements' and 'by the maintenance of good understanding between various groups of Powers' within the framework of the League." The first step was to figure out what worked for Great Britain.[32] Later would come a dramatic, if little known, example of Churchill resisting intervention in

Vietnam, despite an urgent request from President Eisenhower, conveyed by Chairman of the Joint Chiefs of Staff Admiral Arthur Radford, to do so.[33] Churchill would be prepared to suffer the loss of countries, perhaps even whole regions, on the fringes to protect the center. He would not willingly trade British soldiers for Vietnamese whose loss meant little to the real powers that threatened.

Churchill was inclined to fight only when it was necessary and the nation strong. Though famous for leading his country in a fight to the death, Churchill was the person in some senses least likely and least willing to undertake such an engagement. Only when faced with circumstances like those in 1940, when in his judgment the alternative was life under the influence of Nazi Germany, was he unwilling to temporize, compromise, and negotiate.[34] The Second World War was to Churchill "The Unnecessary War"—a war that could have been prevented by acting earlier against Hitler.[35] To fail to prevent such a war, if it could be prevented, was a failure beyond estimation.

The limits that Churchill observed often in his career are implicit in his statement at Fulton that "it is not our duty . . . to interfere forcibly in the internal affairs of countries we have not conquered in war." Given those limits, what help was to be given to all those under the thumb of tyrannies? What was to be done for them? Churchill had something to offer:

> [W]e must never cease to proclaim in fearless tones the great principles of freedom and the rights of man which are the joint inheritance of the English-speaking world and which through Magna Carta, the Bill of Rights, the Habeas Corpus, trial by jury, and the English common law find their

most famous expression in the American Declaration of Independence.[36]

Then he summarizes what those documents say:

All this means that the people of any country have the right, and should have the power by constitutional action, by free unfettered elections, with secret ballot, to choose or change the character or form of government under which they dwell; that freedom of speech and thought should reign; that courts of justice, independent of the executive, unbiased by any party, should administer laws which have received the broad assent of large majorities or are consecrated by time and custom. Here are the title deeds of freedom which should lie in every cottage home. Here is the message of the British and American peoples to mankind. Let us preach what we practice—let us practice what we preach.[37]

So, that is the solution: we who enjoy our freedom "must never cease to proclaim in fearless tones" the good of that freedom. We must say that the people in every country have the right to this freedom. We can distinguish those who have it from those who do not by asking whether the people get to choose their government, speak their minds, and live in equality before stable and dependable laws. And we ourselves will both preach and practice this freedom and the kind of government necessary to preserve it.

This may not seem like much. In the aftermath of world war, and in the presence of a massive Soviet military force occupying much of Eastern Europe, Churchill is promising only to continue to cherish and live by certain principles. Also he is proposing to "never cease to proclaim" those principles—lip service. But lip service is valuable. What one says will affect what one does. If what one says is true and valuable, then sooner or later it will affect what everyone does. Churchill was devoted to government that is "parliamentary," government that proceeds by talking. It had been proved that Churchill was very ready to use force, but also he had often been cautious in its use. He understood that words are weapons too. He would use the principles of freedom as a verbal weapon, partly because force was impractical, partly because words are powerful. Remember that Churchill thought Hitler weak because he was afraid of words. This means that Hitler, too, understood the power of words.

Communist Russia had principles of its own to proclaim. It claimed that in order for all to have enough, all must have the same. It claimed that only a form of dictatorship can achieve this equal distribution. Churchill disputed this claim in his speech at Fulton, and so laid the ground for contesting it in deeds. He said, "I have not yet spoken of poverty and privation which are in many cases the prevailing anxiety." And, "we are plunged in the hunger and distress which are the aftermath of our stupendous struggle; but this will pass and may pass quickly."[38] This passing depends, he says, on success against the marauders of war and tyranny, and then upon "science and cooperation."

Then Churchill turned to one of his oldest authorities, the aforementioned Bourke Cockran, the mentor of his youth.[39] Twenty-three years after Cockran's death, Churchill said, "I have often used words which I learned fifty years ago from a great Irish-American orator, a friend of mine, Mr. Bourke Cockran. 'There is enough for all. The earth is a generous mother; she will provide in plentiful abundance food for all her children if they will but cultivate her soil in justice and in peace.'"[40]

In the *Fabian Essays*, George Bernard Shaw, agreeing with Marx, Stalin, and Lenin on this specific point, wrote that the capitalist is a gambler who plays a zero-sum game in which "the many must lose in order that the few may win."[41] Cockran and Churchill repudiated that view. As they saw it, all may win, and that is a consequential fact because it offers the possibility of harmony: human relations are not a contest in which the advantage of some requires the disadvantage of others. That means in turn that government need not have the authority to allocate resources, at least not comprehensively. A government with such power would be in one sense at war with any citizens who have more than others, effectively with all citizens but the few poorest. And if citizens are not in that contest with one another, then neither are nations. If one must lose so another may gain, citizens and nations are in a contest for resources that only one can win. This situation would mean war abroad and war at home. Churchill rejected it. In so doing, he asserted the principle that nations can get along.

This idea lies behind Churchill's appeal to Stalin in April 1945, a year before the Fulton speech. He wrote a long letter seeking to reach across the divide already growing between East and West:

> There is not much comfort in looking into a future where you and the countries you dominate, plus the Communist Parties in many other States, are all drawn up on one side, and those who rally to the English-speaking nations . . . on the other. It is quite obvious that their quarrel would tear the world to

pieces and that all of us leading men on either side who had anything to do with that would be shamed before history. Even embarking on a long period of suspicions, of abuse and counter-abuse and of opposing policies would be a disaster hampering the great developments of world prosperity for the masses, which are attainable only by our trinity. I hope there is no word or phrase in this outpouring of my heart to you which unwittingly gives offense. If so, let me know. But do not, I beg you, my friend Stalin, underrate the divergences which are opening about matters which you may think are small to us, but which are symbolic of the way English-speaking democracies look at life.[42]

Churchill's argument to Stalin, the builder of the Iron Curtain, was that conflict would cost both sides and therefore was not the best course for either. Even if they did not fight, even if they only suspected, abused, and opposed each other in policy, the "great developments of world prosperity for the masses" would be hampered. That development was possible only "by our trinity."

For Churchill, the world may often be divided into hostile camps, but it need not be. When Churchill asserted that the "earth is a generous mother," he was rejecting socialism, but he was also rejecting inevitable war between man and man and nation and nation. His plan for a United Nations was couched with many reservations, but he meant it too. He thought there was a basis for it in principle. After quoting Bourke Cockran, Churchill came at last "to the crux of what I have traveled here to say": the "sure prevention of war" and the "continuous rise of the world organization" required "the fraternal association of the English-speaking peoples," he said. "This means a special relationship between the British Commonwealth and Empire and the United States."[43]

The people involved in this "special relationship" speak the same language. They are the "English-speaking peoples." They do not occupy a Tower of Babel, and they are not likely therefore to engage in fighting like roosters. Only a few days before the Fulton speech, Churchill had repeated in Miami the famous statement of Bismarck, "that the most important fact in the world was that the British and American peoples spoke the same language."[44] And what do the English-speaking peoples have to say in their common language? Churchill had already said in this speech that we must never cease to "proclaim in fearless tones the great principles of freedom and the rights of man," and these are the "joint inheritance of the English-speaking world." They are found in that list of documents, all written in English: the Magna Carta, the Bill of Rights, the Habeas Corpus, and the Declaration of Independence.

Notice that the "crux" of what Churchill traveled to Fulton to say was a point about the distinction among nations. Churchill came to propose a global strategy aiming to benefit all nations, but the principles key to the strategy were not shared by all nations. The nations that did share them were therefore crucial. They have "faith in each other's purpose, hope in each other's future and charity towards each other's shortcomings."[45] The United Nations, Churchill said, will command "overriding loyalties," but the "special relationship" is not inconsistent with them. "On the contrary, it is probably the only means by which that organization will achieve its full stature and strength."[46]

WHITHER RUSSIA?

From the special relationship, Churchill turned to the part of the speech that is most famous.

He began with good words for Russia. The British want "constant, frequent and growing contacts between the Russian people and our own people on both sides of the Atlantic."[47] Churchill addressed the Russians on behalf of both the United States and Great Britain, and he spoke of them as a unity. Churchill would seek these "growing contacts" and diplomatic relations with the Soviet Union for the rest of his career.

Then Churchill said the famous hard words: "From Stettin in the Baltic to Trieste in the Adriatic, an iron curtain has descended across the Continent." Behind that curtain lay "all the capitals of the ancient states of Central and Eastern Europe. Warsaw, Berlin, Prague, Vienna, Budapest, Belgrade, Bucharest and Sofia." They and their peoples fell into what Churchill called the "Soviet sphere." They were being subjected to police governments. Athens was the only exception. Greece alone would be "free to decide its future at an election."[48] Churchill did not mention it here, but he had intervened in the affairs of Greece forcefully in 1944 to help prevent a communist government being established by force.[49]

Churchill states explicitly that he is trying to avoid the mistakes of the 1930s, when Hitler was not opposed until it was too late to stop him. This implies that the Soviet Union presents the same threat that Nazi Germany had presented. Churchill said:

> Last time I saw it all coming and cried aloud to my own fellow-countrymen and to the world, but no one paid any attention.

Up till the year 1933 or even 1935, Germany might have been saved from the awful fate which has overtaken her and we might all have been spared the miseries Hitler let loose upon mankind. There never was a war in all history easier to prevent by timely action than the one which has just desolated such great areas of the globe.[50]

Churchill said that the Russians were exploiting the favorable position they won by their conquests in the East. They were putting pressure on Turkey and Persia, and they were building a quasi-Communist Party in their zone of occupied Germany. That would cause problems in the British and American zones of occupation. It was not the "Liberated Europe we fought to build up. Nor is it one which contains the essentials of permanent peace."[51] The situation in the East, especially Manchuria, was also difficult, and Soviet Russia benefited from the favorable agreements made for it at Yalta. Russia emerged stronger from all of those events. That was dangerous.

Yet Churchill did not expect war. As there was before the Second World War, so now there was time to make preparations. "I do not believe that Soviet Russia desires war. What they desire is the fruits of war and the indefinite expansion of their power and doctrines." Then he said,

There is nothing they admire so much as strength, and there is nothing for which they have less respect than for weakness, especially military weakness. For that reason the old doctrine of a balance of power is unsound. We cannot afford, if we can help it, to work on narrow margins, offering temptations to a trial of strength. If the Western democracies

stand together in strict adherence to the principles of the
United Nations Charter, their influence for furthering those
principles will be immense and no one is likely to molest
them. If however they become divided or falter in their duty
and if these all-important years are allowed to slip away then
indeed catastrophe may overwhelm us all.[52]

That was Churchill's strategy for the future of the world. It
involved a few principles common to his thinking about war and
politics throughout his life. The free nations must understand,
value, proclaim, and practice their freedom. They must bind
together to constitute overwhelming force. They must keep the
most potent weapons to themselves as far as they are able. They
must build international organizations that are widely inclusive,
and if possible global. They must stand against aggression consistently but not necessarily everywhere. They must understand
the places that are important, fight the battles that they must,
but avoid if at all possible the battles presented upon unfavorable
ground.

The speech began universally, with the marauders of war
and tyranny. It ended in particularity, with particular political principles of freedom, particular nations that practice those
principles, and the association of the strongest of those nations
in a special relationship. Security for the world must be built
upon these strongest free nations, and they must be protected
and protect one another first. Their principles guide and their
strength must support the world organization. In that case, it
could provide a safeguard sufficient to protect the world in a
time when mankind had the ability to destroy itself.

PART TWO

———————

EMPIRE

5

STRATEGY AND EMPIRE

Churchill was an imperialist. He fought to preserve the empire all his life. It occupied for him an essential if not quite central place in the polity of Britain. It was inseparable from his strategic view of British safety and world influence. He thought it essential to the well-being of the British people at home. It occupied for him a space somewhere between foreign and domestic policy, between war and peace, affecting them all in ways profound and beneficial. It presented to him seeming contradictions and therefore dangers, alongside its massive and obvious benefits. It was an element in the trial that he faced.

At Fulton, Churchill said that the special relationship of speech, principle, and power was to include the British Commonwealth and Empire. The empire was to be a senior partner, along with or just beneath the predominant United States. To Churchill, principle and power were related because good principle was a source of power and because power was necessary to survival and to civilization. Civilization was rooted in the rule of law, which protected right through power against lawbreaking at home and aggression from abroad.

The threats that Churchill mentioned at Fulton required massive power to confront, as the world wars and the strength of the Soviet Union had proved. Churchill said later in this speech that "the old doctrine of a balance of power is unsound" in confronting the Soviet Union.[1] This time there must be no appeasement. There must be overwhelming force assembled to deter the Soviet Union. The world had seen in global conflict that large nations, especially when they combine, can exercise devastating force all over the world. The free countries, Churchill thought, must assemble the greatest combination. Their power alone and in combination depended upon their principles. Britain could and must participate, and to do so, it must be in the right.

This connection that Churchill asserts between right and might raises two questions: first, had right made might in the case of Britain? Was the country strong enough to be a senior partner in this relationship that involved both power and principle? In the last paragraph of the Fulton speech, Churchill asked that his audience not be deceived by the appearance of British weakness: by the fact of "46 millions in our island harassed about their food supply, of which they only grow one half, even in war-time, or because we have difficulty in restarting our industries and export trade after six years of passionate war effort."[2] Britain was weak, weak relative to its former self and weak relative to the United States. This was the cost of war.

Throughout his life, Churchill took pride in the global trade and reach of Britain, and also he feared the many things he believed to threaten them. Global power and survival were in his mind separated only by a whisker. During his life, ancient and powerful states were overcome, and Britain came near that fate. In 1903, arguing against tariffs, he objected that they would alienate "farmers of the Western states," vital to the food supply.[3] Later he compared the "artificial position" of Britain, which depended upon "her ships and her seaborne trade," to that of Holland depending upon its dikes, and to that of Egypt depending upon the Nile.[4] He said that socialism threatened the engine by which twenty million people had been "brought into existence,"[5] and they could not be fed and kept alive except with that engine. He said that the navy,[6] defense against air attack,[7] limited government,[8] and sound finance[9] were vital for the same reason. He also said this about the empire, which was to Churchill united by principle and sentiment more than by interest and force.[10] He said all these things many times in many contexts.

Churchill drew a picture of an island nation, crucially separated from the Continent, yet crucially near it.[11] Located near yet still apart from the civilization and force of Europe, it could be both distinct and significant. The island had grown free institutions in part because of that separation; it could defend itself without large standing armies, which weakened the king against the Parliament and thereby allowed authority to spread widely.[12] Because of the proximity of the sea to every part of Britain, the country had built maritime skill and resources, become the preeminent naval power, and traded all over the world. Britain was a tiny place grown mighty and free because of this complex of reasons. And just as these reasons made the nation mighty and free, they also made it fragile, dependent upon all these special factors and their relation.

The empire had grown from this complex of features, and it had become vital to the preservation of them all. For example, the British East India Company, a joint stock company chartered in 1600 to trade in Asia, had acquired India. Churchill wrote of this fact: "To call this process 'Imperialist expansion' is nonsense, if by that is meant the deliberate acquisition of political power. Of India it has been well said that the British Empire was acquired in a fit of absence of mind."[13] The empire in India grew as Britain grew: by commerce, by naval strength, substantially by private action. Churchill favored the empire in India in part because it had grown in this way and was therefore a product of the same forces that made Britain what it was.

The empire made Britain something more than powerful too: it made the country noble. The empire gave the British a service to do for the world, and by doing that service the British could be worthy of their leading station. It established a relation of friendship with the dominions and ultimately with the colonies, and they would together rally to the common cause of the world. The empire was not held together "with bits of string."[14] This may sound naive, even corny, but the voluntary cooperation among the imperial and commonwealth countries was remarkable in the world wars. In 1939 Churchill said to Walter Lippman, an American commentator and public intellectual, that if Britain should falter in the coming war, the burden would fall to the United States: "It will then be for you, for the Americans, to preserve and to maintain the great heritage of the English-speaking peoples. It will be for you to think Imperially, which means to think always of something higher and more vast than one's own national interests."[15] Churchill did not forget the interest of Britain; he even put it first. He conceived that interest to include service to the world.

The empire made Britain powerful in the military sense.

In the Great War, imperial and dominion nations contributed almost 29 percent of British forces and suffered 23 percent of those killed.[16] In World War II, those nations contributed 29.3 percent of the British forces and suffered 47.2 percent of those killed. The casualty rates including wounded for the dominion countries were 1.5 times higher than for the mother country.[17] Britain by itself was a great power in both wars, but much greater when the empire was included.[18]

India alone contributed 1.5 million soldiers during the Great War and another 2.6 million in World War II. All of them were volunteers, the largest volunteer army in history.[19] It is not difficult to see why Churchill, interested not only in the goodness but also in the greatness and force of his country, loved the empire. Its existence permitted him to say at Fulton:

> [D]o not suppose that we shall not come through these dark years of privation as we have come through the glorious years of agony, or that half a century from now, you will not see 70 or 80 millions of Britons spread about the world and united in defense of our traditions, our way of life, and of the world causes which you and we espouse. If the population of the English-speaking Commonwealths be added to that of the United States with all that such co-operation implies in the air, on the sea, all over the globe and in science and in industry, and in moral force, there will be no quivering, precarious balance of power to offer its temptation to ambition or adventure.[20]

The empire and commonwealth were then what Churchill liked to call a "makeweight." Include them, and the whole complex of British freedom and power could be preserved. Freedom and

justice without power *cannot* be preserved; power without freedom and justice *ought not* to be preserved. Britain's strength,
Churchill said many times in many contexts, was in its ability to
join right and might.

RIGHT AND MIGHT

And that raises the second question: did Britain have right on
its side? The empire is a problem, specifically the colonies, especially India. At the moment Churchill spoke in Fulton, Britain
had been locked in a struggle with the Indian National Congress
Party and its eventual leader Mahatma Gandhi since the end
of the Great War, to which India contributed enormous man-
power and resources.[21] In part because of that, Indians began to
claim the right to elect their own governments. They had won
significant concessions in the years between the wars. During
World War II, the Congress Party proved in provincial elections
to be dominant in much of India and strong almost everywhere.
The party demanded self-government through negotiation, civil
disobedience, hunger strikes (especially by Gandhi), demonstrations, riots, and a military mutiny. Having only a small minority
of Parliament at his back and against the opinion of all major
political parties, Churchill had resisted this throughout the
1930s and the war years. In 1943, with Churchill as prime minister, Gandhi had gone on a long hunger strike, and Churchill
had been prepared to let him starve while believing that Gandhi
would not go to that extreme.[22] Moreover the United States,
the indispensable ally, had not liked this and pressed Churchill
repeatedly to grant home rule.[23] Churchill had refused. What
then of these title deeds of freedom?

The contradiction was obvious. Churchill said at Fulton as he had said many times that the United States was crucial to the well-being of the world; that the relationship between the United States and Britain was crucial; that the empire was crucial to Britain. Many in the United States regarded the empire as violating American principles, the principles of universal right and rights. Churchill himself embraced the Declaration of Independence at Fulton and commonly through his life. He said the Declaration was consistent with the British Empire. But the Declaration was written to declare to the British king and Parliament that government is only rightful when the governed may consent. Does that mean that in no case can imperial or colonial rule be justified? Does that mean that Churchill's grand alliance of the United States, Britain, and the British Empire is an alliance made of essentially incompatible parts? In that case Churchill had no strategy. An independent India, governed by Gandhi and the Congress Party, might not have come to the aid of Britain and the rest of the allies in either world war. Would Britain have survived?

IMPERIAL PRINCIPLES

Many historians blame Churchill for his opinion and actions in regard to the empire. One writes that Indian self-rule was "abhorrent" to him.[24] Another writes that he held the view, said to be common to the time, that non-whites could not govern themselves or not so well;[25] and that he evidenced "callousness" in the face of a famine in 1943 in Bengal when more than a million people starved.[26] One biographer wrote that Churchill positively avoided the "Empire's non-white populations."[27] All these points raise the charge of hypocrisy, and they are widely asserted. Are they true?

Churchill did think that in his time the capacity for self-government in what we now call the third or undeveloped world was less than in the developed countries. He said that the Kenyans were like "light-hearted, tractable, if brutish children . . . capable of being instructed and raised from their present degradation."[28] He said that various colonial peoples were not "civilized"; he tolerated, as under-secretary of state for the colonies, the South African government's continued exclusion of non-whites from political equality.[29] He wrote while secretary of state for the colonies: "The Indians in East Africa are mainly of a very low class of coolies, and the idea that they should be put on an equality with the Europeans is revolting to every white man throughout British Africa."[30]

Churchill made his argument about Indian independence at length and for years. It can be stated simply. He argued that India was not a nation, but an "abstraction,"[31] an area of country occupied by many different peoples, only a few millions of whom could read or write.[32] It comprised two main religions, Hinduism and Islam, that were hostile to each other. The Muslims were in the minority, yet still numbered tens of millions and were more warlike: "While the Hindu elaborates his argument, the Muslim sharpens his sword."[33] Churchill believed that there were "fifty Indias."[34] India was divided into myriad princely states, each claiming venerable identity. Its people spoke dozens of languages. Hinduism held the caste system sacred, and therefore the divide between the Brahmin and the Dalit, or untouchable class, was utter. The Brahmins "will not eat with these sixty millions [of untouchables] . . . nor treat them as human beings. They consider themselves contaminated even by their approach. And then in a moment they turn round and begin chopping logic with John Stuart Mill, or pleading the rights of man with Jean Jacques Rousseau."[35]

Britain could not, Churchill said, recognize the "claim to the title-deeds of democracy" of people who "keep sixty millions of fellow countrymen perpetually and eternally in a state of sub-human bondage."[36] None of these tribes, religions, factions, and regions had a legacy of limited government or equal rights. The "political, social, cultural, racial, religious conditions" of India made it certain that any "attempt to apply the democratic institutions of Australia and Canada rigidly and pedantically to India, would produce measureless tyranny and misery, ending in bloodshed and probably utter confusion."[37] The Indians were more numerous, prosperous, and healthy than they had been, and that was in large part a consequence of British rule. If Britain were to leave, these divisions, long held in abeyance and ameliorated by British rule, would erupt into strife, poverty, and death.[38]

On this point, the case of South Africa is related to that of India and may reveal a contradiction. The peace made with the Boers to create the South African republic left whites considerable discretion about how non-whites would be treated, and they were not treated well. One must remember that the Boer War was long and hard, and Britain did things in that war against the South African people that Churchill regarded as wrong.[39] Churchill had written that the war fundamentally concerned the British principle of equal treatment of all races, which he proclaimed as a principle on many occasions.[40]

Churchill and most people in Britain did not like the way

the South African republic treated people of color, but Churchill said that they did not have the power to change it: "Unless we carry public opinion [of white South Africans] with us in procuring the removal of any of these objectionable provisions the result will only be their lawless assertion, which, I believe, would impose more injustice and tyranny on the natives than the regulated assertion which is contained in a statute of law." He also said that "harsh laws are sometimes better than no laws at all."[41]

These points open a world of calculation and knowledge that has been integral to the principle of government by consent since it became the hallmark of modern politics. People have a right to govern themselves; what if the people who exercise that right do not recognize it in others? The American founders, with whom Churchill agreed so often, have much to say about this. James Madison wrote, "In republics, the great danger is that the majority may not sufficiently respect the rights of the minority."[42] Thomas Jefferson said, "All too will bear in mind this sacred principle that though the will of the majority is in all cases to prevail, that will, to be rightful, must be reasonable; that the minority possess their equal rights, which equal laws must protect and to violate would be oppression."[43] The point is precisely parallel to one that Abraham Lincoln made about the feeling in America that whites could not live alongside blacks as equal citizens: "A universal feeling, whether well or ill-founded, cannot be safely disregarded."[44] In another place Lincoln said, "in this and like communities, public sentiment is everything."[45]

This means that government by consent may not be easy to achieve. Its success depends upon many things that are not always present, and for this reason free government is not ubiquitous. Stable, free government, long enduring, is rare. Churchill was aware of this and thought that freedom always hung upon the balance of many factors ever at risk.

Churchill accepted, thinking that he was bound to accept, conditions in South Africa that he encouraged Britain to prevent in India. Of course it is easy to claim a distinction is in the fact that the South African rulers were white, and those they oppressed were not white. If this is true, it can be only a partial truth: neither the Indian Brahmins at the top of the caste system nor the untouchables at the bottom were white.

It would have been better for everyone, Churchill thought, if the Indians had not believed in the caste system, and if the South Africans had treated people of color as equals. But the Indians, or many of them, did believe in it, and the South Africans, or many of them, did not so treat the people of color. Can one convince them? That had not proved easy. Can one force them? That depends upon the resources required to do so. Churchill distinguished the Indian and the South African situations on precisely this point.

Churchill went on to say that the "second limitation" on British action in South Africa was that South Africa achieved self-government, "the greatest and best gift that we can bestow." Self-government can collide with "moral principles," and on occasion it should "be over-borne." Self-government can be given only once, and "once it has been given, it is not good to grudge it."[46] That was one reason Churchill was reluctant to concede self-government to India.

The British had given up the power to compel in South Africa after a hard war. Force was no longer an option. What remained? The only alternative to force is reason. We have seen that Churchill regarded words, lip service, as valuable. He thought that the British Empire, stating its support for equal human rights, would have an influence in South Africa and everywhere else. After saying that "public sentiment is everything," Lincoln added that "he who molds public sentiment goes deeper than he who enacts statutes or pronounces decisions."[47] Churchill and Lincoln believed that words mattered. However the whites of South Africa were going to treat those of color, it would not be worse because of their association with the British.

The situation was different and, Churchill thought, more advantageous in India: Churchill argued that the people of India broadly accepted British rule. This factor is vital. Recall that Churchill favored limited government, and because of that he sought ways to win wars, when they must be fought, as cheaply as possible. For the same reason he sought economical ways to maintain the empire. If Britain exhausted itself, or taxed its people excessively, to win human rights in the colonies, the country would risk losing its position, including its freedom. It was important to Churchill that British rule in India was good for the British as well as the Indians. In 1943 he wrote to Labour Minister Herbert Morrison: "If it were established that we were never to have any advantage from our colonies except that of pure philanthropy, a good many people would argue that we had better spend our money on improving the health and social services of our workers at home."[48] In that same letter Churchill had reminded Morrison that the Boer War involved a difference over the status of the people of color in South Africa.

India was, Churchill thought, economical to manage. Under the Raj, the Indian people were governed mainly by Indians, who made up the majority of the administration, police, and military. Even during the mass demonstrations, for example, in

1931, "hardly any life has been lost or blood shed in the almost ceaseless mob tumult which has occurred in so many places."[49] At the top of India's government was a "very small number of white officials who [had] no personal interests of their own to serve, who [were] quite impartial between race and race, and who [had] built up in 150 years an organization which [gave] these enormous masses peace, justice, and a substantial increase in material well-being, which would have been even greater except for the vast increase in their numbers." Therefore the British had a "supreme moral duty" to remain in India.[50]

But was this duty in fact "supreme"? There are many moral duties: for example, saving Greece from the Nazi invasion; or saving Poland from domination by Stalin, having gone to war to save her from domination by Hitler. These duties proved to be beyond the capacity of Great Britain, at least immediately. Moral duties are done by those who have the power to do them. Churchill was interested in the British Empire in part because it was a source of power to Britain. Britain had plenty of faults, but it was preferable, Churchill argued, to Nazi Germany and to Bolshevik Russia. In relation to those countries, it was good for Britain to have power.

This power, which came partially from India, could be used for good in India. This duty in India, Churchill thought, was possible to discharge without losing other things equally or more valuable. And then the time came when he did not think that. It may be read as sour grapes, but Churchill said to G. D. Birla in 1935, after the Government of India Act passed, "India I feel is a burden on us. We have to maintain an army and for the sake of India we have to maintain Singapore and Near East strength."[51] It mattered to Churchill whether the empire was expensive.

This prudential approach to moral duties, even "supreme" moral duties, may seem to reinforce the indictment of Churchill as a racist in regard to South Africa and India. Churchill acknowledged two things consistently that undercut that indictment. The first is the point about equality. Churchill argued consistently that the British Empire stood for the rights of all, including people of all colors. In *London to Ladysmith* he wrote that the Boer War proceeded from the fact that the British government was "associated in the Boer" mind with the "violent social revolution" of treating the races as equals.[52] He repeated the point in the aforementioned memo to Herbert Morrison: "In fact, our problem with the Boers was originally due to our insistence on the proper treatment of the Kaffirs, and at this moment we withhold native territories from their control."[53] On July 4, 1918, Churchill gave his only Fourth of July speech. He said, "By [the Declaration of Independence] we lost an Empire, but by it we also preserved an Empire." The empire stood for the principles of the Declaration.[54] Speaking of Indian violence against Indians in 1948, he said, "I thought we took the principle of the broad equality of the human race, irrespective of color or creed" in Britain and its empire.[55]

These may have been hypocritical statements, but they were often repeated, and the people of the empire and everywhere else were able to read them and use them in their arguments. Churchill gave effect to these principles in many dealings with the empire. A notable case occurred when, in April 1919, British troops under the command of General Reginald Dyer fired upon an unarmed demonstration at Amritsar in northern India. There were 379 people killed and up to 1,200 wounded.[56] Many drowned in a well, seeking to escape the fusillade. Women and children were killed. Dyer defended himself with reference to the seriousness of the demonstrations: "I understood the position to be that civil law was at an end and that military law would have to take its place for the time being."[57] He had many defenders in Parliament, they too claiming that the law was breaking down.

Churchill was sharply critical of Dyer. He named the "broad lines" to guide British officers when deciding to open fire upon a crowd: Is it attacking anything or anybody? Is it armed? What is the minimum force necessary to secure compliance with the law? Officers should be capable, even in a tense situation before a large demonstration, to make good judgments about these questions. After all, they do harder things in war.[58]

Then Churchill cited a "general prohibition" on British forces: they could not engage in "frightfulness," by which he meant the infliction of "great slaughter or massacre upon a particular crowd of people, with the intention of terrorizing not merely the rest of the crowd, but the whole district or the whole country." He added, "Frightfulness is not a remedy known to the British pharmacopoeia." It was the kind of policy used by the Bolsheviks, and Churchill hated their policies.[59] Churchill did not think that British rule in India or anywhere else rested ultimately upon force, and he opposed the actions of General Dyer because in establishing terror, they implied the rule of force.

If Churchill considered some in the empire "uncivilized," what did he mean by that, and how did it relate to self-government? Remember his definition in his 1938 speech at the University of Bristol: civilization is a society based "upon the opinion of civilians. It means that violence, the rule of warriors and despotic chiefs, the conditions of camps and warfare, of riot and tyranny, give place to parliaments where laws are made, and independent courts of justice in which over long periods those laws are maintained." The strict sense of the term means merely that civilians rule. When that is achieved, as in Britain, "freedom, comfort, and culture" grow. The masses of the people enjoy "a wider and less harassed life"; traditions of the past are "cherished, and the inheritance bequeathed to us by former wise or valiant men becomes a rich estate to be enjoyed and used by all"; there is a great "measure of good will between classes."[60]

Civilization meant then the rule of law. If a people lived in a way and according to beliefs that undermined the equality of all before the law, the effect of placing the people in charge would not be the rule of law or civilization. The effect would be consent of the governed—but only once. According to Churchill's stricter definition of civilization, its possession has not to do with race or color but with culture and opinion.

In the Fulton speech, Churchill spoke of the entitlement of all people to their rights, as he maintained throughout his life. Earlier he had said of the Indians that they were partners with the British in the government of India, and they should be given "responsible government" of the provinces, "territories and populations as large as Germany, France, Poland, Italy or Spain."[61] In 1931 he said that the Indians were *not* inherently "incapable of working modern democratic institutions."[62] In no place did Churchill say that race or color was a qualification for self-government, and he asserted in many places that the Indians were surely capable of it in principle.

The hard fact remains that Churchill wished the British to rule the Indians for the indefinite future against the wishes of many Indians. The advantage of consent of the governed is that it achieves at least this: the government cannot do things to the people that the majority of them do not want. If the British rule the Indians, will they not rule the Indians in their own interest? The British had no perfect record of colonial administration in this regard: they protected the slave trade for more than a century. The Americans had no perfect record either: they held slaves for almost three generations after the Declaration of Independence, although it must be said that slavery was eliminated in most of the Union shortly after the Declaration. These are stains upon the record of two countries that were both powerful and, in other respects, free. Every nation has its stains.

Churchill argued that the British were able to be of service to the Indians—and to themselves—because they had "learned the lessons" of the Declaration of Independence, which are also the lessons of the British "title-deeds" of freedom. The Americans, too, had to learn those lessons. The founders of America were nearly uniform in condemning slavery, unlike the thinkers of the Confederacy who supported slavery and condemned the Declaration of Independence.[63] Slavery was not settled without the violence of the most costly war in American history, which Lincoln described as penance for the failure to live up to the nation's principles, principles established in heaven.[64] Those principles exercised an influence on the nation even when it fell short of them.

These "title-deeds" of freedom, Churchill argued, were not available to the Indians because they did not at the time believe in them, or most Indians did not. The British did believe in them, and they had a constitution effective in implementing and protecting them. This constitution was available also for the protection of the Indians and certain other peoples, until such time as they themselves could protect their rights.

Churchill believed therefore that the British rule of India was good and defensible. His plan was to defend it. Britain should have confidence in its mission in India. It should make plain that "we intend to remain the effective rulers of India in every essential for a very long and indefinite period."[65] He thought that by doing so the British would be of best service to the Indians and to themselves, and the strength of the free countries in the world would be magnified in commerce and in war.

These judgments are much questioned today. Against them is the national popularity of the Congress Party at least from 1936—the first provincial elections—onward. This indicates cohesion where there was also much fragmentation. Against them is the fact that most of India has stayed together, and its democratic forms have held, through many rocky times, and strengthened to become the world's largest democracy. Against them is the national celebration that erupted in 1947 when independence was won.[66] Against them is the opinion of many or most Indians today who write about the matter. Against them is the behavior of Gandhi and Nehru toward the Muslims and the untouchables, both when they had power and when they did not. Churchill admired them for this.[67] Gandhi, it is fair to say, gave his life resisting the violence between Muslim and Hindu: he was shot by a Hindu extremist on January 30, 1948.

There are facts in favor of Churchill's judgments too. India did not remain fully together but was partitioned into three states, two of them Muslim, two of them which face each other in nuclear-armed hostility today. The moment of independence brought violence and death for hundreds of thousands, some say up to one million, and the displacement of millions.[68] The immediate effect of the popular vote for Indians was to make the caste system more rigid.[69] The majority of the Indian people did believe that the caste system was sacred and that some people were too low in the order of things to be touched. That thankfully has improved vastly, and untouchables have served in many high offices. India, it seems, has become a great hope for freedom and justice for its own people and for the world. The happy things about the Indian situation today certainly owe something to British influence.

Also in favor of Churchill is the fact that the empire has given rise to many of the strongest and freest nations in the world, most of them, including India, governed under parliamentary forms unknown to or ill-developed in the region before the British came. Churchill was well aware that the days of imperial control from London were finished at least from the Great War.[70] He did not regret that, so long as those nations remained free and associated with the British Commonwealth.

One part of the problem that Churchill thought the empire helped to solve would continue to press whether there were any empire or no. In the age of confrontation between powerful free nations and powerful tyrannies, many nations are affected that are not fully developed and have not allied with either camp. Those nations are likely to be affected by the policy of the powerful nations, both free and despotic. Churchill argued that the influence of the free nations would be better for them; if they allied with the tyrannies, injustice would be reinforced. Modern history demonstrates that such reinforcement can be overwhelmingly detrimental.

How are the free nations to deal with those countries, when those countries are not possessed of free institutions of their own? One does not have to be an imperialist, cultural or political, to believe that all people have a right to live under laws that protect their freedom. One does not have to be a racist to believe that some peoples cannot achieve that on their own at any given time.

PART THREE

PEACE

6

"LO! A NEW ENGLAND"

Churchill thought that war, ever terrible, had become more so. He thought the same about peace. Ever troubled with injustice and strife, with tyranny and discord, it had become afflicted with the potential for new and more virulent forms of despotism. The cause, he thought, was the same in peace and in war—what we have seen that he calls "mass effects." The essay in which he explains these mass effects thematically gives an account of "modern life," both in war and in peace.[1] In war these mass effects would kill; in peace they would dehumanize. In war they threatened the physical destruction of the free nations; in peace they threatened their souls, their "spirit," which Churchill thought was the decisive thing about humans.[2] For Churchill politics was higher than war, and peaceful purposes were finally, if not always immediately, superior to victory in war. These mass effects, manifested in politics at home, were no less sinister than their manifestation in the world wars. If there is anything clear from the life of Winston Churchill, it is that he regarded it as better to be killed than corrupted.

The causes of these mass effects were partly "unconscious"— they were not guided by anyone's intentions. However they may have begun, they proceeded on their own, outside the management of anyone or any group.[3] At the same time they were partly conscious: there were "conceptions" behind them, conceptions that people held and according to which they acted. The Russian Bolsheviks carried these conceptions to their "utmost extreme."[4] They had their foothold also in British politics, especially in the Socialist movement. That movement was based, Churchill argued, on a new kind of doctrine—a doctrine like the Bolshevik if less extreme. Churchill argued that the basis of socialism was like that upon which Stalin stood, except it was found inside Britain and the British; like that upon which Hitler stood, except speaking English and participating in the ordinary processes of the British Constitution. The danger of socialism was intensified by the fact that Churchill believed he owed the duty of common citizenship to the British statesmen and citizens who followed its doctrines. He recognized that if they came to power through the electoral processes of the British Constitution they were entitled to that power, even if their principles would in his view ultimately subvert that Constitution.

Churchill and British socialism were born and grew up together. British socialism was incubated in the Fabian Society, a group of thinkers and activists led by playwright George Bernard Shaw and social thinker Sidney Webb.[5] Churchill knew these men, corresponded with and wrote about them, and had cordial if also controversial relations with them. These men and others formed the society in 1884, ten years after Churchill's birth. In 1900, the year Churchill entered Parliament, they and others formed the Labour Party, the political instrument that eventually brought socialism to Britain.

Socialism went from strength to strength during Churchill's life: by 1906 it was cooperating with the Liberal Party in many constituencies to prevent the election of Conservatives; in 1910 it elected forty-two members of Parliament; in 1924 it formed a short-lived minority government; in 1929 it gained for the first time a plurality of seats in the House of Commons. In 1945 it defeated Churchill's Conservatives in a landslide and governed for five years with a large majority. True to its word, it national-ized eight major industries, six of which remained under public control for decades. Churchill resisted this tide with all his might and throughout his life, and to a considerable extent he resisted it in vain.

Who were these Fabians against whom Churchill set his face? They were in the main expositors of the historicism of the Left that grew up in Europe in the late nineteenth and early twentieth centuries. Karl Marx lived in London from 1849 until his death in 1883, and many Fabians knew him. On the other hand the Fabians were not Communists or revolutionaries, and they took only limited lessons from Marx.[6] They took their name from the Roman general Fabius Maximus, the great Cunctator (Delayer) who defeated Hannibal by temporizing for years but striking hard when the time was right. The Fabians had their own ideas; they believed in analysis and argument, and they were good at them. In a compliment that he was qualified to pay, Churchill called Shaw the most brilliant living writer of English.[7] Shaw used that ability to compose key sections of the seminal *Fabian Essays in Socialism*,[8] written by seven authors including Shaw and Webb. These essays explain early British socialism with an authority that approaches the authority of *The Federalist* on the Constitution of the United States.

The Fabians were committed to popular rule. In the main, they thought that the ordinary processes of politics would produce a reformed Parliament based on universal suffrage. They believed that such a Parliament would bring the Socialist state into being, certainly and peacefully. In these beliefs they were proved correct, at least in regard to actual events in Britain.

Most Socialists believed that history—an important word—proved that capitalism resulted necessarily in the exploitation of those who labor without ownership. Capitalism must result in the falling of wages to the level of basic human subsistence, which is the necessary stopping point because workers do not compete for jobs after they have died. The Fabians believed that the public ownership of much or most or all of the means of production would solve this problem and achieve more economic equality and a more efficient use of assets.[9]

SOCIALISM, HISTORY, AND NATURE

Socialism means many new things for every human institution and relationship, and it means them according to an overarching idea that at least some Socialists called nature. For socialism, nature is change. Change is "rooted in the nature of human living. Nature herself changes."[10] Change happens over time, and therefore nature is history. History is not so much a story as it is a force. History has a pattern or progress that can be seen and understood, at least at this later stage of history, the stage that makes socialism possible. The world "moves from system, through disorder, back again to system."[11] Through the study of history, we can learn to "class men and ideas in a kind of geological order in time."[12] The Fabians believed mankind was on the verge of the decisive change for the better—change long prepared by the struggles of mankind through history.

Moreover this view of history provided, thought Sidney Webb, an objectivity that modern philosophy had called into doubt. If history works on the human consciousness, then the world in which history unfolds is real, not a figment of our imagination. We can get close to nature because nature is talking to us with force, affecting our minds in ways that give us real knowledge of events outside ourselves. Also our deductions about the world have a basis in evolution: we know things better, even matters of logic, because we know them from an accumulation of experience through the ages and not merely from our rational insight. The former, Webb thought, is much more solid.[13] The process of evolution places us closer to real knowledge and closer, therefore, to the real workings of nature. This answers the question of how the mind is connected to nature. It also raises the question of the mind's independence from nature. What ability has the mind to observe nature objectively?

Like minerals and elements that are formed through geological forces over eons, so humans are formed. Those who live in each age have their characteristics in relation to the historical circumstances or environment of that age. This includes the Fabian Socialists, who were mostly aware that the arguments of historical necessity applied to them as much as they applied to those who came before them. They were aware that their insights and deductions would be replaced or superseded by more advanced insights and deductions to come. They anticipated this and welcomed it; they were progressives. At the same time they understood that they had a special advantage: they knew about history, whereas those before them did not or did not so well. Aware of the ways of history, they were better able to break free from its constraints, or anyway to await patiently its opportunities, which they knew would come.

Behind the patience of the Fabians was optimism. They were living at one of the hinges of history, a pivot toward new things. There was a change in the "content of men's minds. Their standpoints are shifted. Their horizons are suddenly enlarged. Their whole way of considering things is altered, and lo! A new England." And in this process of change England discovered a "new category. We . . . are not merely individuals, but members of the community, nay, citizens of the world."[14] This new understanding of community will work eventually for the transcendence of many limits. All can have enough, and all can have something close enough to the same amount to make real equality. All or most can participate in a richer and fuller life, possess a wider and higher knowledge. At the end all will have time to address even the great books.[15]

This work of capitalizing upon the opportunities of history requires a new and more scientific kind of administration.[16] Public policy must be made rational. Competing interests in the society must be subordinated to the good of the community, brought into harmony to reduce wasted resources and exploitation of some by others. This kind of administration requires a certain technical education to permit the application of the tools of science to public affairs. There is now a mass consciousness, and it is capable of "inarticulate criticism."[17] But this mass cannot articulate, and so its criticism must be articulated for it.

Ministries and administrations led by "national leaders" will do this for them. These leaders can seek "efficiency" in giving the people what they want. They can provide a "National Minimum." They can provide an "efficient education." They can promote "National Efficiency" by subsidies of "twentieth century universities," to study "chemistry and electricity, engineering and business organization in the largest sense." These universities would be "technical," studying science in the sense of art or of making.[18] Those trained in this art are capable of creating "a deliberately planned co-operation in production and distribution for the benefit of all." This will feature "the universal enforcement of the national minimum," the "democratic control of industry," "the revolution in national finance," and "the surplus wealth for the common good."[19] Science is the new rule to guide all common action: "No scheme of Bellers,[20] or Babeuf,[21] or Robert Owen[22] could be resisted, if only their advocates could adduce scientific evidence of their practicability and good tendency."[23]

This process of applying science to human affairs through public administration is essentially experimentation, which is the process that will drive public administration in the future. For this reason, socialism, including the gradualist Fabian socialism, changes as it goes. Socialists hold various opinions. Each person changes his or her mind with time and circumstance, and the plans and platforms of socialism alter as they go. This is something different from the prudential adaptation to circumstances that Churchill understood to be the task of statesmanship. It is rather an adaptation to new truths revealed in new circumstances. One should not look among Socialists for consistency, even in principle, except for a consistent commitment to adaptation, to science, to experimentation.

It is therefore no surprise that the Socialist movement is of many changing minds about what specifically is to be done. Sometimes it thinks that the family should be reconstituted, at least partially socialized; but no, maybe that will not work.[24] Maybe the key is to be found in central administration, unleashed and comprehensive; but no, maybe too much bureaucracy is a problem and voluntary associations must thrive.[25] Maybe major industries should all be nationalized; but no, that goes too far and is inefficient. Maybe instead of comprehensive regulation, the "mixed economy" is all that is needed.[26] Maybe the administration built to accomplish that economy will itself become a danger.

In the self-understanding of Fabian socialism, these changes of mind are not signs of contradiction. Rather they are proof of the openness to evidence, of a commitment to empiricism. Experimentation lights the way. It can make mistakes, even huge mistakes. They are the price of progress. The experiments must be large because the new "category" of community requires that we remake not just this or that government department, but that we remake "society itself." This requires that the "political system and ideas in which [the individualist system of capital production] naturally found expression . . . must go."[27]

The Fabians and their allies looked forward to a climax that would share features with the culminating events foreseen in the Christian faith. The religious foundations of socialism are instructive about its character. Many Socialists were atheists, but others were Christians. Most of the Christians believed that God through Jesus had set about his work through history, here on earth. He was building heaven and a perfect human soul here on earth, and he was doing it through events, including especially the events influenced by socialism.[28]

In the *Fabian Essays*, religion generally and Christianity specifically are indicted for shielding men from the knowledge of their own faults and misdeeds and for making them complacent about the state of things here below.[29] But also Sydney Olivier wrote that the Catholic Church, now "decrepit," had done fine things: it insisted on the duty of helping the poor; it advanced the "widest and freest system of education" the world had known; and above all, with its "revolutionary conception that God was incarnated in Man," it had exploded the "hideous superstition" that the human heart is evil, replacing that with the faith "in the perfectibility of each individual soul" and the idea that "God must be Love" because there is nothing better.[30]

Love is an important theme in the *Fabian Essays*, and it is about to have its day. Up to now the progress, even the advance of democracy, was driven not so much by "love of the many" but by "hatred of the few."[31] But love, Webb wrote, can be liberated, and it can flourish. Love is the social instinct, and it is connected to morality, which comes into being whenever we deal with others. For Sydney Olivier, at least, morality does not seem to be a personal virtue, connected to the nature or proper operation of the human being. It is not a thing like courage, the right disposition toward danger; or moderation, the right disposition toward pleasure. When the individual in solitude exercises morality, that exercise is "indifferent."[32] Only in society can morality be understood. The only teachers of morality are "love, the social instinct, and science, which is ordered knowledge."[33] Love seems to be natural, a driving force in humanity. On the other hand, like everything else, it takes its shape and definition only in society.

When this social instinct of love is liberated, it will be so powerful that philanthropic works will not be honored as they are because they will be seen as simply reasonable—as the path "indicated by common sense toward the satisfaction of the individual passion for the extension of freedom and love."[34] This individual passion will take over for the profit motive when the profit motive is removed. No longer need we work for material gain. "[T]he gold-hunger would disappear upon the certainty of subsistence." It will be replaced by "the desire to excel, the joy in creative work, the longing to improve."[35] When subsistence is assured to all, education can do wonders. The mind can be "trained to appreciate the inexhaustible interest and beauty of the world, and to distinguish good literature from bad." This good literature has become "dirt-cheap," and all can appreciate it. Also they can appreciate "clean and beautiful cities, the joy of the fields, the museum, the art-gallery, the lecture-hall, the drama, and the opera."[36] There will be a leap not only into freedom but also into the cultivation of elevated things. These things will apparently still be considered elevated and refined, even if the ground in reason and faith upon which they were constructed is altered or eroded.

These great things are to be the work of man, not of God, even if they are God's work. The less pious among the Fabians thought that science had shown nature to be "red in tooth and claw." Nature is a cruel and dangerous place. If God made this nature, then he is not benevolent. If he did not make it, then he is not omnipotent.[37] The more pious among the Fabians thought that Jesus had set us an example of a perfect man, an example living among us here and now, commanding us to do the work here and now. All the Fabians, pious or no, thought that the work was to be done on this earth and the gains to be achieved now or soon by our efforts. Anything less would be a disservice to mankind and would tolerate continued misery and wrong. The opportunity is here: it lives in history; it lives in the science through which we understand and by which we can tame ourselves and the world around us.

In regard to means and timing, Fabian socialism was a gradualist movement, proceeding by argument and democratic processes. In contrast to the means it adopted, its aims were far-reaching in every area of human life, especially in key areas where human beings exercise their main responsibilities. These include especially the way we make our livings, the way we raise our children, and the moral sense under which we make our most serious judgments. Socialism meant change in all of these areas; Churchill resisted that change in all of them.

Take, for example, the family. Marx, a precursor of limited influence with the Fabians, called for the abolition of the family on the grounds that under capitalism it had become a system of exploitation of women and children. The family had already disappeared, he wrote, among the proletarians, who had no capital. It would disappear among the bourgeoisie when their capital was removed.[38] In the *Fabian Essays*, socialism was not "concerned with questions of sex or family."[39] On the other hand, the insistence of each family on "having a separate home, and on cooking every day a separate series of meals in a separate kitchen" was the cause of "waste and discomfort." That was being ameliorated because "our growing sense of the individual responsibility and individual rights of wives and children seems already to be lessening both the isolation of these groups and their internal coherency." That is, the "internal coherency" of the family was "lessening." This tendency "must go very much further before society can absorb the family life, or the industries of the home be managed socially." But when the time comes, the British will "cease to feel that an Englishman's home should be his castle."[40]

In *The Intelligent Woman's Guide to Socialism and Capitalism*, George Bernard Shaw wrote that socialism was neutral about kinds of marriage, which were conventional and not, as the church thought, "metaphysical affairs." But social-ism would have a "tremendous effect" on marriage and family. No longer would a "married woman [be] . . . a slave chained to a male one (this is a paraphrase of Marx)." Socialism would end this because it would equalize incomes, liberating unhappy wives and children to leave whenever they pleased. Moreover the state would "concern itself with the question of how many people the community is to consist of, and, when a change is desired, at what rate the number should be increased or reduced." Socialism would eliminate the "overpopulation characteristic of capital-ism."[41] Conception, previously a matter for families to figure out, would then be regulated.

The idea seems to be absent in the *Fabian Essays* that mothers and fathers have the job of raising children, and they do that job better when they are together. Rather, the wish for the "aggran-dizement for . . . family" leads men to seek large incomes.[42] The English family is the scene of "selfish isolation." Fabian author Graham Wallas suggested that children must be weaned from this—an apt metaphor.[43] Some of the Fabians seem to think that children can be raised by the society, and therefore family rela-tionships can be weakened or broken. These relationships are, true enough, constraining. Parenting is not easy, and it takes up much of life. Children are affected by the quality of the parent-ing they get, and there is a wide range of qualities. Family is a lot like property in these regards: it seems necessary, and therefore it constitutes a limit on human life. Also it tends to result in wide differences between people. Socialism, its adherents asserted, would lay the ground for breaking these limits and narrowing these differences.

THE NEW FABIANS

Even as socialism triumphed during Churchill's later career, it encountered difficulties, some of them from Churchill himself. One of those problems was the declining popularity of the 1945 Labour government amid the constant friction produced by nationalization and increasing regulation. These did not go smoothly, which was a disappointment to people who thought a new day had dawned and the Socialist program would win welcome for bringing it nearer. Socialist thinkers worked out theories to adapt to these difficulties and seek to overcome them. In 1949 a group led originally by G. D. H. Cole,[44] who opposed most forms of social coercion, met and began to plan a new series of essays. These were published in 1952 under the title *New Fabian Essays*. They show the flexibility of socialism and also its commitment to experimentation led by scientific administration.

The *New Fabian Essays* are on the whole less optimistic and certain than the *Fabian Essays*. Member of Parliament and intellectual R. H. S. Crossman contributed a particularly thoughtful essay, "Towards a Philosophy of Socialism."[45] The chapter title reveals second thoughts about a Socialist project that had exercised such force in British politics and society.

For Crossman, evolution was inevitable but not necessarily

good. Nature was inadequate: it produced "either a wilderness of weeds or an arid patch of ground." It must be cultivated, and it seemed to supply no standard for the cultivation. To Crossman, exploitation and slavery were the "normal state of man." And today, "the enemy of human freedom is the managerial society," of which the Soviet Union was a pertinent example.[46] The Soviet Union exemplified the fact that the "managerial society" was a "threat." The United States represented something similar, with the power of its corporations. By implication, the bureaucratic Socialist state was another "threat."[47]

In some places Crossman sounded like Churchill. Churchill had spoken of the process of "deglutition" by which Parliament would absorb socialism and, he implied, convert it to something better.[48] Crossman seemed an example of that. Moreover he was an interesting man, distinguished in classics at Oxford, distinguished in World War II, and later editor of the *New Statesman*. Like many in the Labour Party and the Socialist movement, he was working for what he considered an exalted cause. And he did it with wit and style. His writings about life as a cabinet minister helped to inspire the popular television series *Yes Minister*, which exhibits the interplay between the bureaucrat and the elected politician.

Some Socialists, Crossman wrote, despair because of the failures of idealism: they follow the example of Buddha. He favored another example: Prometheus, who "did not believe that any law of nature or divine purpose would automatically give freedom and happiness to his fellow men. Neither God nor history was on his side. It was his duty to steal fire, in defiance of law and order, and to prefer eternal agony to the denial of truth."[49] Crossman was determined not to go back; the experiment must continue because it was the only way to overcome the problems that beset mankind. Crossman knew danger and suffering. He had risked everything for his country in wartime. He was prepared to risk everything still.

Churchill thought that the bold experiments of socialism would call forth more experiments, especially when they failed. He even suggested that the Socialists found failure preferable. In 1947, when the Labour Party reigned supreme, Churchill decried the "confiscatory taxation" applied to "wealth to an extent only practiced in Communist countries" and the fact that daily life was "increasingly subjected to ten thousand Regulations and Controls." He continued, "One could almost wonder whether the Government do not reconcile themselves to the economic misfortunes of our country . . . because these misfortunes give the pretext of establishing even more controls and an even larger bureaucracy. They make mistakes which make things worse. As things get worse they claim more power to set them right."[50] That would not be a fair characterization of the intentions of R. H. S. Crossman, at least. But it was true that Crossman and his colleagues were determined to keep on, whatever the setbacks.

Socialists sought transformations of every human institution under conceptions of right or justice that operated on several levels. Most Socialists believed the Socialist state would be ethical, that is, right and good, because it would make a way for all to live equally well, and it would suppress or overcome the selfishness in man. Some of them focused on economic justice and utility: economic results would come out fairly or equally under socialism, and more would be produced, or anyway more of the right kind of thing. Some of them focused on the qualities of character that would develop under socialism: a wider sympathy, a deeper compassion, a stronger sense of community with one's fellows. Many Socialists were evolutionary Christians, and believed that socialism was a divine plan.[51] Socialism had therefore a basis, in the thinking of its founders, in technical economic science, in morality, and in religion. Some early Socialists emphasized one of these elements and others another. They came together in a powerful movement that rose gradually to dominance and held it for a time. In some ways, it holds that dominance still.

The turning of one of the greatest nations and empires in history to new ideas and new institutions, based on revolutionary hopes, does not seem so remarkable today, for most or all the nations of Western Europe and the United States have to various extents embraced these fundamentals and built institutions upon them. The institutions and the thought of modern liberalism are still evolutionary and egalitarian, and now also they are entrenched in structures of government that approach or surpass half the size, in economic value, of the nations they rule. They are dominant now, just as their founders said they would be. They advanced toward this dominance during Churchill's life and against his opposition.

Nor can one regard those who brought socialism and its companion and successor, bureaucratic rule, to Britain as intending evil. In the minds of many or most of those who did the work, it was an act of love and faith. Many or most of them were people of high character and service. They intended to set many things right that were surely wrong, things that deeply moved Churchill. Millions in Britain worked long hours at debilitating work for wages that hardly supported their families. For them any illness threatened hunger or the breakup of the family. Meanwhile others who worked less in better circumstances enjoyed security and comfort or even opulence. Not only did Churchill regard this situation as wrong; he thought it was politically unsustainable. He meant to do something about it.

But he would not abide socialism.

7

"SOME FORM OF GESTAPO"

Churchill stated his opposition to socialism most prominently and dramatically in a speech on June 4, 1945, in the middle of an election campaign at the end of the Second World War:

> I declare to you, from the bottom of my heart, that no Socialist system can be established without a political police. Many of those who are advocating Socialism or voting Socialist today will be horrified at this idea. That is because they are short-sighted, that is because they do not see where their theories are leading them. No Socialist Government conducting the entire life and industry of the country could afford to allow free, sharp, or violently-worded expressions of public discontent. They would have to fall back on some form of Gestapo, no doubt very humanely directed in the first instance.[1]

Even apart from the context, that was a strong thing to say. The context made it stronger, for there were many reasons why

Churchill would not say such a thing. The Socialists had been
Churchill's coalition partners in the struggle against Hitler.
When Churchill became prime minister on May 10, 1940, he
became the leader of a national government that represented
the three major political parties: Conservative, Labour, and
Liberal. The coalition lasted throughout the war. The leader of
the Labour Party, Clement Attlee, was deputy prime minister
for most of the war, and members of his party were senior in the
cabinet and war cabinet. They made major contributions to the
victory, and largely the coalition operated in harmony. Churchill
abated his statements against socialism during the war. Several
senior Labour members had excellent war records from the
Great War. They were distinguished citizens, and Churchill was
personally drawn to several of them. He was grateful for their
service during the war, and when they did good service after
the war—for example, in resisting the aggressions of the Soviet
Union—he was publicly grateful.[2]

Moreover Churchill had sought to continue the coalition
government, which included all the major parties, until Japan
was defeated. After the proclamation of Victory in Europe Day
on May 8, 1945, Churchill proposed to Clement Attlee that the
coalition continue until the defeat of Japan. Attlee and the other
Labour members of the government proposed instead that the
coalition continue until October. Churchill rejected that proposal because he considered that preparing for a set election
would distract from the Japanese war, which might last, many
thought, into 1946.[3]

Nevertheless, Churchill waged the 1945 campaign on the
assertion that his coalition partners, commanding for years the
greatest or next greatest popular support in Britain, were bound

to become like the Nazis, like the dread force that so many died to defeat. They would even employ the worst techniques of the Nazis, right down to the worst of the worst, the Gestapo. People knew by then that the Gestapo tortured and maimed wherever the Nazi writ ran. They knew it was complicit with the SS in managing factories for the slaughter of millions. Churchill said that his comrades in arms in the Labour Party, presenting themselves for a free vote of the British people, would eventually use the same methods that the Gestapo used. His comments sounded extreme. For whatever cause or causes, the Labour Party won the largest majority in the history of modern British politics up to that time. Labour did not merely beat Churchill's Conservatives in the 1945 election; it overwhelmed them.

There is also the fact that Churchill, in his seventieth year, had at last reached the apex of British politics. He was for the first time in his life accepted as a consensus figure, indeed as a national hero. He could take a victory lap as glorious as any known in British political history. If he was after the honor of a united nation, he could have it now beyond the hopes of an Alcibiades or a Coriolanus. The *Times* encouraged him to campaign in the 1945 election as a nonpartisan "world statesman" and then retire.[4] This seemed advice that Churchill might take, given his history. He had always liked the idea of coalitions of the center, and he was never simply a party loyalist—he changed parties twice during his career. Now he had become a generally beloved man. He spoke once during the campaign to an audience in excess of twenty thousand, and although some heckled, the vast majority received him warmly. The best evidence is that around 80 percent of the British people approved of his performance throughout the war.[5]

Churchill could have had something like the moral position of Paul von Hindenburg after the Great War, when Hindenburg was both war hero and chancellor of Germany. But Churchill seems to have thought that to fail to state his views about socialism in the strongest terms would be to emulate Hindenburg in another way: it would be to welcome a doctrine as vile as Nazism into the government of Britain. He replied to the *Times*, "I fight for my corner," and "I leave when the pub closes."[6] Rather than take his victory lap, Churchill attempted to expel socialism from British politics.

The statement had a galvanizing and divisive effect. Churchill was widely criticized, including by members of his family. His wife read the speech in advance and begged him to take out the passage.[7] Historians have judged that what he said was injudicious, a violation of the position he had won for himself but held for the nation.[8] Here Churchill was being held to a different standard, for Labour leader Attlee and others compared some of Churchill's actions to the Nazis, both before and after Churchill gave the speech; they did not win the opprobrium that descended upon Churchill.[9]

Finally, there is the fact that Churchill had certain agreements with the Socialists, some of which had divided him from his fellow Conservatives in the past. It was not for frivolous reasons that he switched parties in 1904 from the Conservatives to the Liberals. Churchill objected to tariffs, the immediate reason for his switch, because he thought they benefited one class over another. Tariffs were the favored policy of the Tory landowners in the nineteenth century, who controlled the House of Lords and much of the House of Commons. Churchill thought that the aristocracy had used these political privileges to line their own pockets, and like the Socialists he thought this wrong. About this he wrote a letter to his mentor Bourke Cockran on Churchill's twentieth-fifth birthday, when he was prisoner in South Africa. He wrote that he regarded the 1900 presidential election in the United States as a struggle against "vast combinations of capital":

> . . . capitalism in the form of Trusts has reached a pitch of power which the old economists never contemplated and which excites my most lively terror. Merchant-princes are all very well, but if I have anything to say to it, their kingdom shall not be of this world. The new century will witness the great war for the existence of the Individual.[10]

The term "merchant princes" had occurred in the *Fabian Essays,* published ten years earlier. The regulation of large corporations or trusts was an object of progressive politics in America at this time and for decades to follow. The Fabians would go further, to public ownership. The young Churchill, in partial agreement with them, thought that "up to a certain point combination has brought us nothing but good: but we seem to have reached a period when it threatens nothing but evil. I do not want to see men buy cheaper food & better clothes at the price of their manhood. Poor but independent is worth something as a motto."[11] He thought the efficiency of these vast combinations would overcome the individual citizen.

Over a quarter century later, in "Mass Effects," Churchill expressed the same apprehension. He feared that mankind was "escaping the control of individuals." He meant great individuals, the "Master Teachers—Thinkers, Discoverers, Commanders." In addition, he meant everyone and anyone. In the new environment of mass effects, human beings could not manage their individual affairs any better than leaders could manage the great wars. Fewer people had a standing of their own. Fewer could—and here Churchill used a favorite phrase that he took from Rudyard Kipling—"live by no man's leave, underneath the law."[12]

"Powerful companies, which in their turn are swallowed by mammoth trusts" are partly responsible for this. They substitute mass production for the "old family business" where the master was in "direct personal touch with his workmen." Now these people are the "salaried officials of great corporations." They lose "in forethought, in initiative, in contrivance, in freedom, and in effective civic status." These are among many "enormous processes of collectivization which are at work among us."[13] Notice the reference to "civic status." Churchill thought that independent people make more effective citizens. He did not like "merchant-princes" any better in 1931, when he wrote "Mass Effects," than he did in 1899 when he wrote to Bourke Cockran.

Churchill also acknowledged implicitly a point favored by many Socialists: perfect equality of opportunity is impossible. In 1945 he said, "The inherent vice of capitalism is the unequal sharing of blessings. The inherent virtue of Socialism is the equal sharing of miseries."[14] In no case could the world be perfected. There are the thousand chances that affect every life. People have or do not have advantages in parenting. They have or do not have strong bodies and good health. They have or do not have quick or curious or imaginative minds. They meet or do not meet significant and worthy people who help them. Whatever arrangements are made to mitigate the different chances people confront, "life will be pretty rough anyhow."[15]

These opinions of Churchill form part of the foundation

upon which socialism rested. Based on these opinions, Socialists asked the obvious question: blessed with progress, with expanding scientific power, with better forms of organization, why should we not attempt to overcome these disadvantages? The human story is a story of change and progress. Why should we not, if we can, come at last into our own? Why should we not make all these things right, or as many of them as we can? Churchill thought this hope impossible and, worse than impossible, wrong. He thought this pursuit of complete or perfect equality, even of opportunity, would produce not equality but inequality, not justice but injustice, not freedom but grinding tyranny.

Churchill did not withdraw his statement about the Socialists and the Gestapo, despite the criticism and despite the defeat he and his party suffered. Instead, he repeated the charge: in 1947 he said that under socialism the "snoopers of 17 different Departments" would eventually be "assisted by a police Gestapo."[16] During the 1950 election, he said that socialism "leads inevitably to communism" and the "sacrifice of personal individual liberties."[17]

Churchill's Gestapo speech and the line of thought it represents are lesser-known but profound examples of Churchill's magnificent stubbornness—or commitment to principle. Churchill was as relentless in resisting socialism as were its supporters in advancing it. He was as clear in opposition to socialism as he was in his opposition to Hitler and Stalin. He refused to serve with Socialists in any cabinet or coalition, except in the middle of World War II. He rejected the doctrine and its political party root and branch, and right from the start, when he was hardly more than a boy. To understand Churchill requires one to understand the reasons behind this speech.

THE GROUND OF CHURCHILL'S OPPOSITION

Churchill said that the Socialists "did not know where their theories were leading them." They were following theories, like the French painters Churchill describes in "Painting as a Pastime," who painted their tree trunks with side-to-side strokes, whereas in nature trees grow up and down. These painters sacrificed truth for their theories.[18] The truth the Socialists sacrificed was also a truth about nature, about the way of things, even about the whole of things. The Socialists, Churchill thought, would spoil something much more precious than a canvas in pursuit of their theories.

One of Churchill's first statements on socialism is in his previously mentioned novel, *Savrola*, published before Churchill's twenty-sixth birthday. In the novel, the beautiful Lucile, wife of the despot, attends a speech by Savrola, her husband's opponent. A man named Karl, notice the *K,* also attends the speech. As Lucile is leaving the hall, she overhears a man say to Karl that Savrola has spoken bravely. Karl replies that Savrola is a "tool to work with," but adds, "we shall need something sharper." After all, Karl asks, "What does he care about a community of goods?" The other man agrees: "[Or] a community of wives." The wife this other man wants, he says, is the president's wife. Overhearing this, Lucile shudders.[19]

The lesson is clear enough. Community of property is a start, but if we are serious about equality, why should some men have beautiful wives, or some women beautiful husbands, and others not? Why should some children have the advantage of caring, intelligent, and well-placed parents and others not? These are not new thoughts: around 392 BC, Aristophanes wrote a play in which Athens passed a law that the young and beautiful could have no relations with each other until the old and ugly were serviced.[20] Nor have these ideas passed into oblivion: the president of France proposed in 2012 to abolish homework on the ground that it is not fair for some children to have help from their families and others not.[21] The family is a source of inequality of both beginnings and results.

Lucile is a symbol for the state of Laurania, the location of the novel. She is married to the despotic ruler, and she is liberated from him when he falls from power. She is courted in the novel not only by Savrola but also by this unnamed Socialist friend of Karl. Lucile is like the state, something precious and necessary. Under the Socialist everything in the state would be the property of all; the distinction between public and private would disappear, and so not only property but also family would be abolished. Eventually Savrola and Lucile join together, and Savrola becomes the head of the state; but she is not everyone's wife, shared among all. Rather she is to share with Savrola, to be a partner, not a property. As head of the kind of state that Savrola favors, he will exercise great power, but limited power, at the sufferance of independent citizens whose lives and livelihood he does not control. The citizens, joined with each other and with their rulers in citizenship, keep their independence in matrimony and property. Lucile, like the state, has three suitors: the despot, the Socialist, and Savrola, the republican leader. They offer very different ways of living for her and for everyone else. These differences would arise in every aspect of life, personal and civic.

This scene in *Savrola* may be a little crude, and Churchill's novel did not lead him to a shining career in fiction. But the points in that dialogue are serious, and Churchill made them again in other places. In his 1908 election address, for example, he said that in this "bad era" the "love of family and wives and children" are "mere weaknesses." This is bad because we must all be "both a collectivist and an individualist." We have "the police, the army, the navy and officials": in regard to them we are collectivists. On the other hand some things are "sacredly individual." Specifically we do not "eat in common," and we do not "ask the ladies to marry us in common."[22]

In this speech Churchill argued that socialism leaves out "human nature." This term nature is of course a big term, and Churchill used it often. It is the word for the whole cosmos, the word for the physical realm in which we live, the word for the way or essence of all things including the human things, and the word for the source of our rights. It is also literally and figuratively a pregnant term, for it comes from the Latin word for birth. One can see how these meanings are connected: from the seed grows the mature being; the mature being becomes distinguished as fully itself when it achieves the essence of its kind; the accumulation of these beings and the relationships among them make up the panoply of nature and the cosmos.

Today we live in a world in which science can change very much, and so our view of nature does not tend to be as fixed as that stated most often by Churchill. Churchill was aware of the potential of modern science, and he understood that socialism made a plausible claim: the human practice of science is the fulfillment of nature. Churchill agreed with this, as far as it went.

Science is a word of different meanings in different times. It comes from the Latin word that means "to know," a specifically human ability. It takes on a meaning in modernity of a different turn. Its object or chief object became in some thinkers not so much to behold and understand nature as to get the management of it. To a certain modern philosopher, the ancients wasted their time building "imagined republics."[23] Better gains can be had by focusing on *doing*, on getting on with the job, on making a place for ourselves in nature. This follows, naturally one might say, from the situation or nature of man. He lives not by his strength or his speed but by his wits, including his ability to make tools. Better tools and better wielding of them are essential to his survival and his prosperity. It is in his nature to innovate, to be a separate cause in nature alongside nature itself and chance. Why not liberate that ability from the chains of nature?

Churchill wrote in "Mass Effects" that only in science are the thrones of eminence occupied, but they are occupied by a "throng" instead of by individuals.[24] Churchill was ready to use and to foster the tools of science. He regarded them as necessary not only to winning modern war, however much he regretted the way they transformed war, but also to assuring the economic survival of Britain.[25]

Also Churchill thought that when the conquest of nature becomes the signal object, the result will be the conquest of man: in the first case the conquest of most men by a few, and in the second case the conquest of man by nature. The first result is easy to forecast. Churchill wrote in his essay "Fifty Years Hence" that we may soon be able to make people to order, to breed them in laboratories. If we can do that, we can make them better and worse, depending upon the jobs we want them to do. Once we begin this—and it is possible now—we will be making people to suit our convenience. Some will be not just ruling but creating others as tools.

The second is also easy to see. If we conquer nature, it cannot provide a standard for what we do or think. We will be left with our own wills and wishes. But the will unguided is nothing more than appetite, and human appetite can be voracious. What is the hallmark of the white ant except that he follows his appetites? By overcoming nature, we surrender ourselves to it.

Churchill did not think these developments mere hypotheticals: He thought they were upon us in his time. He wrote in "Mass Effects" that the Soviet Union had regressed to the society of the white ant. The Soviet Union was not unique, but Churchill thought it only the "extreme form" of the same tendency in all the developed world. The tendency to universal despotism was present everywhere, Churchill thought, specifically in Britain. In 1945, when Churchill said that socialism would bring a Gestapo, he was saying what he had said for decades.

This is the urgent reason that Churchill worked to protect the rights grounded in our nature, our natural rights. What are these rights? One can see in the various aspects of human nature the various rights that Churchill defended.

Decisively our nature is to reason, to live in the presence of the eternal even if we cannot fully grasp it, to see the being of each thing and be able to place it in its category, to be able because of this perception to speak to one another. Because of this we can communicate things both intimate and abstract with others who may be either familiar or unfamiliar to us. In these ways human nature is different in kind from the other natures we see around us. Having the capacity to do these things as our essence, we have the right to do them. The fundamental liberties of the human being are connected to his rational soul. Whenever Churchill lists the attributes of just government, he always includes the rights of speech, prayer, assembly, and voting that are essentially human. In his strongest condemnations of Nazism, communism, and socialism, he points to their real or alleged violations of these rights.

In other ways human nature is like the natures of other creatures, and in some of those ways it has the same attributes as the others in greater degree. Our nature is to have a long childhood and adolescence, to need our parents for longer and in different ways than other creatures, and thus to be bound to each other in biology more closely than other creatures. Our needs for one another are in these ways deeper than for other creatures. We are or have been drawn close together most profoundly by the fact that we can talk, but also because of these needs for one another that operate through biology.

Like other animals we need material things, a lot of them and constantly. We must get our living from the earth, and if we do not get it, we will die. We have the means to get our living in our bodies and our souls; each of us has these tools, and each of us will die if we do not use them. Nature is apparent in these interactions between the human being and the physical environment, just as it is apparent in the family relationships that characterize human begetting and growth. Churchill saw these interactions, and he thought them fundamental and not transient. In them is found both the importance of the family and the rights of property.

Yet again our nature is to have discretion over these biological matters. We are not required to marry or reproduce; we do not have to care for our children. We do not even have to exercise energy in providing for ourselves. Still we are fashioned to do so, and at least in the older view of nature we will fail as a species to prosper or even to survive without doing so. Our nature is to find a standard in nature, and also it is to be free to disregard that standard—at a cost.

Churchill thought nature was constant. In 1948, he wrote that he knew of "nothing which has occurred to alter or weaken the justice, wisdom, valor, and prudence upon which our ancestors acted." He knew of nothing "that has happened to human nature which in the slightest degree alters the validity of their conclusions." He was speaking of foreign policy here, but he makes the point in the most general terms: he knew of no "military, political, economic or scientific fact which makes me feel that we might not, or cannot, march along the same road."[26] In 1949, Churchill said that you may "chase Nature away, and she returns at the gallop."[27] In this way Churchill harkened to the conception of nature that prevailed in thought for much of human history.

Churchill's differences with socialism proceed from this fundamental difference about nature. He thought that the equality for which socialism aimed was unnatural. He thought that it could not be achieved except by suppressing nature, including human nature, which would require the suppression of humans. He thought that because of this fundamental difference, socialism would result in impoverishment in economics, corruption in personal character, and despotism in politics. He thought that by nationalizing these areas of private life in which most human beings do their most urgent and fulfilling tasks, socialism would truncate the lives of ordinary people. For that reason he regarded socialism as dehumanizing. Aware of and asserting the good intentions of most in the Socialist movement, Churchill argued that their effects, ultimately, would be like the effects of Hitler and Stalin, at least if they stuck to their principles to the last.

THE SOCIAL AND ETHICAL CASE FOR FREE MARKETS

Churchill disputed the economic claims of the Fabians. He thought that economic prosperity proceeded from sources inside each human being, sources that constitute a property of each. The protection of that property enables not only the economy but also the individual to flourish. Socialism would stifle "the spirit of individual daring and initiative," the "wonderful, buoyant and apparently inexhaustible fund of personal energy, thrift and contrivance," which was the chief advantage of the capitalist system. To abandon that would require "in all logic" that one go to the "other extreme and weave the whole industry of the country into one vast structure under State planning." Churchill was against that because "it would be highly infertile, and the mass of the people would be much worse off under an all-embracing bureaucracy."[28] Capitalism, Churchill thought, gave scope for the exercise of the economic excellences. The whole society would benefit. Socialism, on the other hand, lay "down the law that the pace of our advancing social army must be the pace of the slowest and the weakest man."[29]

Churchill thought that industry was good for the nation in several respects and that it reflected and reinforced personal excellence. In an outline for a book, never written, to be entitled *The Creed of Failure*, Churchill summarized Chapter IV, "Capital in Harness," as follows: "Showing how under the present system of high taxation capital is fully harnessed to the service of the nation." He continued:

How businesses are founded, often one on top of the ruins of another; when failure occurs, it is borne by the individual, but success is shared through taxation with the State; on the impossibility of substituting state action for individual enterprise; the risk factor; capital. It is a form of control—the most tolerable and flexible; the only means of automatically approximating the value of individual services.[30]

When Churchill wrote this in 1929, he either had completed or was just about to complete his service of more than four years as chancellor of the exchequer. As chancellor, Churchill was a tax cutter. When he began in 1924, the tax on incomes of £2,000 or below was 22.5 percent. When he finished in 1929 the rate was 20 percent. In 1929, tax rates rose in regular increments as incomes rose; the amount of income above £30,000 was taxed at the peak rate of 50 percent, down from 52.5 percent in 1924.[31] These rates would rise in subsequent years under war and socialism until the tax rate on the highest incomes was 97 percent. They would fall again in later years, especially under Margaret Thatcher, until in 2013 the ordinary income tax rate was 20 percent, and the top rate was 45 percent.[32]

Churchill as chancellor also held the line on expenditures. He fought hard against increases in defense spending, and he supported expansion of social services.[33] Total government expenditures were about the same when he left the office as when he began. During Churchill's second premiership (1951–55), public-sector expenditure fell as a percentage of gross domestic product from 40.2 percent when he took office to 36.3 percent. Current expenditures, those raised and spent in a single year, fell from 32.1 to 29.2 percent of the economy over the same period.[34]

Churchill believed in economy in government. The size of the state was a factor that occupied his thoughts, and he often said that the liberal state requires that most of the money and most of the discretion be in the hands of the people.[35]

Churchill thought that private property united rather than divided people, at least under the right circumstances. These circumstances included a social safety net to help those in need, about which more later, and the prevention of monopoly. The latter reveals that socialism, for all the evil that Churchill saw in it, was not the only manifestation of that evil. He feared concentrations of power in the private as well as the public sector.

When these circumstances prevailed, property rights generated harmony in the society and were therefore not the image but the opposite of war. In this view Churchill again followed Bourke Cockran, who said in 1903, "[Given that the] essential object of war [is] to to injure your neighbor, while the essential object of commerce is to serve him, it surely ought to be self-evident that the terms applicable to the one must become ludicrously misleading when applied to the other." Churchill said effectively the same thing a few months later: "[C]ommerce is utterly different from war, so that the ideas and the phraseology of the one should never be applied to the other; for in war both sides lose whoever wins the victory, but the transactions of trade, like the quality of mercy, are twice blessed, and confer a benefit on both parties."[36]

Limited government and an approximate equal justice were possible, Churchill thought, for the same reason peace among nations was possible. If it was true that the prosperity of one nation did not necessitate the poverty of another, the basis existed for nations to live in amity. Similarly, if the prosperity of one citizen did not mean the impoverishment of another, if both gained their prosperity by serving one another, then the basis for good relations between them was laid in nature itself.

Churchill believed that was especially true for the poor, whose "only chance . . . of enjoying the bounties of nature and science" was an "effective and scientific commercial development." Churchill feared that high taxation of the few would make Britain "not a good country for capital," thereby destroying any chance for the defense of the country, for the improvement of the social safety net, and for the economic growth that alone can ensure a place for all.[37]

Where socialism would concentrate property, Churchill would distribute it. He argued that the "ownership" the people had in state-controlled industries was like the ownership the citizen had in a battleship. A portly gentleman, Churchill related, demanded to board a battleship, and when the sentry challenged him, he said that he was entitled to come on board because he was one of the proprietors. He was not admitted. Churchill said that was a very different situation from "households [in which people] have possessions which they prize and cherish because they are their own, or even a house and garden of their own . . . the result of forethought and self-denial which will be a help in old age or infirmity, or after their death for those they love and leave behind."[38]

Churchill wanted such property to be possessed by expanding millions, which would produce in them the "spirit of individual independence." People possessed of that independence would turn from the "Socialist delusion that one ought to be proud of being totally dependent on the state."[39] This line of thought would be repeated by Churchill's immediate successors. Harold Macmillan, whom Churchill placed in charge of replacing bombed-out housing in the 1951 Conservative administration, pledged as prime minister to see that "as many as possible get a chance to own their own house."[40] Macmillan authorized local authorities to sell off council houses (houses publicly owned and subsidized) to those who lived in them. Margaret Thatcher would later praise this policy and make it a cornerstone of her social welfare plans.[41]

Adjustments to property, Churchill believed, would produce opportunity and wealth in economics, stability and goodwill in politics. Socialism would by contrast reverse the Christian teaching of goodwill. There were strains of socialism in the "Christian era," he admitted, but that was based on the principle "all mine is yours." In 1908, he said the socialism of Victor Grayson, a Socialist member of Parliament, was based on the idea that "all yours is mine." That principle, Churchill said, would breed not heaven on earth, but "spite and jealousy."[42]

THE POLITICAL CASE: THE SOCIALIST ARISTOCRACY

These objections to socialism are fundamental, and they gave rise in Churchill to political objections equally fundamental. They were similar to his opposition to the rule of aristocrats of birth. The grandson of a duke, Churchill argued that both aristocracy and socialism distorted the principle of equality. He favored the monarchy, but only with the understanding that it should rule and not reign.[43] He favored the House of Lords, but insofar as it was a hereditary body, he believed it should be empowered only to comment or delay, not to obstruct the policy of the government as it was adopted in the popular branch, the House of Commons. He said: "'All men are born equal,' says the

American Declaration of Independence. 'All men shall be kept equal,' say the British Socialist party.'[44] But of course they could not be kept equal: nature will return at the gallop. To abandon that standard was to diminish the status of the human being.

Churchill argued that socialism would give rise to a new aristocracy, a term of which he understood the literal meaning, "rule of the best." The British aristocracy was not that, he believed, but rather the rule of only the best born. In response to a statement by Conservative peer Lord Curzon, to the effect that all civilization is the work of aristocracies, Churchill said,

> There was not a duke, not an earl, not a marquis, not a viscount in Oldham who did not feel that a compliment had been paid to him. What does Lord Curzon mean by aristocracy? It is quite clear from the argument of his speech that he did not mean Nature's aristocracy, by which I mean the best and most gifted beings in each generation in each country, the wisest, the bravest, the most generous, the most skillful, the most beautiful, the strongest, and the most active. If he had meant that I think we should probably agree with him. Democracy properly understood means the association of all through the leadership of the best.[45]

In Churchill's understanding of equality, no one is born to rule another. Democracy is preferable because it opens the way for those of talent, the true aristocracy, to rise. This is a test, Churchill implied, that democracy must pass. The hereditary aristocracy can pass down its titles and its property, but it cannot pass down high character and intelligence, anyway not perfectly, sometimes hardly at all.

If some are appointed to rule by birth, others not so wellborn and having better ability are thwarted. Socialism would have the same effect: it would create an aristocracy on other grounds. A state that attempts to equalize things that are not inherently equal will be at war with human excellence. Some people are in fact wiser, braver, more generous, more skillful, more beautiful, stronger, and more active than others. This does not make them different in their rights, if those rights are defined as the right to employ their abilities and gain or lose by their efforts. Both the equality of rights and the differences of human makeup are natural phenomena, and they must be accorded their sway.

The attempt to equalize unequal things would, Churchill argued, produce resistance, which in turn would call forth from socialism more vigorous laws. This cycle would continue until all the rights of the people were gone. We will see in a later chapter that he thought this battle would be waged on behalf of socialism by a bureaucracy, "no longer civil" and "no longer servants."[46]

EDUCATION

How then would Churchill preserve the idea of nature that was being supplanted by the obvious and even necessary triumphs of science? The answer to that was the chief work of his life, outside of war. It begins with the fact that Churchill admitted, and asked the people to admit, that whatever happened, their lives would still be human lives, and therefore filled with struggle. As we have quoted him saying: "Life will be pretty rough, anyhow."[47] In their struggles people exercise their humanity, and they are entitled to them.

Along with these struggles came the relief of what Churchill called "at once the safeguard and the glory of mankind, that they are easy to lead and hard to drive."[48] Humanity is given to freedom, and the strongest protection of that freedom is to be found in a surprising place. In "Fifty Years Hence," a few pages after he has forecast the breeding of human beings for specific qualities, Churchill describes a future state in which people can live as long as they want, enjoy pleasures and sympathies "incomparably wider than our own," and travel anywhere among the planets. "But what was the good of all that to them?" Churchill asks. How can those things answer the "simple question which man has asked since the earliest dawn of reason—'Why are we here? What is the purpose of life?'"[49] Because of the power of these questions, no "material progress" can "bring comfort" to the human soul. And this fact "gives the best hope that all will be well." No matter what happens, our "hearts will ache . . . if [we] have not a vision above material things." Also Churchill wrote in this essay that it is vital that "moral philosophy and spiritual conceptions of men and nations should hold their own amid these formidable scientific evolutions."[50]

Hardly anything about Churchill is more indicative of his outlook than his views of education. He agreed with most everybody in British politics that the state should supply an excellent system of free schools for every citizen or subject of the realm. He favored this while still believing that the "care and education of children is essentially an individual matter."[51] He also had an elevated idea of what people needed to study. Education, he said at the University of Bristol, requires a "detachment from material affairs."[52] One does not discover in Churchill the idea, common today, that education must address the young as factors of production, the purpose being to suit them to a job. In 1943 he expressed hope that British education would become "broader and more liberal" after the war, because "all wisdom is not new wisdom." Then he quoted Benjamin Disraeli: "[N]ations are governed by force or by tradition," and therefore "we must not forget the glories of the past, nor how many battles we have fought for the rights of the individual and for human freedom."[53]

In 1946, a few days before speaking at Fulton, Churchill spoke briefly at the University of Miami. He put in a word for the "late starters" in education, such as himself. He had written in *My Early Life* that it was not until his twenty-second year that the desire for learning came upon him. He proceeded to read many classic books, which he valued ever after. Of the servicemen returning from the war, many of whom would be late starters, he proposed that they gain similar knowledge. He said,

> This is an age of machinery and specialization but I hope, nonetheless—indeed all the more—that the purely vocational aspect of university study will not be allowed to dominate or monopolize. . . . Engines were made for men, not men for engines. . . . Knowledge of the past is the only foundation we have from which to peer into and try to measure the future. Expert knowledge, however indispensable, is no substitute for a generous and comprehending outlook upon the human story with all its sadness and with all its unquenchable hope.[54]

Churchill was all for technical education, but he also made plain that it produced an inferior kind of knowledge. Speaking again of "late starters," he sent a letter of protest to the minister of education in his second administration. She was proposing reductions in the budget for adult education. Churchill wrote,

> There is perhaps no branch of our vast educational system which should more attract within its particular sphere the aid and encouragement of the State than adult education. How many must there be in Britain, after the disturbance of two destructive wars, who thirst in later life to learn about the humanities, the history of their country, the philosophies of the human race, and the arts and letters which sustain and are borne forward by the ever-conquering English language? This ranks in my opinion far above science and technical instruction, which are well sustained and not without their rewards in our present system. The mental and moral out-look of free men studying the past with free minds in order to discern the future demands the highest measures which our hard-pressed finances can sustain.[55]

Churchill was recommending for his fellow citizens the kind of education he provided for himself. The liberally educated address themselves to questions that our souls ache to answer. They tell us the story of the past, the only story we have available to learn. They instruct us in both what and how to choose, and they teach us to measure the circumstances around us in light of the lessons of those who came before.

Churchill thought that people who bear the heavy responsibilities of family, of work, of citizenship ought to be possessed of high knowledge, including knowledge of the past. He did not think the pursuit of such knowledge should wait on some future state in which human concerns were alleviated by revolutionary systems. He thought that here and now, amidst our troubles, is the time to know the best things: the story of unquenchable hope and sadness that is the human story. Human achievement is made on the basis of this hope amidst this sadness.

Sidney Webb wrote that the "perfect and fitting development of each individual" is not the cultivation "of his own personality," but the "filling . . . of his humble function in the great social machine."[56] Churchill would not give the citizens a humble function in any machine. They would rather govern the machine, and they would be encouraged to learn what must be known to do that well.

8

BUREAUCRACY

Churchill said that the Socialist Party could not realize its ultimate aim without some form of Gestapo. The Gestapo, the secret
police, is itself an element of a form of government. This form
fits with a certain purpose of government: to compel the people
to live in a way, and ultimately to *be* in a way, that they were not
then and would not choose. Churchill said that the use of such a
secret police would only come ultimately, that it was not intended
by the existing Socialists, but that they intended an alteration
of the form of the government. They would change, he argued,
not only to what end but also *how* the British government would
operate. Different people would staff the government with a different outlook on their jobs. And there would be more of those
people filling more of those jobs.

The early Socialists included many kinds of people with
many interests. They sought to work their will in all their fields
and with all the peaceful tools available to them. In the end,
they would make a political revolution. They would contrive by

persuasion to win a majority in the House of Commons. Then they would change the law, next they would change the institutions through which law is executed, and by this means they would change the society.

Churchill thought that this change in the number and purpose of the administrative cadre was the key to the Socialist revolution. In his election speech in June 1945, he said,

[A] Socialist Government conducting the entire life and industry of the country . . . would gather all the power to the supreme party and the party leaders, rising like stately pinnacles above their vast bureaucracies of Civil servants, no longer servants and no longer civil. And where would the ordinary simple folk—the common people, as they like to call them in America—where would they be, once this mighty organism had got them in its grip?[1]

Here Churchill invents one of his best phrases: "no longer servants and no longer civil." He thought that civil servants would be transformed into uncivil rulers by a transformation in the principles underlying government. If history is the science by which we understand the development and even the making of mankind, and if that science can tell us how to shape our future and therefore ourselves, then those who know that science must be placed in control.

For that reason Churchill did not understand socialism mainly as a class movement, however it understood itself. In 1924 he said that the political division was no longer based on class. Socialists represented "every class." The Conservative Party represented "the largest mass of British democracy" in the nation.

The fight no longer was between "the few and the many, between privilege and democracy, between aristocracy and the rest. All these issues have long ago been settled."[2] Rather, politics were dominated by an argument between theories. In 1933 he said,

> The worst difficulties from which we suffer do not come from without. They come from within. They do not come from the cottages of the wage-earners. They come from a peculiar type of brainy people always found in our country, who, if they add something to its culture, take much from its strength.
>
> Our difficulties come from the mood of unwarrantable self-abasement into which we have been cast by a powerful section of our own intellectuals. They come from the acceptance of defeatist doctrines by a large proportion of our politicians. But what have they to offer but a vague internationalism, a squalid materialism, and the promise of impossible Utopias?[3]

CHURCHILL AND EXPERTS

The problem, Churchill thought, was seated in intellectualism and expertise, yet he did not reject either thinking or expertise out of hand. Early in the Great Depression, Churchill gave the Romanes Lecture in Oxford. He used the occasion to make a sweeping proposal to appoint economists and other advisors on economics to an elevated place in the government. He proposed to create an "Economic sub-Parliament" to make proposals for economic policy.[4] Troubled and puzzled by the Great Depression and the questions revolving around the gold standard, he thought that the solution to the "problem of prosperity amidst dearth" might be merely technical, in the way that the questions whether radar would work and the atomic bomb would explode were technical questions. In this lecture he was thinking broadly: "Once I have assumed the academic panoply, I present myself before you as a Seeker after Truth."[5] Churchill went to Oxford to speculate, and he concluded by appealing to one of the first and most distinguished universities for help.

The economic problem, Churchill said, presented puzzles that Parliament was incapable of addressing. The puzzles challenged the received wisdom about economic policy: free trade, sound money, good credit, and low taxation. Those things did not seem to be working. Churchill called for them not to be discarded but to be built upon. This would involve some reconsideration.

Churchill's analysis was based on a simple statement of fact. The Great Depression was in many ways a turning point in politics and in economics. Its causes remain controversial among economists as much as among politicians and citizens. Milton Friedman won a Nobel Prize in 1976 for, among other things, explaining the Great Depression as a failure of monetary policy leading to deflation. His explanation gives some color to Churchill's doubts about the return to the gold standard and condemns the decision even as it supports Churchill's instincts.[6] Friedman's views, like those of everyone else, are disputed by credentialed authorities. John Maynard Keynes, a distinguished economist whom Churchill knew, explained the Great Depression and the ways to prevent its coming again in very different ways from Friedman.

The economic problem at the root of the Great Depression cannot be solved, Churchill said, by an "expression . . . of the national will," just as "you cannot cure cancer by majority."[7] Can one cure the economy through a team of researchers? Is the ailment of the economy parallel to this case of cancer? There are limits to the experiments that cancer researchers may perform upon humans and even upon animals. What are the limits that should be placed on economic experiments, which affect property that in turn affects the body? It seems the same organism is affected in cancer and in economic experiments. Who is to decide what experiments may be done? If a group of researchers was given the force to conduct experiments on the economy, it would have supremacy. How would one control a group with the power to control the economy? Churchill regarded this question as both fundamental and essentially political.

The scientific method functions precisely to try a lot of things under strict procedures and careful observation to see what works. Churchill said that it was urgent to know the answer to the question raised by the Depression: "The nation is not interested in politics, it is interested in economics."[8] Well, why not let the people who have the know-how work on it? And because those people must work by trial and error, why not let them experiment on the whole society until they get it right? That was precisely what Socialists proposed: let us try things until we get it right; let us continue to try things so long as circumstances evolve, which endlessly they do. In the Romanes Lecture, Churchill himself was proposing a form of doing that.

Churchill also proposed to divide the political from the economic questions: Parliament would appoint an "Economic sub-Parliament," made up mainly of experts; Parliament would teach them how to debate and argue in parliamentary form; and then the new sub-Parliament would proceed to do just that. If it were able to reach a consensus, it would submit that consensus to

Parliament. The conclusion or consensus by the Economic sub-Parliament would have no "legal force."[9] One would find out in the House of Commons if a political consensus could be reached upon its recommendations.

In this sense, the Romanes speech was a call for help. It concluded: "Let this University bear her part in raising our economic thought to the height of the situation with which we are confronted, and thereafter in enforcing action, without which such thought is vain."[10] Notice the use of "enforcing." The university would help with that, apparently, after Parliament decided.

Those proposals did not come to anything, as many of Churchill's constitutional plans did not. On the other hand, they indicated something about Churchill, and they reinforced the mold. Expert opinion was important to Churchill, but he also regarded expertise beneath the questions properly political. Generals, medical researchers, economists, and such have vital knowledge, and they can do wonders. But they know no more about the questions of politics, the questions proper to the House of Commons, than anyone else. Churchill said, "I decline to admit there are any experts in democracy in this House. We are all elected on equal terms and have a right to equal credit and consideration. We are elected on the widest franchise obtaining in any country in the world, and it is our business to see that the people's rights are not derogated from or prejudiced in any respect."[11]

For Churchill, authority comes from the people, and those in government who understand where authority comes from exercise it best. Politics depends ultimately upon knowledge not of means but of ends, and those who exercise authority in government must contemplate ends. The people, the ultimate

rulers of themselves, require then a different kind of learning than the "purely vocational." Expertise, as we have noted
Churchill saying, is "no substitute for a generous and compre-
hending outlook upon the human story with all its sadness and
with all its unquenchable hope."[12] The questions that have to do
with ends, and with means whenever they are large enough to
alter or compromise ends, are available to all who can think.
Those who live under laws have a right to their say about how
the laws are made and about their content. Churchill objected
that socialism attempts to reduce politics to the sciences, if they
exist, of economic distribution and of social management. To
Churchill, those questions resolve ultimately to the question
of justice and injustice in the full. There is no merely scientific
or technical knowledge of those questions. It is worth repeating that in his strongest statements against socialism, he made
clear that overcoming consent of the governed was not the intention of Socialists. He thought their measures would lead there
nonetheless.

Churchill intended to get the merely technical questions out
of Parliament, out of the place where essentially political questions, questions essentially connected to the common sense and
the moral sense, could be debated in public view.

Of course Churchill relied upon experts all the time.
Professor Frederick Lindemann, whom he elevated to the
peerage as Viscount Cherwell (named for the river that runs
through Oxford, where Lindemann was a physics professor), was
Churchill's adviser for two decades. Beginning a few weeks after
the outbreak of the Great War, Churchill helped to inspire and
sustain the experiments that led to the invention of the tank, but
he did not design it himself: naval engineer Eustace Tennyson

d'Eyncourt and other engineers and military officers did that. Expertise is indispensable.

The need for expertise and technical knowledge is especially acute in war, and it raises the same question as in peace: if the economist knows better, why should he not then rule? If the general knows better, why should he not then rule? Yet in Churchill's opinion experts were not to rule by authority of their expertise. With regard to a commission that looked into the Dardanelles campaign he wrote, "The principle which the Commission lays down about the experts is one of great value. It is that you must always overrule an expert when he is wrong."[13] And in another place: "It was a principle of our Constitution not to employ experts, whether business men or military men, in the highest affairs of State."[14] The highest political questions are not questions to be answered by experts or to be settled by application of the scientific method.

EXPERTISE AND BUREAUCRATIC ARISTOCRATS

Socialism, Churchill thought, must necessarily operate through these experts, trained in public administration, pursuing aims that were, he believed, antithetical to the principles of equal rights and freedom: "Socialism knows that it can only operate through an agency of bureaucracy under the direction of an autocratic sect."[15] This problem of an autocratic sect or a bureaucracy seemed to Churchill fundamental.

Labour rule in the period 1945–51 provided Churchill for the first time with the chance to observe the actual conduct of Socialist administration. He then proceeded to conduct the opposition with the experience of one accustomed to the wilderness. He argued that the reliance upon technical experts inherent in socialism would cost vast sums, would supplant parliamentary government, and would become the enemy of the people.

Churchill thought this expertise would take the form of administrative bureaucracy and was never the friend of parliamentary rule. When he was twenty-one, he objected to taxes imposed on the equipment of British troops in India as a "detestable fruit of bureaucracy."[16] When he was twenty-three, he opined that the courage and wisdom required to solve the problems of India were "rarely possessed by a bureaucracy."[17] At the outbreak of the Great War he described it as a conflict with the "highly efficient imperialist bureaucracy and military organization of Prussia."[18] The Communist system duplicated and exacerbated this form as it was "based on confiscation, bureaucracy and tyranny."[19]

Socialism in Britain would have this same attribute, according to Churchill. Its bureaucracy would have control of property, and therefore "no one could stand against it for a moment." Anyone could be "starved in a moment by the simple order of the Government withdrawing his ration tickets." This was worse than the tsar, the kaiser, or any "Oriental potentate."[20]

The people who work in the civil service, Churchill thought, were a source of stability and constitutionalism in the state when they were organized in the right way, when their powers were within the scope of the Constitution, and when they were not too numerous.[21] On the other hand, members of the civil service were people, too, given to the same partisanship and self-interest as others.[22] When they did not meet the conditions necessary, they interfered with private work, made the economy less efficient, and threatened to remove themselves from popular control. The bureaucracy was sealed off from the pressures for success that faced private enterprises, which must "work on small margins." Bureaucrats were secure in their jobs as long as they "attended at their offices from ten to four in respectable condition."[23]

Their manner of rule, including the way they conveyed information, was impenetrable, "a kind of vague palimpsest of jargon and officialese, with no breadth, no theme and, above all, no facts."[24] They multiplied rules to the point that they could not be read or followed: "If you make 10,000 regulations you destroy all respect for the law. As Burke said . . . 'Those who make professions above the ordinary customs of society, will often be found in practice to fall far below them.'"[25]

When the Labour Party took power in 1945, it launched an aggressive campaign of nationalization. Eventually eight major industries became publicly owned and managed. Churchill charged that Labour had hired 500,000, in another place 650,000, new government officials.[26] The expenditure was enormous, and it made industry less efficient, so the cost must be paid twice.

In their plan to concentrate control, Churchill said Socialists were like the aristocrats of old. In 1946 he told the Conservative Party conference: "We do not wish the people of this ancient island reduced to a mass of State-directed proletarians, thrown hither and thither, housed here and there, by an aristocracy of privileged officials or privileged Party, sectarian or Trade Union bosses."[27]

Churchill thought that the Socialist administration would come to act as the British aristocracy had acted: in its own interest. The members of the aristocracy were mainly landowners, and with their control of the House of Lords and their extensive control of the House of Commons, they maintained taxes on the importation of foodstuffs. That was a transfer of wealth from the poor to the rich. In the nineteenth and early twentieth centuries the ability of the British aristocracy to act in this way was eliminated in a series of steps, some of the later of which were partly accomplished by Winston Churchill. He believed that the remedy for this kind of aristocratic misrule was to enable the governed to consent to the government over them. The rich old families of England could not transfer wealth from the majority to themselves if they had to ask permission first.

Arguing that the Socialist administration would become aristocratic, in the sense of elites who rule of their own authority and not by consent, Churchill saw a populist basis for attacking socialism. This basis would be strengthened, the economy made more productive, and people more independent if property ownership were more widely spread. In the 1950 and 1951 general elections, he waged a campaign for a "property-owning democracy."[28] This theme echoed among Conservative leaders following Churchill, including his immediate successor, Anthony Eden, and Harold Macmillan.

POWER OF THE EXECUTIVE GOVERNMENT

Churchill had long feared the "growing power of the Executive Government."[29] At the outset of his career he fought hard against tariffs, which he never liked even when he endorsed them during the Great Depression.[30] He thought they pitted class against class and concentrated power in government. If the government decided which imported items were to be subject to tariffs and which were not, the "touts of protected industries" would besiege the government.[31] The House of Commons would spend its time debating details. The measures it passed would not be like the acts of Parliament of former days, large pieces of legislation concerning matters of policy and principle. They would be "ukases" (edicts) coming from the great executive departments.[32] If the acts of the government had this character, the House of Commons and the people would be excluded effectively from the making of the law. Experts, not elected, would be the drivers of policy. Bureaucracy under socialism would be worst of all because the all-powerful state would enter "into the smallest detail of the life and conduct of the individual."[33]

Churchill thought that the depreciation of common sense led socialism and its bureaucratic methods to look down on the people it governed. In 1950 he seized upon a statement by a Labour minister to make the point:

> Mr. Douglas Jay has said: "Housewives as a whole cannot be trusted to buy all the right things, where nutrition and health are concerned. This is really no more than an extension of the principle according to which the housewife herself would not trust a child to select the week's purchases. For in the case of nutrition and health, just as in the case of education, the gentleman in Whitehall really does know better what is good for the people than the people know themselves."[34]

Churchill asked, "[W]as there ever a period in the history of this island when such a piece of impertinence could have been spread about by a Minister?" It was not merely that, in the opinion of Mr. Jay, the mothers were to the government as the children were to their mothers. In the opinion of Mr. Jay, the mothers had no more knowledge than had the children what is best to eat. The mothers and the children stood in the same relation to the government. George Bernard Shaw said that socialism would liberate mothers and children from their slavery to fathers. Churchill thought the Socialist state would function like a nanny, except with the power of law at its back, something greater than the power of a father in a patriarchy.

This new kind of government, Churchill believed, changed the status of the individual in nature and in politics. In nature, mothers and fathers have the duty to care for their children, an act of love performed without compensation for two decades or more. Every child needs this care and suffers when he or she does not receive it. It is no mere truism to say that charity begins at home. The mothers and fathers who undertake this charity exercise, within their realm, a set of responsibilities that are large and fateful. When they make their livings and raise their children, they guide their families to the living of fully human lives. If their service can be reduced to an expertise available only to those with professional training, the lives of all those lacking that training are demoted or diminished. Churchill thought it not an elevation but a diminishment of people to subject them to the rigors of administrative progress.

THE ENEMY OF PARLIAMENTARY RULE

As noted above, in 1929 Churchill outlined a book on socialism, never written, entitled *The Creed of Failure*. His summary of chapter III of that book, "Government by Parliament," reads: "About the value and limitations of Parliaments; England their cradle and their citadel; Socialism fatal to Parliamentary system; Reaction against Parliaments; Party organization and Parliament; Effect of the extended franchise; Influence of women."[35]

Notice "Socialism fatal to Parliamentary system." Churchill did not write the book, but he addressed this theme many times. In 1945 he said: "[T]he violent imposition of the socialistic system, such as has now emerged as a demand from the extreme and potentially dominant forces of the Socialist Party, would involve the restriction of Parliamentary Government as we have known it, and the denial of the rights of effectual opposition as hitherto practiced in this country."[36] There was some evidence for this accusation in a statement by Labour politician Stafford Cripps, with whom Churchill served in government during the war, and with whom he often quarreled. Cripps had written in 1934 that parliamentary democracy "in the form in which we know it, is the outcome of the Liberal movement of the nineteenth century, and is not an eternal verity, nor is it even in its present form a useful machine for achieving changes such as we envisage." Further, "We must use the present democratic machinery to achieve power, and when that power is achieved, we must rapidly adapt the machinery of democracy to the needs of our changing society." Further, "The mechanism of [emergency powers granted to Parliament] is not a matter of submission to the electorate, that is a matter for the experts. We want to get the verdict of the nation on the broad points and not on the detail, and we must be in a position to demonstrate clearly after that verdict is given how far it amounts to an imperative mandate for action."[37] Cripps's plans would be based upon the consent of the governed, but they would not follow the parliamentary model.

In Churchill's view, the House of Commons was the heart

of the British constitutional system, and it was not compatible with the centralized and bureaucratic form. He accused the Labour Party of disrupting the work of the Commons. He had made the same accusations against Neville Chamberlain in the 1930s, when he complained that sufficient time was not given for the Commons to debate fully dominion status for India and appeasement of Germany.[38]

Churchill believed and argued that the Socialist government would eventually become the enemy of the people, as the Soviet government became. The Socialist bureaucracy would become an aristocracy, but without the limits inherent in the old aristocracy, defined by birth or lineage and necessarily small in number. The courses of action open to the new aristocracy would be unbounded: how many industries were to be nationalized, how perfectly incomes were to be equalized, how extensive were to be regulations on private life—all of that was to be decided along the way.

In the end, Churchill argued, the worst effects would be on ordinary people. A few months after the 1945 election he said, "It seems impossible to escape the fact that events are moving and will move towards the issue—'The People versus the Socialists.'"[39] Another time he said the people were being reduced to "State-directed proletarians" under an "aristocracy of privileged officials or privileged Party, sectarian or Trade Union bosses."[40] Another time he said that "No Government in time of peace has ever had such arbitrary power over the lives and actions of the British people. . . . No Government has ever combined so passionate a lust for power with such incurable impotence in its exercise."[41] Churchill used the continuation of rationing as proof that the Labour Party was determined to control the people, their consumption, and their lives generally:

177

Look at the restrictions and repressions on every form of enterprise and recovery. Look at the ever-growing bureaucracy of officials quartered permanently on the public. Let us look at Food. The German U-boats in their worst endeavor never made bread-rationing necessary in war. It took a Socialist Government and Socialist planners to fasten it on us in time of peace when the seas are open and the world harvests good. At no time in the two world wars have our people had so little bread, meal, butter, cheese and fruit to eat.[42]

Churchill argued that the Socialist government was artful in deploying its authority to discourage opposition. When the Labour government announced its plan in 1950 to nationalize the steel industry, Churchill remarked, "All this [the steel industry] is to be thrown into disorder not because the Government wants more *steel* but because they want more *power*. Should we be sustained by the electorate we shall repeal the Steel Nationalization Act before it comes into operation." Then he quoted from the Labour election manifesto, which held that the "'Government will be empowered to start new competitive public enterprises in appropriate circumstances.'" The government could use taxpayer money to compete in trade rivalry with any private business it disliked, to ruin any private undertaking in the country. All would feel the need, he said, to "obey their wishes."[43]

That would affect more people than those who owned businesses. Wage earners in state-run enterprises would have a stronger employer than those in private industry:

Now under our present democratic system the wage-earner can of course appeal to his trade union, and also the sacred right of collective bargaining, largely promoted in bygone days by the Conservative Party, comes into play. Then there is Parliament, while it is free, in which the behavior of all employers of labor, either generally or in individual cases, can be brought out and discussed in the full light of day.

But none of this would be possible in a Socialist State, where the central executive authority could not allow itself to be challenged or defeated at any time in any form of Parliament they might allow to exist.[44]

Churchill might have been wrong about this point: State-run enterprises do not have the reputation of being harsh to their employees. But Churchill feared most what he regarded as the full development of the Socialist state, the state that has mastery of the situation, the state against which no one may or can stand. He might have been wrong that such a state is possible in Britain too, but if he was right, his warning about wage earners seems logical and not without precedent. The workers in the Soviet Union and Nazi Germany were conscripted into their work and compensated as powerful people dictated. Those powerful people were compensated better.

To many, these claims by Churchill will sound extreme; to others, a portent of things upon us today. The political questions open today are not so different from the ones that Churchill faced. He meant those arguments and stood by them. His speech in 1945 claiming that the Socialist movement would end up with a Gestapo was not at the time effective, and his subsequent defeat was both humiliating and deeply distressing to him. Nonetheless, as we have noted, he stuck by the point, and in the 1950 election he repeated it:

They [the British people] cannot bear to think that the State will own everybody in their political thoughts and actions, as well as in managing them in their daily political lives. They do not see that their theme of Socialism inevitably leads to Communism and, secondly, that before getting to it they will have to do what they hate to do, and that is to sacrifice the personal individual liberties won so hardly and prized so much. The delicate margin between socialism and Communism was a no man's land, occupied by the crypto-Communists.[45]

In 1950 or today, it would not be good news for the business owner to discover that the state with its resources was thinking of entering competition with him. Any such person, subject to this competition or to comprehensive regulation, would have to consider carefully before criticizing the state.

Why then would the people vote for this kind of government? Churchill wondered about that often. He said in 1924 that the "enthronement in office of a Socialist Government will be a serious national misfortune such as has usually befallen great States only on the morrow of defeat in war."[46] Notice the noun *enthronement*. Britain suffered terribly in the world wars, but it was not defeated. What would lead the people to make such a departure from so much that was settled?

Churchill feared for a long time that they might make this departure. Especially early in his career, he considered it unjust that many British people worked long hours at steady jobs, but lived just above the line of want. A sickness in the family or a job loss would lead to immediate privation, and life was very hard for them even when misfortunes did not strike. Churchill thought that the people were going to do something about this, and unless something constructive were done on their behalf, they would do something destructive. In 1907 he wrote,

> No legislation at present in view interests the democracy. . . . All their minds are turning more and more to the social and economic issue. This revolution is irresistible. They will not tolerate the existing system by which wealth is acquired, shared & employed. They may not be able, they may be willing to recognize themselves unable, to devise a new system. I think them very ready & patient beyond conception. But they will set their faces like flint against the money power, the heir of all other powers & tyrannies overthrown.[47]

Churchill thought in 1907, as he would think later in life, that the people had reason to complain if their nation and many of its people were wealthy while they, working hard and steadily, lived on the edge of a cliff without a safety net. As we shall see in the next chapter, Churchill set out to provide that safety net.

Finally, Churchill seemed to fear something in the people themselves, a tendency that he thought made them vulnerable to the claims of socialism. About that he wrote carefully. Britain was a nation based upon wide suffrage, and soon enough universal suffrage, throughout Churchill's career. Churchill believed this right and supported it. Whether he did or not, he and every politician would have reason to be careful when speaking about the people.

For example, in his essay "Mass Effects in Modern Life" Churchill wrote, as quoted above, that mass effects had their influence upon ordinary as well as extraordinary people. They lost civic standing. They were secure as "salaried officials of great corporations." Their opinions were shaped by the "machinery" of the press and the widespread diffusion of standard views. Education was "universal and superficial," and it produced "standardized citizens, all equipped with regulation opinions, prejudices and sentiments, according to their class or party." Churchill concluded the essay with the argument that we do not have the great peaks of human excellence upon which to gaze. The people today do not have their "frowning crag, their venerated 'El Capitan' or 'Il Duce,' casting its majestic shadow in the evening light." Do we have anything like that today? "We certainly have not."[48]

When Churchill lost the 1945 election, he said several things about it, none of them except one to cast doubt upon the people who voted him out. Historian Brian Gardner considered Churchill's resignation speech as "perhaps the most gracious acceptance of democratic defeat in the English language." Certainly it is lovely:

> The decision of the British people has been recorded in the votes counted today. I have therefore laid down the charge which was placed upon me in darker times. I regret that I have not been permitted to finish the work against Japan. . . . It only remains for me to express to the British people, for whom I have acted in these perilous years, my profound gratitude for the unflinching, unswerving support which they have given me during my task, and for the many expressions of kindness which they have shown towards their servant. [49]

Amidst his repining, Churchill wrote to his friend and colleague Alfred Duff Cooper that there were some "unpleasant features in this election which indicate the rise of bad elements."

He added, "Conscientious objectors were preferred to candidates of real military achievement and service." Members of Parliament "who had done the most to hamper and obstruct the war were returned by enormously increased majorities." And, "None of the values of the years before were preserved." Churchill was wounded by the vote of the soldiers, which went heavily against him, saying they voted with "mirthful irresponsibility." One general told him that the "shortage of cigarettes and some questions of leave were the deciding factors."[50]

For Churchill socialism grew from causes of injustice that had festered in the British past. Also he feared that it reflected change in the people. He had feared this change all his life because he regarded the people rightful to rule and also the most likely to rule well. At that moment of defeat he wrote the gloomiest things of which there is record about the people.

Yet he did not abandon them. When Churchill's doctor, Lord Moran, accused the British people of ingratitude, Churchill replied, "Oh no, I wouldn't call it that. They have had a very hard time."[51]

Nor did he abandon hope. He had a plan, a strategy, to cope with these mass effects, the intense one of socialism and the more general ones that he thought afflicted the nation.

9

THE SOCIAL REFORMER

Churchill's strategy to banish socialism from British politics included the continuous rejection of socialism in principle. It also included efforts to take better care of the poor, the old, and the sick. The attempt to do this placed him right where politics occurs: between the upper and nether millstones. Like every politician he lived in that place and struggled not to be crushed.

Churchill did not favor redistribution for its own sake: he believed that unequal results, economically and otherwise, were a requirement of justice, written in the nature of man. At the same time he favored policies that would take money from richer taxpayers to support those who had less, when those who had less met misfortune and old age. He thought this was right. He looked for ways to do it that would not undermine the freedom of the society, its limited government, and free markets. These included especially social insurance that was mandatory and required contributions from the beneficiary.

He often called these policies "a minimum standard of life

and labor."[1] He favored this partly but not only because it was a weapon against socialism. He also favored it because he thought the poor, or many of them, were worthy of help, even in some sense entitled to that help.

THE CASE OF THE POOR

In 1901, fewer than three months in Parliament, Churchill found a study by social reformer Benjamin Seebohm Rowntree, the son of Quaker Joseph Rowntree, one of the founders and head of the company that continues to make Rowntree's chocolates under the ownership of Nestlé. Seebohm managed the company after his father. The Rowntrees practiced what they preached, running their company as a Christian duty: they paid well, provided employee benefits in ways little known at the time, and limited work to the eight-hour day. Father and son were interested in social reform, and they founded and maintained several institutions, some of them charitable and others political, to study and encourage social reform.[2]

Seebohm conducted and published a study of the town of York, where the company was based. Entitled *Poverty: A Study of Town Life*, it is built upon data gathered from and about several tens of thousands of residents of York.[3] The book is almost five hundred pages long, and it is entirely descriptive. It found that more than half the families of York were living in poverty; that is, they lacked "the necessities to a healthy life." Twenty-eight percent were in serious poverty, meaning they lacked urgent necessities such as sufficient food.

Churchill wrote a review of the book that he did not publish. It described the condition of the poor of York in terms both sympathetic and ironic. The people of York "endure all the privations which are usually associated with a state of siege." Some families are in "primary poverty": they do not have enough money from their regular earnings to purchase sufficient food to sustain themselves. Others are in "secondary poverty": they earn enough to feed themselves, but some misfortune or mistake temporarily placed them in the same condition.[4] Both groups are wasting away physically. They go through cycles of relative sufficiency to desperate want. Unemployment or illness is to them immediate disaster. Children bring extra burdens that sink many below the level of sufficiency. The poor of York pay a high percentage of their income for rent, and so the worst places to live are snapped up first: existence in a hovel leaves more money for food.

At the end of his essay Churchill wrote ironically: the British Empire is large, but there is no place for these people in it. They would have a better chance of happiness if they had been born "cannibal islanders of the Southern seas." The scientific advances of the modern world have not helped them. Granting that "nations exist and peoples labor to produce armies with which they conquer other nations," he believed that poverty and insecurity were bad policies to achieve that end. These poor people of York are not strong enough to stand in the ranks and defend the empire. Too bad such things have to come to the attention of busy statesmen, but let us take the trouble to feed these people so they can stand up straight in the military ranks when they have to fight.[5]

Churchill's irony was only partial. Two years earlier he wrote that to "keep our empire we must have an Imperial stock. . . . Where is the glory of a starving peasant arrayed in purple and in cloth of gold? That is the imperialism of modern Russia," not the "imperialism of Tory Democracy."[6] He observed, "I see little glory in an Empire which can rule the waves and is unable to flush its own sewers."[7]

The book moved Churchill, who wrote that it "impressed me very much,"[8] and he built his early politics around an effort to address the situation it described. First as a Tory Democrat[9] and then as a Liberal—Churchill crossed over to the Liberal party in 1904, and roughly the first decade of the century is considered his "radical period"—he aimed for the "social progress of the great mass of the people."[10] The "main end of modern government," he said, is the "improvement of the condition of the British people."[11] The young Churchill thought that most people in Britain had a chance of "happiness and the means of maintaining physical health." But a small class was being left behind, and that was a "disgrace to civilization and an injury to an Imperial State."[12] That was a greater danger than any revolution. No "policy of negation" would suffice. After Churchill lost his seat in Parliament in Dundee in the election of 1922, he commented, "[W]hen one thinks of the kind of lives the poorer people of Dundee have to live, one cannot be indignant at the way they voted."[13]

Churchill considered the issues of the unfortunate in light of the sacrifices that all citizens make on behalf of the nation. Especially in war, the sacrifices were heavy. In many cases they were borne by the community as a whole. In World War II, for example, the public reimbursed those whose houses were lost to bombing. But the burdens also fell disproportionately upon individuals. Those who lost their homes could not be fully paid for their inconvenience or have their possessions fully restored.

Those who were wounded or lost their lives could not be paid for that, or not fully, nor could their loved ones, except in the coin of honor. On May 26, 1940, Churchill sent an order to Brigadier Claude Nicholson, commanding at Calais. Churchill effectively told him to fight his position to the death, even though it was already untenable, because he was holding up the German advance toward Dunkirk and the British forces escaping from there. Later Churchill could hardly eat his dinner and reported that he felt "physically sick."[14] The force of 4,000 under Nicholson's command was nearly wiped out. Nicholson was captured and died within two years in a German prisoner-of-war camp. The bravery of Nicholson and those 4,000 helped save many others, including the father of my wife, who left Dunkirk beach among the last to escape. Lieutenant Colonel Denis Houghton went on to have a long life and a family, including now several grand-children. Nicholson had a wife, a son, and a daughter, and he never saw them again.[15] These are the costs of war, which is a feature of political life. This particular war had a profound effect on the opinions of the British people.[16]

A MAN OF THE MODERN LEFT?

Churchill often compared his support for the social safety net to these costs of war, suggesting for example that the rescue of the poor was like a military rearguard action.[17] It did not seem right to him to ask the dread sacrifices of war from a people and then leave some of them in want in time of peace while most prosper. He was only partly sarcastic when he suggested that the poor should be fed enough so they could stand up in the ranks. To this degree, he made an argument similar to the one made by British

Socialists. Churchill thought the people had some right or claim in justice to health care and to other elements of the minimum standard.

There were other similarities between Churchill and the Fabians and also to the American progressives. In his book about his father, *Lord Randolph Churchill*, he wrote that the dominion in Britain of the middle class had begun in the first major extension of the franchise in 1832 and reached its culmination in liberalism, meaning government for all and by all. "Slaves were free. Conscience was free. Trade was free. But hunger and squalor and cold were also free; and the people demanded something more than liberty."[18] He thought that the "ever-growing complexity of modern civilization, and the standard of administrative efficiency expected by the public, add to the cost of every service and create the need for new services and more improvements on existing service."[19]

In an essay published on March 7, 1908, entitled "The Untrodden Field in Politics," Churchill argued that the Liberal party had not "abandoned in any respect its historic championship of liberty." It had also become "acutely conscious of the fact that political freedom, however precious, is utterly incomplete without a measure at least of social and economic independence." He called for a "scientific treatment" of the remaining social and economic questions.[20]

This anticipates the argument that Franklin Roosevelt, who was of course to become important to Churchill and Britain, would make in his famous 1932 Commonwealth Club Address. There Roosevelt attempted to ground modern administrative government in the principles of the Declaration of Independence.[21] He did this by arguing that the right to property could not be fully effective if one's property is in jeopardy. Therefore the state must guarantee that one's property will not be lost. Of course the state cannot make any such guarantee unless it has access to sufficient property, in principle any amount necessary. This means that private possession of property becomes subject to the needs of others as determined by the force of law. Roosevelt would continue and develop this line of thought into a proclamation of new kinds of rights, rights to include not just economic opportunity but economic well-being. Like Churchill when he was in this vein, Roosevelt argued that these new rights will be the completion of the old ones. Civil liberties, including property rights, will be more fully secure when the citizen is secured against the loss of his property.

This is a clear departure from the argument of, for example, James Madison, when he connected the right to property to all human rights, including worship, speech, and the press: "as a man is said to have a right to his property, he may be equally said to have a property in all his rights." In his definition, "property" means "every thing to which a man may attach a value and have a right; and *which leaves to every one else the like advantage*" (emphasis in original).[22] We may all speak, or pray, or assemble, or hold our own property, and all at the same time, and without depriving anyone else of the "like advantage." The new economic rights, as suggested here by Churchill and later by Franklin Roosevelt, require that some must sacrifice property so that others may not lose theirs. In those cases the state arbitrates who keeps and who gains property, and to that extent it replaces the free market.

From the beginning of his career, Churchill cites many reasons to fear this ability in government. In opposing tariffs, he says again and again that tariffs will divide the country into classes and will fill the lobbies of Parliament with the "touts of protected industries."[23] If one judges in purely economic terms, to transfer wealth from the rich to the poor rewards poverty and discourages wealth, and it creates interests in the society that have powerful effects in politics.

In 1910 Churchill said that he looked forward to working with the Conservatives, whom he had left to join the Liberals, "for a better, a fairer, and more scientific organization of the social life of the people, for the due correction of the abuses of wealth and monopoly, for religious equality, and for industrial progress."[24] This would make the government bigger, about which Churchill had reservations both then and later. Nonetheless he embraced the opening of a new domain for government action and the deploying of the tools of modern science in that domain. These are fundamental tenets of the modern Left, and Churchill regarded them as true or partially true.

The need for these reforms was reinforced, Churchill believed, by the knitting together of the world economically. Competition, currency rates, tariffs changing anywhere in the world could cause a mill to close and the worker to lose his job. "What is the use of preaching to the humble bread-winner of the cottage home the old virtues of thrift and self denial? All the thrift and self-denial he can practice in a lifetime would be of no avail" in the face of world influences.[25] A national plan is necessary, Churchill thought, because new conditions in the world required new government programs and even structures.

Finally we have seen that Churchill had his own fears of the "money power, the heir of all other powers & tyrannies overthrown."[26] He believed that the British aristocracy, in substantial control of both houses of Parliament for most of the nineteenth century, had saddled the other classes with the cost of its "upkeep."[27] As we have seen, he thought that large business enterprises altered the attitudes, even the characters, of their employees compared to the business owner and his employees operating on a small scale with customers who are also neighbors.

All these points are central tenets of Fabianism in Britain and of progressivism in the United States. Churchill upheld these things in common with them both.

OR NOT OF THE MODERN LEFT?

What can one make of Churchill's virulence against the Socialists if he had so many things in common with them? The answer lies in that point about nature that Churchill made repeatedly in his criticisms of socialism and bureaucracy. One can see it, for example, in an essay he published in the middle of his radical period. It was a review of *The Jungle* by Upton Sinclair, an American novel inspired by progressivism—Jack London called it "the Uncle Tom's Cabin of wage slavery"—that gave rise to groundbreaking legislation to regulate the food industry and other legislation to regulate factory conditions. Both the tone and the content of Churchill's review are instructive. The tone is ironic, distant from the pathos of the book. The novel, he wrote, was animated by "one purpose and one purpose alone . . . to make the great Beef Trust stink in the nostrils of the world, and so to contaminate the system upon which it has grown to strength." This is part of a strategy to effect the "bodily capture of the Democratic party and the installation in its place of a thorough and unshrinking Socialist organization."[28] Churchill had no sympathy with that.

Churchill had another plan. He proposed instead that "vast and intricate fabric of Factory Law, of Health Acts, of Workmen's Compensation, upon which Parliament is swiftly and laboriously building year by year and month by month." The justification for these measures was plain enough "so that a child may see it, so that a fool may see it, so that a knave may see it."[29] Not only Parliament, but also Churchill, was busily at work as a member of the Liberal Party upon just those reforms.

Then Churchill made a point about the power of government:

> A National or Municipal Beef Trust, with the United States Treasury at its back, might indeed give more regular employment at higher wages to its servants, and might sell cleaner food to its customers—at a price. But if evil systems corrupt good men, it is no less true that base men will dishonor any system, and while no bond of duty more exacting than that of material recompense regulates the relations of man and man, while no motion more lofty than that of self-interest animates the exertions of every class, and no hope beyond the limits of this fleeting world lights the struggles of humanity, the most admirable systems will merely succeed in transferring, under different forms and pretexts, the burden of toil, misery, and injustice from one set of human shoulders to another.[30]

The people who ran the Beef Trust, being people, were likely to include some who would abuse any absolute control they possessed. To convert the Beef Trust into a Municipal Trust (that is, a government trust) was to create a larger and stronger authority than any private trust. People would run it, too, and at least some of them would be "base men." Churchill was looking for a way to prevent people from being abused. He was prepared to fight monopoly in private corporations to do that. He was not prepared to trust the government to act better in possession of power than people do when they have private power. James Madison wrote that government is necessary because men are not angels, and limits on government are necessary because angels do not govern men.[31] Churchill believed this too.

Moreover Churchill believed that the free market system advantaged the poor as much as those who thrived in it, and for many reasons. The "only chance the struggling millions of whom we read in Mr. Rowntree's book," he said, "and whom we see in our own constituencies, ever have of enjoying the bounties of nature and science, lies not in any socialistic system of taxation, not in any charitable enterprise, or charitable immunity from taxation, but, solely and simply, in an effective and scientific commercial development."[32] In 1899 Churchill promoted "all legislation" to "raise the standard of comfort and happiness in English homes," but not any that would impair "that tremendous energy of production on which the wealth of the nation and the good of the people depend."[33]

Churchill did not think that an able-bodied person, the working man "in good health and young, or in the prime of his life, and in employment at good wages," should be regarded as an "object of compassion." Only when misfortune came upon him, including prolonged unemployment, was he to be regarded as a subject of relief.[34] Churchill argued in 1943 that there must be "no idlers or drones," even among the rich. "Idlers at the top make idlers at the bottom. No one must stand aside in his working prime to pursue a life of selfish pleasure. There are wasters in all classes."[35] He would discourage the rich idlers by taxing income from investments more; and of course in Britain the income tax was progressive, as were the death duties. Wanting people to work, Churchill was distressed by unemployment, especially during the Great Depression. He pitied the unemployed if they were looking for work: "Leaving out the lazy or the sulky, consider only the ordinary hard-working man who cannot get a job, who has been for many months—and in our country sometimes for years—without anyone requiring his services . . . he himself is nothing but a drone. If there is food in the pot it is not he who has put it there . . . it is his very existence which is challenged by the age in which he lives."[36]

PUBLIC CHOICE AND PRIVATE CHOICE

Believing these things, Churchill was required to control the social safety net at the same time he promoted it. There were effects both political and economic to consider, effects upon both the material well-being and the character of the people. Churchill thought about those deeply, and he thought that the answer lay in social insurance. He thought it the best way to stabilize the conflict between rich and poor, protect limited government, and help those in need.

It was no good, Churchill thought, to rely upon private insurance, because the people who bought it were people likely to be those with immediate claims.[37] This is of course the nature of insurance: it is easy to sell life insurance to people who have cancer, but it is hard to make a living in the insurance business if they are the only customers. Insurance companies make their money by selling to a lot of people, only a few of whom will have claims in any given period for which premiums are collected. Insurers do not mind as much, as a purely business matter, if the cancer rate rises in general as they do if it rises among their customers. The situation of the political community is different, because cancer patients without insurance are still citizens. It would be better if everyone bought insurance: rates would be lower and tragic situations avoided. It would be better if everyone worked hard. But some do not, and those who suffer the resulting tragedies may make claims upon the community for relief, and if their claims are ignored they may join together to take what they need by political force. Socialism may look good to them. These points were apparent to Churchill, and he favored mandatory social insurance to be purchased by all workers. He would bring "the miracle of averages to the rescue of the masses."[38]

For example, the medical coverage under the National Insurance Act of 1911, driven by David Lloyd George with Churchill's support, required employees who made less than £160 a year to pay four pence a week into the insurance fund. Richer people, it was thought, did not need the insurance and were not covered. Employers were required to pay three pence a week. The taxpayer contributed two pence. The money was deposited in "friendly societies"—private financial institutions. People got books of stamps that showed how much they had. Therefore people could look at the accounts, feel ownership in them, and watch the money grow.[39]

The employee contributions into these plans make them more like the free market, but they are not the free market. The distinction between the employer and employee contributions was more apparent than real. Both the employer and the employee contributions raised the cost of employment, and both shifted income from current to future purposes. For employees who lived on tight margins, this could be a serious loss, and that would provide a reason not to purchase insurance if they were given the option. The same can be said for the employer. Moreover the act did not cover the unemployed. The taxpayer component of the act was therefore a transfer of wealth from current to future purposes; from the unemployed to the employed, to the extent that the unemployed paid taxes; it was in all cases a transfer from all taxpayers to the beneficiaries of the system.

None of this was unknown to Churchill. In 1930 he wrote an essay, "The Abuse of the Dole," admitting that the employer contributions were, to "orthodox economists," really "deductions from real wages." He continued that by 1930 the cost of social insurance to both employers/employees and the taxpayer had risen. And by then, Churchill wrote, people were using the insurance more. Employers were reducing the hours of their employees to preserve their eligibility for unemployment benefits. Employees were making claims not only when they were unemployed, but when they were given longer holidays because business was slow. They felt justified in doing this—whereas a generation ago they would not have—because it was common practice ("all the loafers are drawing it"), because they had a legal right, and because they had paid into the fund. Therefore it avoided the "odious taint of being a 'dole.'" Churchill regarded these abuses as "minor" or perhaps not even abuses.[40] It was an insurance scheme, and people were making their claims. The problems could be managed.

Churchill was especially interested in the political benefits of social insurance. In 1909 he regarded the "simultaneous waste of extreme wealth and of extreme want" as cause for "deep anxiety" and as a threat to the whole empire.[41] This division inside Britain was more threatening than any foreign or imperial danger. Also, the Socialist movement sought to capitalize on this division to revolutionize the country. Churchill's advocacy of social reform and his opposition to socialism are coincident both in time and intensity. The way to close the division, he believed, was to provide a floor under each citizen, substantially with funds that he, the employee, contributed. In 1925 Churchill wrote to Neville Chamberlain, then Minister of Health, about their common effort to expand social insurance: "the whole principle of contribution is valuable: It avoids pauperization and the stigma of doles; it will promote each man's self-respect and make him value his pension the more when he gets it."[42]

Serving as chancellor of the exchequer at the time of this letter, Churchill sought to close the gap between the classes by giving them all a stake in the society and its governing structures. He wrote to Prime Minister Stanley Baldwin that he was seeking cuts in direct taxation—paid more heavily by richer taxpayers—to defray the cost of employer contributions to social insurance. The treasury could not afford, he continued, to cut indirect taxation (which struck lower-income people equally with the rich) at the same time it was expanding social insurance. But cutting direct taxation "might well be taken as an equipoise in the general scheme of the Budget."[43] Businesses and their owners would pay less in taxes, but more in contributions to social insurance for their workers (and themselves). He wrote King George V that his two main objects as chancellor were "security for the wage earning population and their dependents against exceptional misfortune," and "encouragement to the enterprise of the nation by the remission of taxes upon income."[44]

The net effect would be a relatively smaller government in most respects, with relatively larger expenditure on social insurance. Social insurance was tied to the welfare of individual workers, who had invested alongside the government in that welfare. It would therefore be hard to change the weight of taxation back toward other purposes. Churchill imagined a government that taxed and spent in ways that provided a minimum standard of living for all its workers, most of the cost of that provided by the workers themselves.

In Churchill's mind, there was no alternative to social insurance. In March 1925, having been chancellor for four months, he spoke with a deputation from the National Confederation of Employers Organizations. They made excellent points about the excessive burden industry was carrying. The leader of the deputation, Lord Weir, said: "'Many of us believe that thrift and self-help have been a big asset in the past, and the habit of work has been a pretty big influence in building up the character of our people . . . and we really believe that the incidence of these measures is beginning to impair that character."[45]

Churchill agreed. He said that "the first great aim" was to reduce taxation in the country. Also he agreed that social insurance "may well be" making the workers "to a certain extent less self-reliant"; increasingly "they expect to have things done for them."[46]

On the other hand, he continued, there was no choice. It was necessary in 1909 and 1910 to implement social insurance against disease and unemployment. Under the plans that were implemented, the workers have contributed "vastly the greater

proportion" of the cost. The workers had accepted the direct taxation of their wages "cheerfully," an important fact about which
there had been apprehension at the time.[47]

Churchill had sensed in his radical period that the British
people wanted more security against the trials of life. Also he
sensed and feared a rising tide of socialism. He had been working
since those days to give the people what they wanted on certain
terms. He wanted them to contribute "vastly the greater proportion" of the cost—to bear most of the cost themselves, rather
than passing it on to others. To the industrialist deputation in
1925 Churchill said, "when we feel that they are not self-reliant
because the burden has been taken from them, to a large extent,
they are bearing their burdens themselves." In other words,
if they are paying for most of it, the reserve that accumulates
makes them independent, not dependent. The insurance system
would even help to commit the people to a system in which they
helped themselves: "[social insurance] eventually must have the
effect of attaching the minds of the people, although their language and mood in many cases may not seem to indicate it—it
must lead to the stability and order of the general structure."[48]
The "general structure" included capitalism, the lowest possible
taxation, and thriving free markets.

The system Churchill devised depended heavily upon working and savings: the former provided the latter. It did not set
up entitlements, but rather savings plans, the savings deducted
from wages and supplemented by the taxpayer. For those who
had no wages, there was an employment relief, assuming that
one had been employed previously. The Labour Exchanges
helped to make sure that workers knew whether and where jobs
were available. The government, responsible for unemployment

insurance, learned from those exchanges whether a worker was refusing work. Benefits had a time limit, and they were low and did not compete with low-paid employment.[49] This system may look stingy today, when transfer payments are more generous, but its benefits supplied things that did not exist, or exceeded things previously existing. Also they solved one part of the problem: they did not operate at a level to make them economically preferable to work.

When the benefits ran out, one fell back upon the family, friends, private charity, or the poor Law, which had yet more serious incentives to find work. In its original form it was designed to keep people from starving and also to present worse conditions than could be bought with the lowest-paying jobs. The Poor Law of 1834 had required an able-bodied person to live in a workhouse to receive assistance, although this was modified gradually to allow "outdoor relief." The poor law survived until 1948, when it was rescinded by the Labour government. Over the previous decades it had been extensively superseded by the social reforms of both Liberal and Conservative governments. Churchill's purpose was to keep people out of the grasp of the poor law, and he was extensively successful, though there were setbacks.[50] As chancellor, Churchill sought cuts in expenditures in many places, including especially the military and the navy, in order to afford tax cuts, and expanded social insurance. In 1926 these cuts affected the duration of unemployment insurance, which forced some people onto the mercies of the poor law.[51] In 1928 Churchill and the cabinet implemented a plan to relieve industry and agriculture of local property taxes, which he said enabled local government to treat those businesses as a "milch cow to provide revenue for extravagant local schemes."[52] He took pride in the fact that the plan as he proposed it avoided "the measureless evils which would follow from the Central Government taking upon itself the direct and continuous care of able-bodied unemployed and unemployables and their families."[53] In social reform as elsewhere, Churchill tried to keep the size of government under control.

In 1937, Churchill wrote that much of what he sought had been achieved. The British people, he wrote, are tied together by "deep associations arising from long-gathered tradition, and also from a very strong and just realization of all we have to lose." These had been reinforced by the "new machinery" of social insurance, which is organized in a familiar "system of tripartite contribution whereby workmen, employers and the State all pay to a central fund." This appeals to the "core of good sense and fair play which counts so much in our country." Also, he continued,

> The ordinary British subject feels not only that he is a citizen of a great country, but that he is provided for and safeguarded to an extent which no other Government can show. For this reason he becomes an active partner in the maintenance of the Empire and the social system, without which the Empire could not endure. If England had to cry for help to her children at home and abroad, she would not cry in vain.[54]

"There lies the march," Churchill concluded, "and those who valiantly pursue it need never fear to lose their hold upon the heart of Britain." Churchill was after that heart; he did not want to lose it to socialism.

KIND AND DEGREE

The difference between Churchill's social reform and socialism was of both kind and degree. Of kind, it was a difference
in understanding of human nature, and this involved a difference about the purpose and operation of government. Churchill
regarded this difference as fundamental. He thought it would
reduce ultimately to the difference between just and unjust government, between freedom and tyranny. He did not believe that
any administrative class, however educated, could be trusted
with the kind of power that he feared it would gather, the kind
that the doctrines of socialism and scientific historicism justified
and required. The members of that class would still be human,
and men are not angels.

Churchill was prepared to accept that the people would
depend upon the state in new ways under his social insurance
policies. He was prepared to accept that this would not be wholly
good for them. He thought that the damage would be offset by
public acceptance of and attachment to the "general structure"
that provided the social insurance. Under this structure, the
people who received the benefits would pay for most of them.
The able-bodied would have to work. Taxes would be kept
within bounds, and free markets and property rights would be
protected. The social insurance system would operate in some
ways separately from the regulatory and taxing authority of
the government, and so the government would remain limited.
This, as we shall see, would permit the British Constitution to
continue to operate through Parliament, especially the House of
Commons, fully representative and focused upon national and
imperial issues. And socialism would be forestalled.

This difference of kind gave rise to differences of degree in the size and scope of the social welfare state. Sometimes the difference of degree was lesser and sometimes greater, but it was always present. Churchill supported the social safety net with conviction, but the limits he sought to place upon it also stemmed from conviction. For him, work, profit, property, and the free market were not necessary evils, but important goods, expressions of human capacities and human rights. The limited government that sheltered these essential liberal institutions was good in part because it did shelter them.

"The inherent vice of capitalism," we have seen him say, "is the unequal sharing of blessings. The inherent virtue of Socialism is the equal sharing of miseries."[55] He regarded capitalism as a virtue with potential vices. He regarded the virtue of socialism as no virtue at all. The inequality of result that flowed from free markets was partially a vice for Churchill because it laid the ground for political dissension, ultimately for socialism. It was more profoundly a virtue for Churchill because it was an expression of human nature. There were higher expressions of that nature, Churchill thought, than the economic virtues. They were to be found in the right service to conscience both public and private, in the duties of citizenship in peace and war, in the courage and justice those duties demanded, and in the right kind of knowledge and the learning necessary to it. These goods—economic, moral, and intellectual—formed for Churchill a seamless web. He sought to foster and protect that web with all the tools he could contrive. His strategy reached as far, in a different direction, as the strategy of the Fabians. "Lo, a new England," hoped Sidney Webb. According to different standards, Churchill hoped for that too.

Churchill was not fully, and perhaps not ultimately, successful in implementing this strategy. Yet he kept at it with the same determination that drove him in war, and on the same convictions.

10

THE CONSTITUTIONALIST

Churchill wrote that a Municipal Trust would be more dangerous than the Beef Trust. Something must be done, he thought,
for the victims of the Beef Trust and its kind, but whatever power
is raised to do it is by definition a greater power. That greater
power will also be directed and staffed by human beings. How
shall that power be organized? This is a problem of constitutionalism, a constant theme in Churchill's speaking and writing.

Think for a minute of the broad meaning of the term *constitution*. It is related in etymology to the words *statue* and
statute, which come from a Latin word that means to set a thing
firmly in place. When we make a statue, we set it somewhere
firmly so it will not fall over. When we make a law, we make it
to last. And if it is to last, those who live under it must follow it.
Because laws have a way of reaching everywhere, either directly
or indirectly, a people's laws will reflect everything about them.
This broad sense of the term *constitution* is the reason why the
best books about politics—those of, say, Plato or Aristotle or

Montesquieu—have a lot to say about institutions that we today regard as social and not political.

In this broadest sense of the term *constitution*, Churchill proposed the social safety net as a constitutional arrangement. Apart from the justice he thought it would do, it would also tie the classes of British society together and connect them to the welfare of the country. When Churchill said that the "minimum standard" might rise with the level of wealth in the nation, he was speaking to an audience of citizens. He wanted people to think that all of them benefited when the economy was prosperous, even if some benefited more than others.

In this sense, the free market economy is just like the social safety net. They are constitutional arrangements designed to protect one kind of life rather than another. Churchill saw these two arrangements as working together to protect a kind of life, that of liberty under law. Living that life, people for the most part take care of themselves, their families, their neighbors, their country. Churchill thought that this kind of living was the best for human beings, whose lives cannot be perfect, but who can be upright and successful at meeting the challenges of life.

Churchill said that civilization begins with the institutions of limited government and the rule of law. In the immediate sense, civilization is a political term calling for a liberal kind of politics in which the military is not all and civilians control the government. In liberal society we do not think of nonpolitical things as political, yet in one way they are: the regime that depends upon a private institution such as property, family, or religion will not do well unless those private institutions do well. When the Socialist Party adopts a different attitude toward religion or toward family, it takes a different view of the constitution every bit as much as when it adopts a different attitude toward property. We have seen how Churchill traced the war-fighting strength of Britain to its private institutions. He did that at the outset of a generation in which Britain would be fighting for its life, and it would need that strength, every ounce of it.

Churchill was trying to marry two things that are not commonly regarded as eligible for mating. For him, the free market is a necessary condition of the liberal society, the pursuit of individual satisfaction and also (do not forget) of individual excellence. It makes possible limited government because state allocation of goods would be an essentially limitless form. The social safety net becomes the free market's partner because it performs a task Churchill believed necessarily a common undertaking: helping those who suffer misfortune. It does more: it breeds loyalty to the liberal state with its capitalist ways.

That is the match he proposed. It is, in the broad sense, a constitutional match. It affects powerfully the arrangement of offices and honors in the nation. For example, knighthoods go to captains of industry and leaders of trade unions as well as to soldiers, scholars, and artists. Churchill's constitutionalism would set things up in a certain way and set them up firmly.

THE CHALLENGE OF LIBERAL GOVERNMENT

This broad definition of the term *constitution* operates in tandem with the ordinary sense of the term, which is also not narrow. In this more ordinary sense we mean the principles, rules, and procedures that lie behind and give shape to the making and enforcing of the law. In any country that is a just political union, there is always such a constitution. Each one varies with and helps to define its regime.

For example, the liberal (in the classic sense) regime is confined to using a lot of indirect methods. The family, property, and religion are important to that kind of regime, and yet they cannot be incorporated into the government. A free country where people lack industry will be poor and weak; a free country where the family does not function will have a lot of children dependent on its government; a free country where religion teaches oppression will have oppressive voters. What we mean by *liberal* in the liberal regime is "free" and also independent. We mean people doing as they please to a large extent with their own property, their own spouses and children, their own consciences and duties to God. For a liberal statesman to support these things means in large part to protect them in their independence. At the same time, liberal regimes that have thrived in modern times are given to wars every bit as fierce, and much larger and more costly, than the wars of ancient times. If these private things are the source of their strength, they need them to thrive.

One danger, then, for constitutions in these modern and liberal times is how they can remain liberal. Churchill believed that this danger was acute in his time. It became so partly because of the great wars of his lifetime, and partly because doctrines arose in modern social science to demand the comprehensive regulation of the society. Churchill, opposing those doctrines, was loyal to the liberal constitutional arrangements of the British Constitution, as that constitution had come to be understood over history.

Take a case from the 1930s, when Hitler loomed and Churchill's main object was to provoke the British government to build more weapons and to look for allies—first France and then Russia, then finally and especially the United States. Nonetheless Churchill wrote a long essay, "What Good's a Constitution?" published in Britain in 1935 and in the United States in 1936, about the constitutional controversies under way in America. He had very much to say about American politics, and also indirectly about the doings of Franklin Roosevelt, who would become his much-admired friend.[1]

The question of constitutionalism, Churchill wrote, raised the larger question of whether the state was above the citizen, or the citizen above the state. The question was answered in favor of the state in Russia, Germany, and Italy. Most nations, whether free or despotic, answered in favor of the state in time of war. But at the present time, Churchill continued, the argument was made that "economic crises are only another form of war, and as they are always with us, or can always be alleged to be with us, it is claimed that we must live our lives in a perpetual state of war." Socialism, he continued, was not so dangerous when proponents presented themselves with "an international guise as creators of a new world order, like the beehive or the ant heap, with a new human heart to fit these novel conceptions."[2] Churchill echoed phrases he had written four years earlier about the Bolsheviks in "Mass Effects in Modern Life," writing now about the Nazis in Germany and the Socialists in Britain.

Socialism was more formidable, he continued, when it was "grafted not upon world ideals but upon the strongest forms of nationalism." When socialism became patriotic, in other words, it gained new force. It co-opted the political loyalties that provided the basis of any nation. That happened in Germany. The Nazis were able to overwhelm the Weimar Constitution until it became only a "scrap of paper." Now in Germany "the tyranny of the ruling junta extends into every department of life. Friends may not greet each other without invoking the name of Hitler." The "very meals that a family eats in the privacy of its home are regulated by decree."[3] Here recall that in the *Fabian Essays* family meals at home are regarded as inefficient, something to change, not by force, but over a long time.

This tendency was not confined to the totalitarian states. Churchill wrote: "In the United States, also, economic crisis has led to an extension of the activities of the Executive and to the pillorying, by irresponsible agitators, of certain groups and sections of the population as enemies of the rest. There have been efforts to exalt the power of the central government and to limit the rights of individuals." Mobilized behind this reversal of the American tradition was the "selfishness of the pensioners, or would-be pensioners, of Washington, and the patriotism of all who wish to see their country prosperous once more."[4]

In other words, the doctrine that united ideology, whether of the Left or the Right, with patriotism gained power among the patriots and among the ideologues of that stripe. The passions unleashed by this kind of government became effective, Churchill wrote, when it was wedded to the "sense of public duty" that "rides high in the hearts of all men and women of good will." Then "handcuffs can be slipped upon the citizens and they can be brought into entire subjugation to the executive government."[5] Coupled with those doctrines, the love of country becomes a tool of despotism.

In his first inaugural address in 1933, Franklin Roosevelt had said that he would treat the challenge of putting people back to work as an "emergency of a war." He called upon the people to "move as a trained and loyal army willing to sacrifice for the good of a common discipline." We must be prepared to "submit our lives and property to such a discipline, because it makes possible a leadership which aims at a larger good."[6] In his second inaugural four years later, Roosevelt would say that in pursuit of that larger good, "We are beginning to wipe out the line that divides the practical from the ideal; and in so doing we are fashioning an instrument of unimagined power for the establishment of a morally better world."[7] Notice "unimagined power."

What Churchill was prepared to do in war, Roosevelt was prepared to do in peace. Churchill objected that an economic crisis cannot "ever truly be compared with the kind of struggle for existence by races constantly under primordial conditions." He did not think "that modern nations in time of peace ought to regard themselves as if they were the inhabitants of besieged cities." And because peace is the typical state, or so one hopes, Churchill feared that the conditions of the armed camp would prevail most of the time, at least in principle. "One of the greatest reasons for avoiding war," he wrote, "is that it is destructive to liberty."[8] So, too, is the waging of war in peacetime upon domestic evils.

Churchill raised the question about whether a fixed constitution is a "bulwark or a fetter."[9] In *The World Crisis*, he had stated objections to the American Constitution, specifically about its inflexibility and the power it invests in the executive: "The rigid Constitution of the United States, the gigantic scale and strength of its party machinery, the fixed terms for which public officers and representatives are chosen, invest the President with a greater measure of autocratic power than was possessed before the war by the Head of any great State."[10] In 1926 and elsewhere he praised the British Constitution for its flexibility: "the whole advantage of our position has been that we have been able to get on without writing things down on paper."[11] He said this in relation to the development of the empire, where Britain was ruling some peoples differently than it ruled the British people at home.

Churchill went on in *The World Crisis* to say that the American Constitution makes it difficult to focus the people's attention on national affairs, in part because of emphasis on federal features. Also it frees the winning party from concern with the opinions of the loser; it invests authority of a direct and personal kind upon the president; it produces presidents who are not well known to the people who vote for them; and it concentrates power in political parties, especially the president's. Churchill wrote this passage just before some highly critical passages he placed in the book about Woodrow Wilson. He said that Wilson was previously unknown and was first and last a "Party man."[12]

Such criticism of the American Constitution was not unique for Churchill. In 1932, he said in the House of Commons that the US Constitution worked like a machine, and it created "what is virtually a hiatus in the relations of that great country, the vast, intricate vital relations of that great country, with the outside world."[13] Churchill was unhappy, as he had been since the conclusion of the Great War, that the United States demanded full repayment of war debts, especially British war debts. He argued that the European Allies had fought longer and suffered worse in the war that became our common cause when the United States entered it. The debts should be forgiven, at least partially. And he saw that separation of powers in the United States was part of the obstacle to forgiveness: some in Congress or the executive branch might agree, but they could not come together. The American Constitution was thwarting a purpose of Churchill, and he was impatient with it.

In "What Good's a Constitution?" Churchill took a different view, accepting and even praising the rigidity of the American Constitution, as he supported the forms and restraints of Britain's. He published this essay in the year of Roosevelt's Second New Deal, which featured the Works Progress Administration and the Social Security Act. In May 1935, the month before the essay's publication in England, the United States Supreme Court decided *Schechter Poultry Corp. v. United States*, a case that challenged the constitutionality of the most sweeping piece of New Deal legislation: the National Industrial Recovery Act of 1933.

This act gave the federal government, through its newly created National Recovery Administration (NRA), power to fix wages and prices across the economy and to regulate extensively in new ways. The *Schechter* case arose when the NRA claimed that the Schechter family was selling sick poultry, which led to the popular name of the case, the Sick Chicken Case. The Supreme Court struck down the National Industrial Recovery Act, which destroyed the NRA. The court was unanimous in its opinion. Chief Justice Charles E. Hughes stated one of the key grounds for the decision, and it has a profound bearing on questions of governance in the United States today: Hughes argued that the Constitution gives legislative power solely to Congress, and it cannot delegate that power to the president, any entity, or anybody outside itself.

Roosevelt was sharply critical of the decision. He proposed in the Judicial Reform Bill of 1937 that the size of the Supreme Court be enlarged by one new member for each current member over seventy years old. This court-packing scheme was never passed, but the court reversed itself in the 1937 case *National Labor Relations Board v. Jones and Laughlin Steel* and came to approve New Deal legislation of sweeping powers, if less sweeping than those of the NRA.

Churchill defended the Supreme Court's *Schechter* decision. He regarded the "fixed Constitution" of the United States as a "bulwark" of freedom and not as a "fetter." He wrote of the institution of judicial review:

> [W]e now watch the workings of a written Constitution enforced by a Supreme Court according to the letter of the law, under which anyone may bring a test case challenging not merely the interpretation of a law, but the law itself, and if the Court decides for the appellant, be he only an owner of a few chickens, the whole action of the Legislature and the Executive becomes to that extent null and void.[14]

Churchill continued that the American Constitution is very difficult to amend, and so it remains a guardian of the people's freedom against the stress of events.

As noted, this praise of the American Constitution runs in a different direction from Churchill's earlier criticisms of it. He sometimes regretted the flexibility of Britain's unwritten Constitution and feared that it would not be able to restrain socialism. But it has something else on its side: age. The supremacy of Parliament was first established, he writes, amidst party controversies between the Whigs and the Tories in the seventeenth century. The Whigs believed in parliamentary supremacy as a fundamental principle, and the Tories were agreeable because they did not like the king, James II, and his religion. Because of this interplay of principle and interest, not unlike the interplay that James Madison sought to foster in the operation of the US Constitution, both parties had a long tradition of "jealous care for constitutional rights." This has been passed down to modern times, guarded by the people and also "by our permanent civil service"[15]—that is, when it is civil and when it is a service.

Churchill notes that the British and the Americans have something in common too. The founders of America encouraged the people to a "frequent recurrence to first principles" as they are stated in the "grand, simple affirmations of the past," such as the Declaration of Independence. Such documents defend "civilization," which Churchill judged by "simple tests." Then he summarized what makes a government just and free: "What is the degree of freedom possessed by the citizen or subject? Can he think, speak and act freely under well-established, well-known laws? Can he criticize the executive government? Can he sue the State if it has infringed his rights? Are there also great processes for changing the law to meet new conditions?"[16]

The American Constitution, Churchill wrote, is one of the finest achievements in history because it guarantees these freedoms. He quoted a "leading member of the Convention of 1787": "To control the powers and conduct of the legislature . . . by an overruling constitution was an improvement in the science and practice of government reserved to the American States."[17]

Churchill perceived the advantages of the American Constitution. The difference between the British and the American Constitutions is not, at least from the point of view of the American framers, found in its age but in its source. The American people, voting in their states, ratified their Constitution by a process invented and used for that purpose only. No law passed under the Constitution can have the same authority as the Constitution itself because the Constitution is the direct product of the sovereign people. That is why the Constitution can restrain the ordinary actions of government. That is why the Supreme Court has the authority to void a law passed through both houses of the legislature and signed by the executive. None of the great documents that make up the British Constitution may claim this authority.

Churchill admired this ability of the American Constitution to restrain, and he admired it increasingly throughout his life. In 1923 he said that Britain was exposed to unparalleled "difficulties and risks," having "neither the rigid constitutional safeguards which dominate the United States nor their vast party organizations and machinery"; "neither the logical electoral system of France nor her carefully balanced system of counter-checks against revolutionary change"; nor the federal system of Germany or America to "relieve the strain upon the central organism." Nor had it any referendum, "as in Switzerland."[18] Britain was disadvantaged without the "rigid, fixed Constitutions or fundamental laws that cannot be altered except by a two thirds or three quarters majority." Also Britain could not match the "strong Second Chambers" found in many countries.[19]

At the same time, Churchill admired the claims of venerability and flexibility available to the British Constitution. In this vein he echoed the point of Edmund Burke that the British Constitution was a "partnership not only between those who are living, but between those who are living, those who are dead, and those who are to be born."[20] This is reinforced in the language of the great documents of the British Constitution: the Magna Carta, the Petition of Right, and the Bill of Rights, which appeal to British practices long established—and those documents are very old. To the extent that the people and their representatives respond to this argument, it is a restraint upon the government of the day and upon the people. The election of the Socialist government, he warned, would be a sign that the Constitution's power was waning.

To Churchill, the British Constitution is two things. First, it is hallowed, venerated, and flexible. Second, it is an expression of principles that abide, principles that can be known to reason. This idea of an evolutionary and historical constitution may contradict the idea of a constitution of fixed purpose. Churchill reconciled this contradiction through a reading of the history of the British Constitution: it has a direction. It has proceeded through the "toilsome marches of the generations" toward the British people's "hearts' desire."[21] It is the result of a "famous chain of events which has made us what we are"; this chain has given us "our Parliament, our Habeas Corpus, our rights and many freedoms, our tolerances, our decencies."[22] This is an emulation of the Whig interpretation of history, and for Churchill as for the Whigs it is an expression of something peculiarly British, but also an expression of a movement toward the right way of governing, determined by principles that apply generally over time and place.

Churchill regarded this story of the British Constitution with reverence and awe. He thought it among the greatest political developments in history. It produced a way of governing that was beautiful and good. Churchill spent his life participating in this form of government. He fought for it in war and in peace.

BEATING HEART OF THE CONSTITUTION

To Churchill, the form of the British Constitution includes a representative legislature, the greatest talking body in the world, which is also the home of the executive government; a monarch, the symbol of sovereignty, who formerly exercised executive authority; and an independent judiciary that made a common law over the centuries.

For Churchill the center of the British Constitution is an activity involving about six hundred and fifty people. They meet in a famous chamber, not quite big enough to seat all of them. They meet to talk. There are rules to organize this discussion and a Speaker to represent those rules with authority. The activity carried on in this chamber is the form of talking known as debate: interruptions are constant, confrontation is often excited and sometimes hot, and points are made and rebutted in direct opposition to one another. Each speech and each speaker are factors, and whatever is said changes things in unpredictable ways. Being interrupted, as he was so often, Churchill once raised his voice to quiet the opposition: "I am expressing my opinion. When my hon. and gallant Friend is called, he will express his opinion. That is the process which we call Debate."[23] This is also the process by which the greatest parliamentary government proceeds, the process by which the first and in Churchill's mind greatest of the free peoples decides what they shall do. This activity guards the freedom of that people, and it makes them strong.

During the Great War, he said of this activity: "This little place is what makes the difference between us and Germany. It is in virtue of this that we shall muddle through to success and for lack of this Germany's brilliant efficiency leads her to final disaster. This little room is the shrine of the world's liberties."[24] On May 10, 1941, the Germans bombed the House of Commons chamber into a ruin. It happened on precisely the one-year anniversary of Churchill's coming to power. The Commons met for several years in the House of Lords Chamber. Plans were being made to rebuild it, and Churchill made a speech in favor of building it back the way it was. Of course there was a move to make it more commodious and comfortable. Churchill replied that "we shape our buildings, and afterwards our buildings shape us."[25]

Two features of the shape were fundamental, Churchill said. The chamber was oblong. One must choose upon which side to sit. He could not move by "insensible gradations from Left to Right." It was a choice hard to make. Churchill noted with some pride that he altered his choice twice. The second characteristic was that it was too small to seat all the members. When it was not so well attended, still it seemed full, and its deliberations gained the appearance of importance. When an important matter was under consideration, it was overcrowded, and that conveyed the excitement and significance of the occasion. It achieved "a sense of crowd and urgency."[26] A year later he said: "If you want to reduce the power of Parliament, let it sit every day in the year, one-fifth part filled, and then you will find it will be the laughing-stock of the nation."[27]

Members and the people who elected them take it seriously. The shape and size and configuration of the Commons, which shaped those who entered it and those who elected them, operated as part of the British Constitution and in the manner of a constitution. It influenced its members to act in certain ways.

In his speech on rebuilding the Commons, Churchill said that Britain was fighting the war in part to see Parliament

continue as a "strong, easy, flexible instrument of free Debate."
He stated the conditions:

> The vitality and the authority of the House of Commons,
> and its hold upon an electorate based upon universal suf-
> frage, depend to no small extent upon its episodes and great
> moments, even upon its scenes and rows, which, as everyone
> will agree, are better conducted at close quarters. Destroy
> that hold which Parliament has upon the public mind and
> has preserved through all these changing, turbulent times,
> and the living organism of the House of Commons would be
> greatly impaired. You may have a machine, but the House of
> Commons is much more than a machine; it has earned and
> captured and held through long generations the imagination
> and respect of the British nation.[28]

The House of Commons had a "code of its own which everyone knows, and . . . means of its own of enforcing those manners
and habits which have grown up and have been found to be an
essential part of our Parliamentary life." It was able to face "the
possibility of national destruction with classical composure."[29] It
could change governments, and it did. It could take up any and
every question that was presented to the British public, debate it,
and contrive solutions that accorded with the public will. It was,
Churchill thought, the greatest of governing institutions.

The House of Commons was Churchill's home. He lived in
it, worked in it, and thrived in it for more than fifty years, most
of them as a member of profound influence. He even attended
the Commons in his later years and retirement, though he did
not speak. Today when members enter the Commons they pass

a statue of Churchill on the left, one of his shoes shining brightly because members polish the bronze by touching it for eloquence on the way in. To the suggestion from the Queen that he accept a dukedom, the highest peerage available outside the monarchy, Churchill declined partly in the name of his loyalty to this chamber.[30] He considered it the beating heart of the British Constitution.

THE WORK OF THE PEOPLE

According to Churchill, the legitimacy of the House of Commons derived from the manner of its selection. Members were elected and sustained by millions of people who went to the polls after weeks of debate that arrested the attention of the nation. Members must remain in close contact with the people through frequent elections and through regular communication with their constituents.[31] If Parliament should make a change in the franchise, it must be followed immediately by an election.[32] The people were the guardians "over every institution of the realm which really ministers to the needs of the whole nation."[33] The House of Commons was the "mirror of the opinions and wishes of the Nation." Because of this, it had in its power "control of the Executive Government."[34]

The representative character of the Commons was won by "the eloquence of statesmen like Mr. Fox and Mr. Gladstone," but also by "fierce and bloody fighting in actual war."[35] The authority of the Commons stemmed from its representative nature.[36] Churchill worked hard and successfully to curtail the authority of the House of Lords in the 1911 Parliament Act, and he said doing so was necessary because the House of Lords was unrepresentative.[37] In that contest between the Lords and the Commons, the "will of the people, as expressed by their accredited representatives," shall and must prevail.[38]

In comparison to despotic systems, the British government was reliably the protector of freedom because it was based on elections in which the people chose "freely and fairly the party they wish to have in office," and they could change their minds at any time.[39] In war, Churchill said in a speech to the American Bar Association, some freedoms of ordinary people may be temporarily curtailed or suspended, but only when "special powers [are] granted by the elected representatives of those same people by Congress or by Parliament, as the case may be." These powers do not belong to the "State or Government as a right. Their exercise needs vigilant scrutiny, and their grant may be swiftly withdrawn."[40] The American Constitution and the British Constitution, beginning with the Magna Carta, therefore overlap.

The people of Great Britain authorized this activity in the House of Commons. They were the source of its authority, and the constitutional system began with them. During the Second World War, Churchill said, "At the bottom of all the tributes paid to democracy is the little man, walking into the little booth, with a little pencil, making a little cross on a little bit of paper—no amount of rhetoric or voluminous discussion can possibly diminish the overwhelming importance of that point."[41]

Because choices by the little man in the little booth were fundamental, the little man must have information. His representatives owed him "candor." It was a "constitutional misdemeanor" for statesmen to fail to state to the nation "plainly and squarely the fiscal principles by which they propose to stand."[42] Governments may continue while they are strong with the people's mandate and while they operate within the scope of that mandate.[43] They must stay constantly "in close and harmonious contact with the constituent bodies which return them.[44]

The people had work to do in this system, and they must do that work in order to vindicate their authority. They must attend to politics with interest and care. During the 1909–11 controversy over the "People's Budget"—that is, the controversy over taxes and social welfare programs—Churchill was proud that his constituents "scarcely cared to hear about anything else" than the constitutional issue.[45] The Constitution depends upon a "union of consenting minds," minds "aiming at the same objective"; despite any division among them they must "feel that the greatness and glory of Britain and the happiness of her people have always been, and are still, the objective on which they are marching."[46] The people must carry on an "enlightened, active political life" expressing a "considered, instructed, organized public opinion. . . . [C]itizens in every class" must make "ceaseless political exertion . . . in all parts of the country."[47]

One can see why politicians would like citizens to pay attention to politics: it makes them famous. Churchill allowed that politicians even like to be caricatured in cartoons: "They are quite offended and downcast when the cartoons stop. They wonder what has gone wrong, they wonder what they have done amiss. They fear old age and obsolescence are creeping upon them. They murmur: 'We are not mauled and maltreated as we used to be. The great days are ended.'"[48]

Churchill developed the fear that the great days had ended. He recalled his boyhood:

Politics seemed very important and vivid to my eyes in those days. They were directed by statesmen of commanding intellect and personality. The upper classes in their various stations took part in them as a habit and as a duty. The working men whether they had votes or not followed them as a sport. They took as much interest in national affairs and were as good judges of form in public men, as is now the case about cricket or football. The newspapers catered obediently for what was at once an educated and a popular taste.[49]

Britain in those older days had a "vigorous, active, law-making citizenship."[50] Churchill regarded that as a pillar of British strength and freedom.

Churchill feared, and sometimes said he observed, that this civic spirit was dissipating. The British people became more passive as the government did more for them. Britain achieved universal suffrage in 1928 when the voting age for women was lowered to twenty-one, the same as for men. As the franchise was extended, voter participation declined. He thought that stemmed in part from the fact that voting was no longer a privilege, a special responsibility. Available to all, it was taken for granted. In 1935 he called for voting to be made mandatory; failure to vote would carry a fine.[51]

At the same time he called for improving "the quality of the franchise." He was forthright about it, as about most things, and he campaigned for it in public. He would make "a difference between the householder or head of the family and his or her children, or dependents." Everyone, man or woman, "who pays the rent and the rates of any dwelling in which more than two persons habitually reside" would be given a second vote. He said that would make the franchise available to everyone, and it would cut across rank, class, party, wealth, age, and sex. It would strengthen the influence of those who "face the real problems of national life with a responsibility quite different from that of lodgers of all kinds."[52] Of course it would also give further influence to those who paid for government against those who received from it.

This position was a change. Churchill was generally, early and late, in favor of extending the franchise for all. For South Africa, for instance, he endorsed the principle of "one vote, one value." In 1906 he said that "the only safe principle . . . is that all men are equal, and that voting power, as far as possible, should be evenly distributed among them."[53] He favored women's suffrage in principle consistently, even when suffragettes twice attacked him and more often interrupted his meetings; even when he and others were worried that women's votes would disadvantage his party; even when, before the extension of the franchise to all men, giving women the vote would exclude most women and favor the more wealthy.[54]

This means that during the course of his career Churchill had doubts, and he went back and forth. Generally in his early days he believed that the extension of the franchise to all, or at least all men, if accompanied by a system of relief for the poor, would win the people to the Constitution, to limited government, and to free markets.

In 1908, during his radical period, he went as far as to say that the Constitution was "mainly British common-sense" and that the real security of property was in the "class struggle," which was constant. He described a process of "perpetual friction" that never "breaks into violence." On this process depended

the security of property. The British, he said, are "always changing," and after each change reach a "higher level," yet with the
"harmony of our life unbroken and unimpaired." This friction
was not simply a matter of class: "There have always been men
of power and position who have sacrificed and exerted themselves in the popular cause." That was why there was little class
hatred in Britain despite the "squalor and misery which we see
around us." That was the "evolution of democracy." Like nature,
"we change always very slowly."[55]

Rarely did Churchill suggest the evolution of nature. In
this same speech he accused socialism of "leaving out human
nature."[56] Seldom, early or late, did he depreciate the importance
of the Constitution in relation to anything. Here is an exception.
It expresses a hope, which he held for decades, that the extension of the franchise and of the social safety net would wed the
British people to their Constitution and away from socialism,
and these would be sufficient. In 1924, a few months after he
was appointed chancellor of the exchequer, Churchill wrote to
his wife in optimism about the new administration under Prime
Minister Stanley Baldwin: "A strong Conservative Party with an
overwhelming majority and a moderate and even progressive
leadership is a combination which has never been really tested
before. It might well be the fulfillment of all that Dizzy [Benjamin
Disraeli] and my father aimed at in their political work."[57]

These hopes reflected Churchill's view of how the
Constitution should alleviate conflict among the classes. At its
best, the British system of representation united the people and
the members of the House of Commons in an intense national
debate whenever decisive issues arose. While the Commons
sometimes debated things small, local, or private, Churchill

believed it worked best debating large and fundamental matters of public business. He favored and helped to arrange home rule for Ireland—which his father resisted—in part because the Commons was not "sufficiently representative of the local and provincial life of the nation."[58] That was part of the reason he proposed a "sub-Parliament" to debate economic policy. That was also why he favored the creation of local Parliaments for Scotland, Wales, and the large centers of England.[59] He believed these federalist innovations would liberate the House of Commons to do what it did well: debate the national and imperial issues of justice that are decisive and can be understood and debated by the people as a nation.

For those reasons, Churchill thought that bureaucratic rule was a threat to the work of the Commons. It could not debate and decide the endless details that administrative government regulated and decided. Only cursory oversight would be possible. As we have seen, Churchill thought the sheer numbers of regulations alone would destroy respect for law. No one could follow the making of that many or be part of the process. The Labour Party in the 1945 election allowed that it would, according to Churchill, "pass Laws simply by resolutions of broad principle in the House of Commons, afterwards to be left by Parliament to the executive and to the bureaucrats to elaborate and enforce by departmental regulations."[60] Churchill believed that was the road to the Gestapo.

THE DANGERS OF EXECUTIVE POWER

The House of Commons is the home of the executive government. The executive power was taken, over time, from the monarch, the sovereign king, who wielded it for centuries. By gradual steps he was required to choose his ministers from the Commons, and finally he was required to choose them as the Commons directed.

Now the monarch reigns and is the symbol or holder of British sovereignty, and Churchill believed it vital that he or she continue in this station. Ministers must talk with the monarch on a regular basis. Queen Elizabeth must sign laws to make them law. She issues an invitation to Buckingham Palace to invite a potential prime minister to form a government. The prime minister surrenders his office to her when he is replaced. She tells Parliament and the nation the plans of the government at the opening of Parliament and does so from a throne in the chamber of the House of Lords. All of this matters. The monarch is the living symbol of the history of the British Constitution; she is "the most effectual barrier against one-man power or dictatorship arising whether from the Right or from the Left," Churchill said in 1937. "It has never been more valid and precious to democracy than it is at the present time."[61] "Nations," he continued, "are driven by force or tradition." He quotes Disraeli further:

> Here in this country we have seen tradition and custom giving us a decency and a security in our national life which no iron law, however brutally enforced, has been able to give to other countries. Long may it be the function of the Monarchy, sustained as it will be by Parliament and by the masses of the nation, to give that element of unity, of the present with the past, which, when all is said and done, is the greatest hope of our freedom in the future.[62]

But the Monarch does not rule. Churchill thought that was as it should be.

The British people and their leading political parties had, Churchill thought, become deeply attached to these arrangements by the process of political conflict. The people of Britain, by long exercise of their control of the government and by long exercise of their personal liberties, shared this conviction. It was the abiding strength of the British Constitution. The Crown had become the symbol of those convictions, which included the subordination of the Crown.

Despite the fact that the executive government rests in the House of Commons, Churchill did not understand the British government to be unitary in the sense praised by many American writers, especially among the founders of the progressive movement.[63] In their view the people place a party in the majority, and therefore it automatically controls both the legislative and the executive branches. It is therefore liberated to act in a way that makes vigorous government possible. Churchill thought rather that the activity of debate in the Commons is a constant superintendent of the government, and he was impatient with attempts by the executive to override this process of debate.[64]

In Britain the executive sits right there in the House of Commons, its ministers members of the legislature. It holds the executive authority of the nation. The government enforces the laws, keeps the secrets of the state, deploys force, and chooses actions that may be lethal at any point. Its members respond to crises, command respect, and even become famous. The ministers sit in the most distinguished place, to the Speaker's[65] right, not on one of the backbenches but on the front or Treasury Bench. Before them is a table, and they are the only ones who have a place upon which to keep their notes or behind which to stand. On the table sits the mace, the symbol of the authority of the monarch, who is the symbol of the authority of the British nation. Other members sit upon the backbenches, the government upon the front. They are powerful and important. They have authority strong enough to affect any member, to reward or punish.

On the other hand, these members of the government are simply members of the Commons. They are placed in their positions by a majority of those in the Commons, who selected and installed them and who may choose others when they please. The backbench Conservative members of Parliament, for example, have long been organized as a standing committee, the 1922 Committee. Whenever 15 percent of the members write to the chairman requesting a vote of confidence in their leader, who is the prime minister when the party is in power, that vote is held promptly, and it results from time to time in a change of leadership.[66] The Labour Party has similar arrangements. Churchill takes pride in the fact that the Commons can change governments and has "changed them by heat of passion."[67]

Each week when the Commons sits, time is planned for ministers to answer questions, often hostile, from members of their own party and especially from the opposition. These questions lead to other questions. Some of them are asked upon advance notice, and ministers in the government send their functionaries scurrying to get the answers. The press is constantly watching. What members say is recorded. Even before the electronic age, note takers were charged to produce a precisely faithful account of everything said. Charles Dickens

served in this function.[68] This account is made available free
of charge for public inspection, and the record of the proceed-
ings exists to the early nineteenth century. Members of the press
take notes or make electronic recordings, and every day they
publish or broadcast them. The potential for embarrassment is
ever present. No single person is in control of the activity of
debate. Members of the government are not simply participants:
they are the prime targets. Whenever the government seeks to
pass an important or controversial bill, which is constantly, the
ministers must participate in the debate, and they are watched
with particular attention. If they stumble, it is noted to their
shame and potential demotion.

As early as 1904 Churchill warned against the "growing
power of the Executive Government" and of the "consequent
decline of the Parliamentary authority."[69] But there is a built-in
corrective. The members of the Commons, elected by millions, go to Westminster to "support, correct, and control the
Executive Government." This executive does "direct affairs,"
but only by "virtue of the support of the majority of those
members," and this is given only "from day to day."[70] President
Roosevelt and his close colleague Harry Hopkins, for instance,
congratulated Churchill during the war that he had certainty
of support of his legislature. Churchill replied that the support
could be withdrawn and he could be dismissed on any day.[71]
The House of Commons is a test that the executive in Britain
must pass daily when the Commons is in session. Margaret
Thatcher herself, one of the longest-serving prime ministers,
was removed from the premiership by pressure from parliamentary members of her party and not by the loss of an election
by that party.

THE BENEFIT OF DIVIDED GOVERNMENT

The third element of the British Constitution was in Churchill's view the judiciary. In all cases between parties the judges are independent. The judiciary decides those cases on its own authority and finally. In his many lists of respected rights in free governments, Churchill constantly mentioned the independence of the judiciary as a hallmark. In other words, Churchill understood the British system as one of separation of powers: "There is not an official of the state who is unchecked or uncontrolled."[72]

Over the course of centuries British judges developed the common law, a treasure available to the world and used in many of its English-speaking parts. This common law proceeds from and also protects the independent judiciary, not subject to the control of monarch or Parliament in its decisions over individual cases. It and the judges who act under it are the protectors of the individual from the whole power of the state. It guarantees the grand features of trial by jury and habeas corpus. The first means that ordinary citizens, not those who exercise governing authority, determine the guilt or innocence of their peers. The second means that a judge may command that the executive deliver a detained person before him for adjudication.

Churchill sometimes regretted that the British judiciary does not have the power to protect the Constitution from legislative and executive encroachment as the American judiciary does. According to Churchill, the renowned jurist, Sir Edward Coke, argued that the common law and its traditions were the fundamental protections of Englishmen. But in the course of the English Revolution, when Oliver Cromwell reigned as Lord President, the idea of the supremacy of Parliament took root. Coke's "claim that the fundamental law of custom and tradition could not be over-borne, even by Crown and Parliament together, and his dream of judges in a Supreme Court of Common Law declaring what was or what was not legal, had been extinguished in England forever."[73] The important point for Churchill is that judges keep their remaining power to apply the law through the cases that come before them and thereby protect the individual and the rule of law. Though the judiciary cannot strike down an act of Parliament, it can, at least at the margins, interpret the laws in these cases to place the most constitutional construction on them.

Churchill admired the division of powers in the American government, but he thought they were copied from much older British practices. In 1950 he said:

> [T]he division of ruling power has always been for more than
> 500 years the aim of the British people. The division of power
> is the keynote of our parliamentary system and of the consti-
> tutions we have spread all over the world. The idea of checks
> and counter checks; the resistance to the theory that one man,
> or group of men, can by sweeping gestures and decisions
> reduce all the rest of us to subservience; these have always
> been the war cries of the British nation and the division of
> power has always been one of the war cries of the British
> people. And from here the principle was carried to America.
> The scheme of the American Constitution was framed to pre-
> vent *any one man or any one lot,* getting arbitrary control of
> the whole nation.[74]

We can see how Churchill understood the British Constitution by his attempts to reform it. When he said that

Crown, Lords, and Commons served as restraints upon one another, he was aware that the restraints weakened over time; the power of the House of Lords was reduced in 1911 by his own hand among others. Churchill wanted to strengthen the House of Lords by giving it a new basis of legitimacy. In 1925, as chancellor of the exchequer in the Conservative government, Churchill made a serious play to restore bicameralism to Britain by restructuring the House of Lords and making it representative of the people. He based much of his proposal on the recommendations of the Bryce Report of 1918, the product of a joint conference of members of the two houses of Parliament chaired by Lord Bryce, a Liberal politician.

Churchill outlined his plan in a cabinet memo. He began by rehearsing the debates over the Parliament Act of 1911, which established two things: that the House of Lords could not veto money bills, and that it could veto no other bills for more than two successive years. This meant that a majority party could pass any legislation it pleased in the life of a single Parliament as long as it kept control of the House of Commons for two years. Those changes were hard won. The Liberals won two successive elections in 1910 over the issue. After the second, King George V agreed that if the Lords rejected the measures, he would appoint enough Liberal peers to secure its passage. Many of the hardest things Churchill said about the aristocracy were said during this fight.

In his 1925 memorandum, Churchill repeated his arguments from that time: the House of Lords, unrepresentative, was acting in a partisan way. This behavior thwarted the will of the people. Yet it acted, unwittingly, to the advantage of the Liberal Party government, of which Churchill was then a member. In

his opinion the "action of the House of Lords and the antagonism to it in the country were the main cause of the continued
Liberal ascendancy in the years before the war, in spite of the
preponderating Conservative instincts of the English people."
Churchill argued that he and his fellow Liberals did not object
that the House of Lords was putting a "brake on the wheel" so
much as that it placed this brake in the hands of one particular
political party.[75] He proposed a brake that was neutral among
political parties, including Labour, and neutral among the various classes and interests.

The new House of Lords, he said, must have "continued contact with Constitutional equality." He meant that all parties must
have a fair chance to have influence in a stronger House of Lords.
Also he meant that the stronger House of Lords must rely indirectly upon popular support for its authority. The people must
indirectly elect the members, as direct election would give the
House of Lords "a different measure of the same kind of authority" as the House of Commons.[76] Churchill intended a body that
would behave differently, especially more slowly and deliberately,
than the House of Commons. If the House of Lords were elected
directly, it would be sucked into the "whirlpool of popular election." He proposed a "Chamber of Elder Statesmen."[77] In other
words, he proposed a body with the same character and goals as
those originally intended for the US Senate.[78] This new House of
Lords would act as a "Chamber of review." It would have power
of "Referendum,"[79] that is, it could delay implementation of a law
passed by the House of Commons pending a vote of the people.[80]

Given the fact that all authority comes from the people
in Great Britain, the new House of Lords must in some way
draw upon that authority. Churchill proposed that the House

of Commons select the members of the House of Lords from a panel of eligible candidates, primarily senior and accomplished political figures. Churchill also planned to include the largely conservative aristocracy. From this panel, numbering about 1,200 members who had indicated their willingness to serve if selected, the House of Commons would elect a House of Lords with 315 members. In this case the House of Commons would be "doing the House of Lords the service, which only they can do, of putting them in contact with the authority of the electorate."[81] Any members of the peerage who were not selected would be free to attend the meetings of the House of Lords, to participate in its debates, but not to vote. That would help to keep alive the traditions of the peerage and the good those traditions brought to British politics. Elected members would serve twelve years.

At the same time that many Americans were attempting to make the American government operate more like the British, Churchill was attempting to make the British government operate more like the American. Churchill sought to emulate the achievement in which James Madison took pride in the writing of the US Constitution. Madison wrote in *The Federalist Papers* that the powers of government are entirely derived from the "great body of the people," and yet these powers are divided and arranged in ways that will provide both stability and reason.[82] Britain would have a popularly elected government in all of its major parts, and that government would proceed in whatever direction the people wished it to go. But it would not respond instantly. The long-standing opinions of the people would be elevated above those of any given moment. Churchill saw this as a chance to protect the British Constitution and prevent rapid conversion of the British government and economy to socialism.

The Conservative government of 1924–29 did not implement these proposals, and thereafter Churchill's opportunity was gone. The next ten years were consumed chiefly in resistance to the proposals from Labour, National Coalition, and Conservative governments to grant dominion status to India and more especially to the appeasement of Hitler. That was followed by war. That was followed by six years of opposition while socialism was extensively implemented in the nation. That was followed by his second premiership, in which he had a narrow majority elected by 200,000 fewer voters than supported Labour.[83] By then Churchill was growing old.

One must consider how Churchill believed statesmen were to operate under the British Constitution. When Churchill said that "we shape our buildings, and then they shape us," he was explaining the importance of institutions. Buildings, like constitutions, are part of the organizing form of things. Churchill's affection for the shape of the House of Commons was of a piece with his affection for the British Constitution. In his view the House of Commons was the radiating center of that Constitution. To preserve the House of Commons was to preserve the British Constitution and vice versa.

Politics is not in the end institutions. In the end it is what people say and do. The constitutions and buildings that shape us are shaping an activity, not a static thing; an activity of people, not of automatons. Political institutions are powerful and yet we have the ability to stand outside them. That is why they change. That is why they can be created and destroyed.

Citizens and the statesmen who represent or control them carry on the activity of politics. Representative statesmen are, to the extent they represent, obeying forms of law that make it possible for an absent and preoccupied people to control them. These representatives have the power to use force on those they represent. They have reason to want their independence from any control: they are of a controlling disposition, or they would not be where they are. This is the point with which we began this book. Let us return to it here to say a word about Churchill and the British Constitution.

First, it must be admitted that Churchill did not get his way fully about the Constitution. The House of Lords was not in his time, and has not been since, reconstituted into a powerful and effective second chamber. The activity of the House of Commons was diminished in his day for just the reason he feared: so much of the job of governing came to happen outside it in agencies that the Commons created. This trend has now gone much further. Government in Britain, the United States, and much of the West is more expansive, more expensive, and less trusted (at least in the United States) than it was in Churchill's day.[84] Not many people defend bureaucracy, and yet we have more of it.

Churchill was an assertive human being. He took over the British government at the moment of the near-certain defeat of the nation, and he led the nation to victory. Moreover, he prevented a negotiated settlement that some around him supported. He argued that the settlement would amount to defeat, and it was better to pay the cost of war, frightful though it was, than risk association with Nazis. Those were commanding acts, of a piece with things that Churchill did on battlefields many times.

One can see the opposite spirit at work in Churchill's attempts to strengthen and enhance the House of Commons and the British Constitution. He was a great orator but not in the mode of Adolf Hitler. He did not favor the address to stadiums full of frenzied admirers or to millions on television or radio—and on radio he was effective.[85] His place was the House of Commons, facing his opponents or often sitting on the same side as they. There is an equality about that kind of oratory. One may be interrupted at any moment by anyone. Everything one says is contested. It is a process of back and forth, speaking and hearing in turn, ruling and being ruled in turn. In attempting to preserve this kind of government, Churchill was promoting himself, sure enough, for he excelled at it. Also he was demoting himself, because to be effective in the Commons was to be a servant of the Commons and of those it represents. He wrote that he had spent an entire year trundling from town to town, urging people to vote for him. He liked the meetings best when he was heckled.[86]

If his plans to reconstitute the House of Lords into a strong body had been realized, Churchill personally would have grown weaker. As it was, to pass something through the House of Commons where he sat and argued was to pass it into law. To add another body was to weaken the Commons in which he sat and therefore to weaken his own power.

Churchill represents a curious phenomenon, a man who used his considerable talents and boundless ambition to build up institutions that he could not ultimately dominate. Moreover he seemed to want those institutions to be dominated ultimately by those whom they governed. He said to Violet Bonham Carter that he was not a worm, but a glowworm.[87] He chose to serve a people, most of them not so talented or so ready to sacrifice as he. When they rejected him, he carried on in their service, according to his own lights, seeking agreement with them.

Churchill's eloquence was cultivated to this goal. He shone when speaking in the Commons, and he shone when speaking

on the platform in front of voters. He was never a media phenomenon except during the war, and then it was to him secondary.[88]
Moreover he wrote constantly, including his speeches, a stream
of articles for the press, and dozens of books. This writing is
often sublime. It is built out of common terms that are known to
all, especially terms hallowed through time in the English language. He was explaining himself to people in their multitudes.
He spoke and wrote in a way that they could understand.

In opposing Socialist and bureaucratic rule, Churchill was
opposing one kind of strong government in support of another.
The kind he favored dealt with relatively few subjects, chosen
for their moment and elevation. The subjects could be discussed in the plain language of justice and injustice, of right and
wrong. They could be debated at the same time in the House
of Commons and in the country. He believed this kind of government could be sustained through the conversion of Britain
to popular rule and would thrive thereafter. In that way Britain
would be whole, still mighty, and now democratic and including
everyone. This may have been a dream. If so, he dreamed it and
worked for it.

One of the darkest passages Churchill ever wrote is in
his essay "Mass Effects in Modern Life." He described the
Bolsheviks, who like the Nazis sought to treat people like beasts
and so reduce them to insects. He said those ideas were not confined to those monstrous tyrannies but had their seed also in the
scientific approach to politics that was spreading in his time and
in his country. He regarded socialism as the point of that spear,
and it gained strength throughout his life. He feared that this
doctrine was changing the people of Britain and reducing the
scope for freedom and for excellence.

"Mass Effects" ended in a reverie for a lost time when there were heroes. Of course Churchill could not know that, as he wrote in 1931, the most heroic time was still to come. He said that in this new day, armed with science, Britain had reached an upland, above the peaks it had struggled so long to ascend. There was no mountain upon which to gaze upward. He was making a point about the loss of heroes and the loss we suffer without them.

This dark passage from "Mass Effects" contains the lines: "In Soviet Russia we have a society which seeks to model itself upon the Ant. There is not one single social or economic principle or concept in the philosophy of the Russian Bolshevik which has not been realized, carried into action, and enshrined in immutable laws a million years ago by the White Ant." This passage is followed immediately by one of the most optimistic he ever wrote: "But human nature is more intractable than ant-nature. The explosive variations of its phenomena disturb the smooth working out of the laws and forces which have subjugated the White Ant. It is at once the safeguard and the glory of mankind that they are easy to lead and hard to drive."[89]

This is both an observation and an expression of faith. It led Churchill to support the British Constitution, the only way possible he believed for a modern Britain with its millions to participate together in the activity of self-rule. It led him to think that he could explain it to them, that they would understand, and, in understanding, rise up to claim it once again for their own. He showed them how, by making that claim. He gave testimony to his faith that mankind can be led better than driven.

CONCLUSION

Churchill's Trial and Ours

Churchill faced a trial of war. It can be argued that he failed that trial. He tried to find a way around the trenches in the Great War; he failed, millions died, and he suffered disgrace. He tried to prevent the war with Hitler; he failed, and war raged until Europe was broken, and Britain, still independent and free, was reduced.

On the other hand, Britain was not overcome, against all odds. Moreover, the policy Churchill proposed for confronting the Soviet Union was largely if not fully implemented. Deterrence, the special relationship, the alliance among the free nations, and containment were parts of Churchill's Cold War strategy, a strategy that eventually succeeded. Furthermore, the cultivation of free markets and representative government based entirely upon popular sovereignty and consent of the governed, which he championed vigorously, remain even today the basis of Western societies. These made those societies much more powerful even than the resolute Soviet despotism, and they won the day.

Churchill faced a trial of peace. It can be argued that he failed that trial. Like most Western countries, Britain is today a bureaucratic state. When Churchill retired from public office, a larger majority of the resources of the nation were left to "fructify in the pockets of the people"[1]—a phrase Churchill favored. Today the British government consumes 43.3 percent of the gross domestic product, exclusive of the cost of regulation.[2] The specific qualities of a liberal society as Churchill conceived it turn upon the relationship between public and private, upon the dominance of the citizens in their private capacity over the government. The government is bigger now.

Today the vast majority of laws or rules in Britain are made outside Parliament in administrative agencies. They have power to reach nearly anywhere, and formerly private matters are now closely controlled by the regulatory state. Martin Loughlin writes,

During the 20th century the number of Bills enacted in a parliamentary session has hardly changed. What has altered dramatically is the length and complexity of this legislation. In 1900, Parliament enacted 63 Acts amounting to fewer than 200 pages of the statute book. In 1950, only 51 Acts were passed but these took up over 1,000 pages. By 2000, the 45 Acts passed filled nearly 4,000 (larger-sized) pages of the statute book. And this is just the tip of the iceberg. The volume of executive legislation passed during the 20th century has grown tenfold: from around 300 Statutory Instruments (SIs) of under 1,000 pages in 1900 to 3,500 SIs amounting to over 10,000 pages in 2000. Since 1972, Parliament's powers with respect to legislation have been further circumscribed by its commitment to recognize European Union laws and to amend UK law to ensure compliance. Today, it is clear that only in a purely formal sense can Parliament be said to legislate. Legislation must be promoted through and approved by Parliament, but it may be more accurate to say that Parliament does not in any substantive sense legislate; it mainly legitimates.[3]

One may argue, as some do, that the social welfare state, many features of which Churchill supported, planted the seed that has grown into this tree. On the other hand the state in most every free nation today, being a more comprehensive entity than ever before, claims authority to redefine many of the rules that Churchill regarded as written in nature.

It is true that in the Western countries, bureaucratic though they are, people may still write and speak as they please, mostly. If the bounds between church and state are adjusted at the expense of the church, still people may pray as they wish and worship together on Sunday wherever they please, and they surely have a wider freedom not to be exposed to worship than they enjoyed previously. This may mean that Churchill was wrong about the tendencies of socialism and of the bureaucratic state. Everywhere that kind of state is successful and enjoys the prestige of intellectual support. Against that there is Churchill's warning, just like another from James Madison,[4] that a state so powerful will come to own the people under its domain. It may be too early to settle this question.

If Churchill was right about these tendencies, the fact that the disasters he predicted have not appeared has something to do with his successes. He managed after six years of fierce opposition to regain control of Parliament and change direction.

The bureaucratic state was not nearly as far advanced when he retired as it is today.

The tendencies that Churchill feared in war are also still very much with us. Nuclear weapons have proliferated and threaten imminently to proliferate further among tyrannical nations. War is more terrible in potential today than ever, and should it break out on the general scale it will be more destructive than has been seen. Moreover individual attacks by terrorists, often complicit with despotic governments, may one day make some city or cities disappear in a flash of catastrophe. No one can read Churchill's "Shall We All Commit Suicide?" without understanding its contemporary implications.

THE LESSONS OF CHURCHILL

Churchill spent his life aware of these "mass effects" in war and in peace, and in resistance to them. Prudence being what it is, we cannot know with certainty what Churchill would say if he were alive today. He has been dead for fifty years at the time of this writing. But we can identify the themes of his life and study how he applied them in the practical situations of his day from the richest available record for any statesman.

Churchill taught that war is dangerous always but especially in modern times. He taught that despotic governments are not to be trusted, even if they are to be negotiated with, compromised with, traded with. He taught that free peoples must work together to guard their freedom, and to do so they must recognize each other for the friends in principle that they are. Churchill taught that when these free peoples are threatened by armed despotism, they should seek unity and also overwhelming force, including especially military force. That was the best way to prevent war, imperfect though it was. He taught that we should be cautious in going to war and employ a strategy that envisions a victory worth the cost. He taught that this rule does not apply the same where life and freedom are at stake from aggression. In that case, and only that, it is better to die fighting.

Churchill taught that one should be on the side of the people. "Trust the people" was his lifelong refrain. Another was "tell the truth to the British people." As people are not beasts, he thought they had the right to govern themselves. He also thought that they are the best judges of their own interest and, given time and the right constitutional arrangements, they would make the best decisions for themselves that are humanly possible. He thought them a much better guide to the fundamentals of political life than the trained experts produced by the academy.

Churchill thought the British people courageous: he even said that he preferred the kind of war in which British civilians bore part of the brunt of battle to the awful trenches of the Great War, when young men perished in millions and their families were left in safety to grieve for them. He thought the free countries especially well adapted to this kind of war, despite its terrors. He thought that statesmen must understand the propriety and advantage of the people's authority and should calculate their actions to benefit them and to sustain their authority for the long term. He thought that the best way to confront the modern ideologies that beset free government was to explain to the people that these ideologies were the enemy of ordinary people, first and foremost. At the end of his career, in the only election that he won to become prime minister, he made this strategy work, and he gave those who held these ideologies one of their most significant setbacks.

Churchill taught that free markets are "twice blessed" because they confer benefits on both parties in every transaction.[5] He taught that "trade . . . is the way in which peaceful peoples earn their livelihood,"[6] and if people are allowed to ply their trade in free markets under the rule of law, nearly all can prosper.[7] Churchill taught that a modern society, with all its wealth, must use some of that wealth to ameliorate the condition of those who suffer misfortune and serious poverty. He taught that there must be safeguards to prevent this arrangement from building a society populated by drones, or a society dominated by bureaucrats, which two things he thought moved hand in hand. Churchill taught that this could be accomplished in ways that did not empower the state to overcome or own the people. He taught that every part of government, including national defense and war strategy, including the "machinery" of social welfare, should be subjected to the search for economies. He taught that civil servants should be both civil and servants, and he taught that their constant accountability to elected politicians, themselves made civil and servants by the process of election, was the only guarantee of that.

Churchill taught that constitutional rule, based upon the people alone, with arrangements to solicit from the people their most considered advice and to protect the rights of all, was vital. He taught that government must be representative, that debate must be open and free. He taught that powers must be separated. He taught that powers over local things should be exercised locally. He taught that government must be limited. In other words, his views on constitutionalism echoed those behind the American Constitution, which he admired.

Churchill taught that the heart of constitutional rule in Britain is the activity of talking in the House of Commons. He sought to defend that activity from the executive arm of the government, which was to be its creature. He sought to defend it from domination by trivia or excessive delegation to experts. He gave participation in this activity his first attention, and it is no accident that he was successful at it. He thought this activity in the House of Commons was rooted in the opinions of the British people whom Parliament, both Houses, must represent. He thought that activity also echoed into every corner of the land and into the mind of each citizen who paid attention. He thought opinions were elevated by talking, which meant debate and argument. He taught that citizens must pay attention to debates and arguments, or others will rule them.

Churchill taught that statesmanship, in some obvious senses the opposite of constitutionalism, must realize that this constitutionalism is necessary. The greatest statesmen, willful, ambitious, strong, and artful, work within its bounds and in support of its continuation. Statesmen who combine that mixture of talent and conviction are very rare, like great generals much rarer than the "largest and purest of diamonds."[8] They should be appreciated and supported—and also contested—when they are present, and they should be remembered and studied when they are gone.

Churchill taught that constitutionalism and limitless government could be recognized by their opposite fruits. He gave often and concisely, sometimes beautifully, summaries of the happy results of constitutional rule. Under a good constitution, people may speak their minds, have security in their property, and elect rulers who are beholden to them. Under such a constitution people may pray and worship as they please, free to "live by no man's leave underneath the law."[9] Under such a constitution, the law is predictable, easy to understand, not frequently changed, and the product of public deliberation. The laws that legislatures pass are carried out by executives who are watched by other branches, whose actions upon individuals are subject to review by independent judges, and who themselves are accountable to the people. Such a constitution features a separation of powers sufficient to make sure no exercise of power is arbitrary.

Churchill taught that these constitutional arrangements are the foundation and the guarantee of civilization itself. Civilization, like government, is an activity, a form of community. It begins with the rule of law under the control of civilians. It proceeds to its first goal, the safeguarding of people in their homes and with their families, living fully human lives in care of themselves and others, participating in the common rule of all. It culminates in the beautiful things to know and to see, in art, in science, in learning.

Churchill taught that people are not to be regarded or used as instruments or merely as factors of production. He taught that the discipline, self-restraint, courage, and charity that make a nation civilized and strong must be located in the people, and if people have these things, they can and will care for themselves and for their nation, including their fellow citizens who suffer misfortune and privation. If the people do not have them, all is lost. He taught that they must be encouraged to learn the things that are highest and that bring out their best, things beyond themselves and their use. He taught that "engines were made for men, and not men for engines."[10] He taught that ideologies, whether at home or abroad, whether gradualist or sudden, whether moderate or extreme, would lead ultimately to the same despotism if they are followed. He taught that ideologies are ugly things, and though he never called himself wise, he was guided by wisdom, and he sought to protect the pursuit of that wisdom.

OPPORTUNITY AND DISASTER

Churchill taught these things, for he was as much a teacher as a statesman, as much given to explaining as he was to convincing. He left behind a record of speech and writing that is unsurpassed among statesmen in quantity and in quality. When he was young, he declared the importance of learning to do this. He consumed his life in producing words. It is no accident that we remember so many of those words.

Churchill had many grave and solemn things to say and to do. When we read them we may think we live in a dark age, a "bad age," as Churchill said. To dwell too much on that would be to forget the young Churchill striding confidently about the armored train under fire or the old Churchill giving his speeches in defiance of Hitler. It would be to forget the old Churchill, whipped in the 1945 election and encouraged to resign a great man, gathering himself instead to make the same arguments again after almost fifty years of repetition, providing a model of opposition politics in humility before the will of the people. This is the Churchill holding up the V sign in the bombed ruins of London. This is the real Churchill. He grows bigger, not smaller, when one knows that he was worried and afraid, when one knows that he made mistakes and became desperate—almost.

Such are the courageous. To know the full Churchill is to understand the combination of boldness and caution, of assertiveness and humility necessary to statesmen. To know the full Churchill is to learn that one should be happy, for the virtues are called virtues because they make one so, especially in adversity, which is bound to come.

Like many old men, Churchill at the end of his life sometimes spoke of how much the world had changed and how his views seemed old-fashioned. They did and do seem old-fashioned to many. But his case for them was not ultimately that they were old or that they were fashionable, but that they were blessed with the truth established in the nature of things. Therefore he thought that fashion would conform to them sooner or later and not they to fashion.

We live in the same modern world that Churchill occupied. In some ways it provides greater opportunity for more people in more lands than has ever been known. Churchill hoped for this. Also he warned that achievements and opportunities have dangers and potential disasters as their companions. "We pay for every pleasure and every triumph we have in this world,"[11] he wrote. The power we have to make us comfortable and secure can be used to kill us and make us slaves. The art is to prevent that, and the art begins with knowing the danger is real.

Many today admire Churchill for his gallantry in war, his eloquence, his liberalism in the original sense, and his conservatism in the same sense. They have reason to think that Churchill was right when he warned that modern conditions make things so large and power so great that mere humans cannot control them. They have reason to think that he was right when he warned that the accumulation of strength by man over nature means only, as Churchill's contemporary C. S. Lewis wrote, and as the Socialist R. H. S. Crossman agreed, the power of some men over others.[12] This means that in some sense Churchill failed: he did not eliminate the mass effects of which he warned. Churchill resisted this kind of thinking. Human problems are not to be overcome for all time, at least not by humans. And yet still it is true, as he said in his final words to the cabinet upon his resignation as prime minister: "Man is spirit."[13]

If we take the grim lessons from Churchill as truth, we are also required by consistency to listen to the rest of his advice. We should remember that fearing war, he fought it with courage and skill, and he and his country won. We should remember that fearing these modern ideologies, he opposed them with tireless and eloquent argument at immense trouble to himself, and he held them back and even rolled them back. We should remember that all is not lost until all is lost, and fifty years after Churchill died, all is not lost. If he was right about the dangers, the fact that we are in a position to confront them owes partly to him. We should remember the last words of his last major speech in his beloved House of Commons: "never flinch, never weary, never despair."[14]

Churchill's trial is also our trial. We have a better chance to meet it because we had in him a statesman.

ACKNOWLEDGMENTS

I must thank my teachers, especially three of them. The late Harold S. Rood and Harry V. Jaffa introduced me to the study of Churchill long ago in my first year of graduate school. They approached this subject in their constant way, as if there might be something of abiding truth and value to be found there. They looked for it both seriously and skeptically, and the limits on the benefits they gave me are all in me. Professor Jaffa died this January, and I join his family, his students, and many others in mourning the loss of a mind as powerful as any I have met.

I dedicate this book to Sir Martin Gilbert. Sir Martin is the greatest of the Churchill biographers and one of the greatest of historians. I was privileged to study and work with him intensely for three years and less intensely for four decades after that, until his incapacity that ended this February in his passing. His absence is a blow to all who study Churchill or anything else in history. He was an electric personality, quick, learned, good of heart, and to see him is to delight. I am privileged to carry on in his stead the completion of the document volumes of the official biography, a plan we made over many years to prepare for his being unable.

I thank my colleague of these thirty years and more, Douglas Jeffrey, whose ability to edit, grounded in a deep understanding, is the best I know. His deft hand is apparent to those who know in better books than this one, and he has improved and enriched this one everywhere.

Kyle Murnen led several young people who have helped me beyond any telling in the writing of the book. Kyle is both a student and a colleague of mine, and there is very little that his intellect and character do not equip them to do. I am deeply grateful to him and to Aaron Kilgore, Soren Geiger, Kevin Bishop, Sam Ryskamp, Mary Meyer, Victoria Bergen, Andrew Reuss, Julia DeLapp, Julia Kilgore, and John Shannon.

If wisdom is the accumulation of knowledge about elevated things, then in his decades of work on Winston Churchill, Richard Langworth has become wise. He has lent that wisdom to me in reading this book. His comments are insightful, thorough, and always helpful, just as he is.

Christopher Harmon, Patrick J. Garrity, and my colleague Matthew Spalding made comments on the text that were helpful and encouraging. They are people of learning who have better things to do, and I am in their debt.

I thank my editor at HarperCollins, Joel Miller. His importunities are the reason I have written this book so long intended, and his advice has made it better. Kristen Parrish and Heather Skelton succeeded Joel in this project, and I have benefited from working with them again. Dimples Kellogg copyedited the book, and she has a genius for the work.

Portions of chapter 2 are taken from an essay I published in the excellent *Claremont Review of Books*. I thank the Claremont Institute for its permission to reprint.

I am privileged to teach courses on Churchill and related subjects to many intelligent students, and I thank them for the countless things they have taught me. One day one of them will write a book on Churchill better than this one, and I look forward to reading it. I live and work in a fine community of learning, and its faculty and staff are an inspiration to me. They influence whatever is good in this book.

I thank my wife of many decades, the lovely and good Penny, whom I met first as a colleague in the employ of Martin Gilbert. We have produced four children, Kathleen (formerly Katy, but she is now a scholar), Henry, Alice, and Tony. To their goodness I owe the stability in my life and most of its joy. Katy's husband, Daniel O'Toole, made helpful if also critical comments on one of the chapters, and it is better for them. His father-in-law does not seem to intimidate him.

Larry P. Arnn
Hillsdale, Michigan
July 2015

APPENDIX I

Fifty Years Hence

*First published in *Strand*, December 1931
The great mass of human beings, absorbed in the toils, cares and activities of life, are only dimly conscious of the pace at which mankind has begun to travel. We look back a hundred years, and see that great changes have taken place. We look back fifty years, and see that the speed is constantly quickening. This present century has witnessed an enormous revolution in material things, in scientific appliances, in political institutions, in manners and customs. The greatest change of all is the least perceptible by individuals: it is the far greater numbers which in every civilized country participate in the fuller life of man. "In those days," said Disraeli, writing at the beginning of the nineteenth century, "England was for the few and for the very few." "The twice two thousand for whom," wrote Byron, "the world is made" have given place to many millions for whom existence has become larger, safer, more varied, more full of hope and choice. In the United States scores of millions have lifted

themselves above primary necessities and comforts, and aspire to culture—at least for their children. Europe, though stunned and lacerated by Armageddon, presents a similar if less general advance. We all take the modern conveniences and facilities as they are offered to us without being grateful or consciously happy. But we simply could not live if they were taken away. We assume that progress will be constant. "This 'ere progress," Mr. Wells makes one of his characters remark, "keeps going on. It's wonderful 'ow it keeps going on." It is also very fortunate, for if it stopped or were reversed, there would be the catastrophe of unimaginable horror. Mankind has gone too far to go back, and is moving too fast to stop. There are too many people maintained not merely in comfort but in existence by processes unknown a century ago, for us to afford even a temporary check, still less a general setback, without experiencing calamity in its most frightful form.

When we look back beyond a hundred years over the long trails of history, we see immediately why the age we live in differs from all other ages in human annals. Mankind has sometimes travelled forwards and sometimes backwards, or has stood still even for hundreds of years. It remained stationary in India and in China for thousands of years. What is it that has produced this new prodigious speed of man? Science is the cause. Her once feeble vanguards, often trampled down, often perishing in isolation, have now become a vast organized united class-conscious army marching forward upon all the fronts towards objectives none may measure or define. It is a proud, ambitious army which cares nothing for all the laws that men have made; nothing for their most time-honored customs, or most dearly-cherished beliefs, or deepest instincts. It is this power called Science which

has laid hold of us, conscripted us into its regiments and batteries, set us to work upon its highways and in its arsenals; rewarded
us for our services, healed us when we were wounded, trained
us when we were young, pensioned us when we were worn out.
None of the generations of men before the last two or three were
ever gripped for good or ill and handled like this.

Man in the earliest stages lived alone and avoided his neighbors with as much anxiety and probably as much reason as he
avoided the fierce flesh-eating beasts that shared his forests.
With the introduction of domestic animals the advantages of
cooperation and the division of labor became manifest. In the
Neolithic times when cereals were produced and agriculture
developed, the bleak hungry period whilst the seeds were ger-
minating beneath the soil involved some form of capitalism,
and the recognition of those special rights of landed proprietors
the traces of which are still visible in our legislation. Each stage
involved new problems legal, sociological and moral. But progress only crawled, and often rested for a thousand years or so.

The two ribbon States in the valleys of the Nile and the
Euphrates produced civilizations as full of pomp and circumstance and more stable than any the world has ever known. Their
autocracies and hierarchies were founded upon the control and
distribution of water and corn. The rulers held the people in an
efficiency of despotism never equaled till Soviet Russia was born.
They had only to cut off or stint the water in the canals to starve or
subjugate rebellious provinces. This, apart from their granaries,
gave them powers at once as irresistible and as capable of intimate
regulation as the control of all food supplies gives to the Bolshevik
commissars. Safe from internal trouble, they were vulnerable
only to external attack. But in these states man had not learnt

to catalyze the forces of nature. The maximum power available was the sum of the muscular efforts of all the inhabitants. Later empires, scarcely less imposing but far less stable, rose and fell. In the methods of production and communication, in the modes of getting food and exchanging goods, there was less change between the time of Sargon and the time of Louis XIV than there was between the accession of Queen Victoria and the present day. Darius could probably send a message from Susa to Sardis faster than Philip II could transmit an order from Madrid to Brussels. Sir Robert Peel, summoned in 1841 from Rome to form a government in London, took the same time as the Emperor Vespasian when he had to hasten to his province of Britain. The bathrooms of the palace of Minos were superior to those of Versailles. A priest from Thebes would probably have felt more at home at the Council of Trent two thousand years after Thebes had vanished than Sir Isaac Newton at a modern undergraduate physical society, or George Stephenson in the Institute of Electrical Engineers. The changes have been so sudden and so gigantic that no period in history can be compared with the last century. The past no longer enables us even dimly to measure the future.

The most wonderful of all modern prophecies is found in Tennyson's "Locksley Hall":

> For I dipt into the future, far as human eye could see,
> Saw the Vision of the world, and all the wonder that
>   would be;
> Saw the heavens fill with commerce, argosies of
>   magic sails,
> Pilots of the purple twilight, dropping down with
>   costly bales;

Heard the heavens fill with shouting, and there
    rain'd a ghastly dew
From the nations' airy navies grappling in the
    central blue
Far along the world-wide whisper of the south-wind
    rushing warm
With the standards of the peoples plunging thro' the
    thunderstorm;
Till the war-drum throbb'd no longer, and the
    battle-flags were furl'd
In the Parliament of man, the Federation of the
    world.
Slowly comes a hungry people, as a lion creeping
    nigher,
Glares at one that nods and winks behind a slowly-
    dying fire.

These six couplets of prediction, written eighty years ago, have already been fulfilled. The conquest of the air for commerce and war, the League of Nations, the Communist movement—all divined in their true sequence by the great Victorian—all now already in the history-books and stirring the world around us today! We may search the Scriptures in vain for such precise and swiftly-vindicated forecasts of the future. Jeremiah and Isaiah dealt in dark and cryptic parables pointing to remote events and capable of many varied interpretations from time to time. A Judge, a Prophet, a Redeemer would arise to save his chosen People; and from age to age the Jews asked, disputing, "Art thou he that should come or do we look for another?" But "Locksley Hall" contains an exact foretelling of stupendous events, which many of those who knew the writer lived to see and endure! The dawn of the Victorian era opened the new period of man; and the genius of the poet pierced the veil of the future.

There are two processes which we adopt consciously or unconsciously when we try to prophesy. We can seek a period in the past whose conditions resemble as closely as possible those of our day, and presume that the sequel to that period will, save for some minor alterations, be repeated. Secondly, we can survey the general course of development in our immediate past, and endeavor to prolong it into the near future. The first is the method of the historian; the second that of the scientist. Only the second is open to us now, and this only in a partial sphere. By observing all that Science has achieved in modern times, and the knowledge and power now in her possession, we can predict with some assurance the inventions and discoveries which will govern our future. We can but guess, peering through a glass darkly, what reactions these discoveries and their applications will produce upon the habits, the outlook and the spirit of men.

Whereas formerly the utmost power that man could guide and control was a team of horses, or a galleyful of slaves; or possibly, if they could be sufficiently drilled and harnessed, a gang of laborers like the Israelites in Egypt: it is today already possible to control accurately from the bridge of a battle cruiser all the power of hundreds of thousands of men: or to set off with one finger a mine capable in an instant of destroying the work of thousands of man-years. These changes are due to the substitution of molecular energy for muscular energy, and its direction and control by an elaborate, beautifully-perfected apparatus. These immense new sources of power, and the fact that they can be wielded by a single individual, have made possible novel methods of mining and metallurgy, new modes of transport and undreamed-of machinery. These in their turn enable the molecular sources of power to be extended and used more efficiently. They facilitate also the improvement of ancient methods. They substitute the hundred-thousand-kilowatt turbo-generators at Niagara for the mill-wheel of our forefathers. Each invention acted and reacted on other inventions, and with ever-growing rapidity that vast structure of technical achievement was raised which separates the civilization of today from all that the past has known.

There is no doubt that this evolution will continue at an increasing rate. We know enough to be sure that the scientific achievements of the next fifty years will be far greater, more rapid and more surprising, than those we have already experienced. The slide-lathe enabled machines of precision to be made, and the power of steam rushed out upon the world. And through the steam-clouds flashed the dazzling lightning of electricity. But this is only a beginning. High authorities tell us that new sources of power, vastly more important than any we yet know, will surely be discovered. Nuclear energy is incomparably greater than the molecular energy which we use today. The coal a man can get in a day can easily do five hundred times as much work as the man himself. Nuclear energy is at least one million times more powerful still. If the hydrogen atoms in a pound of water could be prevailed upon to combine together and form helium, they would suffice to drive a thousand horse-power engine for a whole year. If the electrons—those tiny planets of the atomic systems—were induced to combine with the nuclei in the hydrogen the horse-power liberated would be 120 times greater still. There is no question among scientists that this gigantic source of energy exists. What is lacking is the match to set the bon-fire alight, or it may be the detonator to cause the dynamite to explode. The Scientists are looking for this.

The discovery and control of such sources of power would cause changes in human affairs incomparably greater than those produced by the steam-engine four generations ago. Schemes of cosmic magnitude would become feasible. Geography and climate would obey our orders. Fifty thousand tons of water, the amount displaced by the *Berengaria*, would, if exploited as described, suffice to shift Ireland to the middle of the Atlantic. The amount of rain falling yearly upon the Epsom race-course would be enough to thaw all the ice at the Arctic and Antarctic poles. The changing of one element into another by means of tem-peratures and pressures would be far beyond our present reach, would transform beyond all description our standards of values. Materials thirty times stronger than the best steel would create engines fit to bridle the new forms of power. Communications and transport by land, water and air would take unimaginable forms, if, as is in principle possible, we could make an engine of 600 horse-power, weighing 20 lb. and carrying fuel for a thousand hours in a tank the size of a fountain-pen. Wireless telephones and television, following naturally upon their present path of development, would enable their owner to connect up with any room similarly installed, and hear and take part in the conversation as well as if he put his head in through the window. The congregation of men in cities would become superfluous. It would rarely be necessary to call in person on any but the most intimate friends, but if so, excessively rapid means of commu-nication would be at hand. There would be no more object in living in the same city with one's neighbor than there is today in living with him in the same house. The cities and the countryside would become indistinguishable. Every home would have its garden and its glade.

Up till recent times the production of food has been the prime struggle of man. That war is won. There is no doubt that the civilized races can produce or procure all the food they require. Indeed some of the problems which vex us today are due to the production of wheat by white men having exceeded their own needs, before yellow men, brown men and black men have learnt to demand and become able to purchase a diet superior to rice. But food is at present obtained almost entirely from the energy of the sunlight. The radiation from the sun produces from the carbonic acid in the air more or less complicated carbon compounds which give us our plants and vegetables. We use the latent chemical energy of these to keep our bodies warm, we convert it into muscular effort. We employ it in the complicated processes of digestion to repair and replace the wasted cells of our bodies. Many people of course prefer food in what the vegetarians call "the second-hand form," i.e. after it has been digested and converted into meat for us by domestic animals kept for this purpose. In all these processes, however, ninety-nine parts of the solar energy are wasted for every part used.

Even without the new sources of power great improvements are probably here. Microbes which at present convert the nitrogen of the air into the proteins by which animals live, will be fostered and made to work under controlled conditions, just as yeast is now. New strains of microbes will be developed and made to do a great deal of our chemistry for us. With a greater knowledge of what are called hormones, i.e. the chemical messengers in our blood, it will be possible to control growth. We shall escape the absurdity of growing a whole chicken in order to eat the breast or wing, by growing these parts separately under a suitable medium. Synthetic food will, of course, also be used in the future. Nor need the pleasures of the table be banished. That gloomy Utopia of tabloid meals need never be invaded. The new foods will from the outset be practically indistinguishable from the natural products, and any changes will be so gradual as to escape observation.

If the gigantic new sources of power become available, food will be produced without recourse to sunlight. Vast cellars in which artificial radiation is generated may replace the cornfields or potato-patches of the world. Parks and gardens will cover our pastures and ploughed fields. When the time comes there will be plenty of room for the cities to spread themselves again.

But equally startling developments lie already just beyond our finger-tips in the breeding of human beings, and the shaping of human nature. It used to be said, "Though you have taught the dog more tricks, you cannot alter the breed of the dog." But that is no longer true. A few years ago London was surprised by a play called *Roosum's Universal Robots*. The production of such beings may well be possible within fifty years. They will not be made, but grown under glass. There seems little doubt that it will be possible to carry out in artificial surroundings the entire cycle which now leads to the birth of a child. Interference with the mental development of such beings, expert suggestion and treatment in the earlier years, would produce beings specialized to thought or toil. The production of creatures, for instance, which have admirable physical development with their mental endowment stunted in particular directions, is almost within the range of human power. A being might be produced capable of tending a machine but without other ambitions. Our minds recoil from such fearful eventualities, and the laws of a Christian civilization will prevent them. But might not lop-sided creatures of this type fit in well with the Communist doctrines of Russia? Might not the Union of Soviet Republics armed with all the power of science find it in harmony with all their aims to produce a race adapted to mechanical tasks and with no other ideas but to obey the Communist State? The present nature of man is tough and resilient. It casts up its sparks of genius in the darkest and most unexpected places. But Robots could be made to fit the grisly theories of Communism. There is nothing in the philosophy of Communists to prevent their creation.

I have touched upon this sphere only lightly, but with the purpose of pointing out that in a future which our children may live to see, powers will be in the hands of men altogether different from any by which human nature has been molded. Explosive forces, energy, materials, machinery will be available upon a scale which can annihilate whole nations. Despotism and tyrannies will be able to prescribe the lives and even the wishes of their subjects in a manner never known since time began. If to these tremendous and awful powers is added the pitiless sub-human wickedness which we now see embodied in one of the most powerful reigning governments, who shall say that the world itself will not be wrecked, or indeed that it ought not to be wrecked? There are nightmares of the future from which a fortunate collision with some wandering star, reducing the earth to incandescent gas, might be a merciful deliverance.

It is indeed a descent almost to the ridiculous to contemplate the impact of the tremendous and terrifying discoveries which are approaching upon the structure of Parliamentary institutions. How can we imagine the whole mass of the people being capable of deciding by votes at elections upon the right course to adopt amid these cataclysmic changes? Even now the Parliaments of every country have shown themselves quite inadequate to deal with the economic problems which dominate the affairs of every nation and of the world. Before these problems the claptrap of the hustings and the stunts of the newspapers wither and vanish away. Democracy as a guide or motive to progress has long been known to be incompetent. None of the legislative assemblies of the great modern states represents in universal suffrage even a fraction of the strength or wisdom of the community. Great nations are no longer led by their ablest men, or by those who know most about their immediate affairs, or even by those who have a coherent doctrine. Democratic governments drift along the line of least resistance, taking short views, paying their way with sops and doles and smoothing their path with pleasant-sounding platitudes. Never was there less continuity or design in their affairs, and yet towards them are coming swiftly changes which will revolutionize for good or ill not only the whole economic structure of the world but the social habits and moral outlook of every family. Only the Communists have a plan and a gospel. It is a plan fatal to personal freedom and a gospel founded upon Hate.

Certain it is that while men are gathering knowledge and power with ever-increasing and measureless speed, their virtues and their wisdom have not shown any notable improvement as the centuries have rolled. The brain of a modern man does not differ in essentials from that of the human beings who fought and loved here millions of years ago. The nature of man has remained hitherto practically unchanged. Under sufficient stress—starvation, terror, warlike passion, or even cold intellectual frenzy—the modern man we know so well will do the most terrible deeds, and his modern woman will back him up. At the present moment the civilizations of many different ages co-exist together in the world, and their representatives meet and converse. Englishmen, Frenchmen, or Americans with ideas abreast of the twentieth century do business with Indians or Chinese whose civilizations were crystalized several thousands of years ago. We have the spectacle of the powers and weapons of man far outstripping the march of his intelligence; we have the march of his intelligence proceeding far more rapidly than the development of his nobility. We may well find ourselves in the presence of "the strength of civilization without its mercy."

It is therefore above all things important that the moral philosophy and spiritual conceptions of men and nations should hold their own amid these formidable scientific evolutions. It would be much better to call a halt in material progress and discovery rather than to be mastered by our own apparatus and the forces which it directs. There are secrets too mysterious for man in his present state to know; secrets which once penetrated may be fatal to human happiness and glory. But the busy hands of the scientists are already fumbling with the keys of all the chambers hitherto forbidden to mankind. Without an equal growth of Mercy, Pity, Peace and Love, Science herself may destroy all that makes human life majestic and tolerable. There never was a time when the inherent virtue of human beings required more strong and confident expression in daily life; there never was a time when the hope of immortality and the disdain of earthly power and achievement were more necessary for the safety of the children of men.

After all, this material progress, in itself so splendid, does not meet any of the real needs of the human race. I read a book the other day which traced the history of mankind from the birth of the solar system to its extinction. There were fifteen or sixteen races of men which in succession rose and fell over periods measured by tens of millions of years. In the end a race of beings was evolved which had mastered nature. A state was created whose citizens lived as long as they chose, enjoyed pleasures and sympathies incomparably wider than our own, navigated the inter-planetary spaces, could recall the panorama of the past and foresee the future. But what was the good of all that to them? What did they know more than we know about the answers of the simple questions which man has asked since the earliest dawn of reason—"Why are we here? What is the purpose of life? Whither are we going?" No material progress, even though it takes shapes we cannot now conceive, or however it may expand the faculties of man, can bring comfort to his soul. It is this fact, more wonderful than any that Science can reveal, which gives the best hope that all will be well. Projects undreamed of by past generations will absorb our immediate descendants; forces terrific and devastating will be in their hands; comforts, activities, amenities, pleasures will crowd upon them, but their hearts will ache, their lives will be barren, if they have not a vision above material things. And with the hopes and powers will come dangers out of all proportion to the growth of man's intellect, to the strength of his character or to the efficacy of his institutions. Once more the choice is offered between Blessing and Cursing. Never was the answer that will be given harder to foretell.

APPENDIX II

What Good's a Constitution?

*First published in *Collier's,* August 22, 1936

No one can think clearly or sensibly about this vast and burning topic without in the first instance making up his mind upon the fundamental issue. Does he value the State above the citizen, or the citizen above the State? Does a government exist for the individual, or do individuals exist for the government? One must recognize that the world today is deeply divided upon this. Some of the most powerful nations and races have definitely chosen to subordinate the citizen or subject to the life of the State. In Russia, Germany and Italy we have this somber, tremendous decision, expressed in varying forms. All nations agree that in time of war, where the life and independence of the country are at stake, every man and woman must be ready to work and, if need be, die in defense of these supreme objects; and that the government must be empowered to call upon them to any extent.

But what we are now considering is the existence of this principle in times of peace and its erection into a permanent system to which the life of great communities must be made to conform. The argument is used that economic crises are only another form of war, and as they are always with us, or can always be alleged to be with us, it is claimed that we must live our lives in a perpetual state of war, only without actual shooting, bayoneting or cannonading.

This is, of course, the Socialist view. As long as Socialists present themselves in an international guise as creators of a new world order, like the beehive or the ant heap, with a new human heart to fit these novel conceptions, they could easily be beaten, and have been very effectively beaten both by argument and by nature. But when new forms of socialism arose which were grafted not upon world ideals but upon the strongest forms of nationalism, their success was remarkable.

In Germany, for instance, the alliance between national patriotism, tradition and pride on the one hand, and discontent about the inequalities of wealth on the other, made the Weimar Constitution "a scrap of paper." Either of these two fierce, turbulent torrents separately might have been kept within bounds. Joined together in a fierce confluence, they proved irresistible.

Once the rulers of a country can create a war atmosphere in time of peace, can allege that the State is in danger and appeal to all the noblest national instincts, as well as all the basest, it is only in very solidly established countries that the rights of the citizens can be preserved. In Germany these rights vanished almost overnight. Today no one may criticize the dictatorship, either in speech or writing. Voters still go to the poll—in fact, are herded to the polls like sheep—but the method of election has become a fantastic travesty of popular government. A German can vote for the régime, but not against it. If he attempts to indicate disapproval, his ballot paper is reckoned as "spoiled."

The tyranny of the ruling junta extends into every department of life. Friends may not greet each other without invoking the name of Hitler. At least on certain days, the very meals that a family eats in the privacy of its home are regulated by decree. The shadow of an all-powerful State falls between parent and child, husband and wife. Love itself is fettered and confined. No marriage, no love relation of any kind is permitted which offends against a narrow and arbitrary code based upon virulent race prejudice.

Nor is this all. Even in the sphere of religion the State must intervene. It comes between the priest and his penitent, between the worshipper and the God to whom he prays. And this last, by one of the curious ironies of history, in the land of Luther.

To rivet this intolerable yoke upon the necks of the German people all the resources of propaganda have been utilized to magnify the sense of crisis and to exhibit sometimes France, sometimes Poland, sometimes Lithuania, always the Soviets and the Jews, as antagonists at whom the patriotic Teuton must grind his teeth.

Much the same thing has happened in Russia. The powerful aid of national sentiment and imperialist aspirations has been invoked to buttress a decaying Communism.

In the United States, also, economic crisis has led to an extension of the activities of the Executive and to the pillorying, by irresponsible agitators, of certain groups and sections of the population as enemies of the rest. There have been efforts to exalt the power of the central government and to limit the rights of individuals. It has been sought to mobilize behind this reversal

of the American tradition, at once the selfishness of the pensioners, or would-be pensioners, of Washington, and the patriotism
of all who wish to see their country prosperous once more.

It is when passions and cupidities are thus unleashed and, at
the same time, the sense of public duty rides high in the hearts
of all men and women of good will that the handcuffs can be
slipped upon the citizens and they can be brought into entire
subjugation to the executive government. Then they are led to
believe that, if they will only yield themselves, body, mind and
soul, to the State, and obey unquestioningly its injunctions,
some dazzling future of riches and power will open to them,
either—as in Italy—by the conquest of the territories of others,
or—as in America—by a further liberation and exploitation of
the national resources.

I take the opposite view. I hold that governments are meant
to be, and must remain, the servants of the citizens; that states
and federations only come into existence and can only by justified by preserving the "life, liberty and the pursuit of happiness"
in the homes and families of individuals. The true right and
power rest in the individual. He gives of his right and power to
the State, expecting and requiring thereby in return to receive
certain advantages and guarantees. I do not admit that an economic crisis can ever truly be compared with the kind of struggle
for existence by races constantly under primordial conditions.
I do not think that modern nations in time of peace ought to
regard themselves as if they were the inhabitants of besieged cities, liable to be put to the sword or led into slavery if they cannot
make good their defense.

One of the greatest reasons for avoiding war is that it is
destructive to liberty. But we must not be led into adopting

for ourselves the evils of war in time of peace upon any pretext whatever. The word "civilization" means not only peace by the non-regimentation of the people such as is required in war. Civilization means that officials and authorities, whether uniformed or not, whether armed or not, are made to realize that they are servants and not masters.

Socialism or overweening State life, whether in peace or war, is only sharing miseries and not blessings. Every self-respecting citizen in every country must be on his guard lest the rulers demand of him in time of peace sacrifices only tolerable in a period of war for national self-preservation.

I judge the civilization of any community by simple tests. What is the degree of freedom possessed by the citizen or subject? Can he think, speak and act freely under well-established, well-known laws? Can he criticize the executive government? Can he sue the State if it has infringed his rights? Are there also great processes for changing the law to meet new conditions?

Judging by these standards, Great Britain and the United States can claim to be in the forefront of civilized communities. But we owe this only in part to the good sense and watchfulness of our citizens. In both our countries the character of the judiciary is a vital factor in the maintenance of the rights and liberties of the individual citizen.

Our judges extend impartially to all men protection, not only against wrongs committed by private persons, but also against the arbitrary acts of public authority. The independence of the courts is, to all of us, the guarantee of freedom and the equal rule of law.

It must, therefore, be the first concern of the citizens of a free country to preserve and maintain the independence of the courts of justice, however inconvenient that independence may be, on occasion, to the government of the day.

But all this implies peace conditions, an atmosphere of civilization rather than militarization or officialization. It implies a balance and equipoise of society which can be altered only gradually. It is so hard to build the structure of a vast economic community, and so easy to upset it and throw it into confusion. The onus must lie always upon those who propose a change, and the process of change is hardly ever beneficial unless it considers what is due to the past as well as what is claimed for the future.

It is for these reasons among many others that the founders of the American Republic in their Declaration of Independence inculcate as a duty binding upon all worthy sons of America "a frequent recurrence to first principles." Do not let us too readily brush aside the grand, simple affirmations of the past. All wisdom is not new wisdom. Let us never forget that the glory of the nineteenth century was founded upon what seemed to be the successful putting down of those twin curses, anarchy and tyranny.

The question we are discussing is whether a fixed constitution is a bulwark or a fetter. From what I have written it is plain that I incline to the side of those who would regard it as a bulwark, and that I rank the citizen higher than the State, and regard the State as useful only in so far as it preserves his inherent rights. All forms of tyranny are odious. It makes very little difference to the citizen, father of a family, head of a household, whether tyranny comes from a royal or imperial despot, or from a Pope or Inquisitor, or from a military caste, or from an aristocratic or plutocratic oligarchy, or from a ring of employers, or a trade union, or a party caucus—or worst of all, from a terrified and infuriated mob. "A man's a man for a' that." The whole point is, whether he can make head against oppression in any of its Protean shapes, and defend the island of his home, his life and soul. And here is the point at which we may consider and contrast the constitutions of our respective countries.

It is very difficult for us in England to realize the kind of deadlock which has been reached in the United States. Imagine, for instance, the gigantic India Bill, passed through Parliament and for two or three years in active operation throughout the whole of India, suddenly being declared illegal by the law lords sitting as a tribunal. Imagine—to take an instance nearer home—some gigantic measure of insurance as big as our widows' pensions, health and employment insurance rolled together, which had deeply interwoven itself in the whole life of the people, upon which every kind of contract and business arrangement had been based, being declared to have no validity by a court of law. We simply cannot conceive it. Yet something very like that has occurred on your side of the Atlantic.

In our country an act of Parliament which, upon the advice of the ministers responsible for it, has received the royal assent is the law of the land. Its authority cannot be questioned by any court. There is no limit to the powers of Crown and Parliament. Even the gravest changes in our Constitution can in theory be carried out by simple majority votes in both Houses and the consequential assent of the Crown.

But we now watch the workings of a written Constitution enforced by a Supreme Court according to the letter of the law, under which anyone may bring a test case challenging not merely the interpretation of a law, but the law itself, and if the Court decides for the appellant, be he only an owner of a few chickens, the whole action of the Legislature and the Executive becomes to that extent null and void. We know that to modify the Constitution even in the smallest particular requires a two-thirds majority of the sovereign states forming the American Union. And this has been achieved, after prodigious struggles, on only a score of occasions during the whole history of the United States.

American citizens or jurists in their turn, gaze with wonder at our great British democracy expressing itself with plenary powers through a Government and Parliament controlled only by the fluctuating currents of public opinion. British Governments live from day to day only upon the approval of the House of Commons. There is no divorce between the Executive and the Legislature. The ministers, new or old, must be chosen from men and parties which in the aggregate will command a majority in the House of Commons. Parliament can, if it chooses, even prolong its own life beyond the statutory limit. Ministers may at any time advise the King to a sudden dissolution. Yet all classes and all parties have a deep, underlying conviction that these vast, flexible powers will not be abused, that the spirit of our unwritten Constitution will be respected at every stage.

To understand how this faith is justified, how the British people are able to enjoy a real stability of government without a written Constitution, it is necessary to consider the beginning of party politics in Britain. Whigs and Tories were almost equally concerned to assert the authority of Parliament as a check upon the Executive. With the Whigs this was a matter of fundamental principle; with the Tories it was a question of expediency. James II was a Catholic and his efforts to further the cause of his co-religionists alienated the great bulk of the Tory party, who were loyal to the Church of England. Then from the advent of

William of Orange to the accession of George III, with a brief interval in the reign of Queen Anne, the Crown could do nothing without the Whigs and the government of the country was predominantly or exclusively in the hands of that party.

The Tories were thus vitally interested in preserving and extending the rights of the parliamentary opposition. In this way a jealous care for constitutional rights came to mark both the great parties of the State. And as to all men the Constitution represented security and freedom, none would consent willingly to any breach of it, even to gain a temporary advantage.

Modern times offer respect for law and constitutional usage. Nothing contributed so much to the collapse of the general strike ten years ago as the declaration by great lawyers that it was illegal. And the right of freedom of speech and publication is extended, under the Constitution, to those who in theory seek to overthrow established institutions by force of arms so long as they do not commit any illegal act.

Another factor making for stability is our permanent civil service. Governments come and go; parliamentary majorities fluctuate; but the civil servants remain. To new and inexperienced ministers they are "guides, philosophers and friends." Themselves untouched by the vicissitudes of party fortunes, they impart to the business of administration a real continuity.

On the whole, too, popular opinion acts as a guardian of the unwritten Constitution. Public chastisement would speedily overtake any minister, however powerful, who fell below the accepted standards of fair play or who descended to trickwork or dodgery.

When one considers the immense size of the United States and the extraordinary contrasts of climate and character which differentiate the forty-eight sovereign states of the American Union, as well as the inevitable conflict of interests between North and South and between East and West, it would seem that the participants of so vast a federation have the right to effectual guarantees upon the fundamental laws, and that these should not be easily changed to suit a particular emergency or fraction of the country.

The founders of the Union, although its corpus was then so much smaller, realized this with profound conviction. They did not think it possible to entrust legislation for so diverse a community and enormous an area to a simple majority. They were as well acquainted with the follies and intolerance of parliaments as with the oppression of princes. "To control the powers and conduct of the legislature," said a leading member of the Convention of 1787, "by an overruling constitution was an improvement in the science and practice of government reserved to the American States."

All the great names of American history can be invoked behind this principle. Why should it be considered obsolete? If today we are framing that constitution for a "United States of Europe" for which so many thinkers on this side of the ocean aspire, fixed and almost unalterable guarantees would be required by the acceding nations.

It may well be that this very quality of rigidity, which is today thought to be so galling, has been a prime factor in founding the greatness of the United States. In the shelter of the Constitution nature has been conquered, a mighty continent has been brought under the sway of man, and an economic entity established, unrivalled in the whole history of the globe.

In this small island of Britain we make laws for ourselves.

But if we had again attempted to apply this flexibility and freedom to the British Empire, and to frame an Imperial Constitution to make laws for the whole body, it would have been broken to pieces. Although we have a free, flexible Constitution at the center and for the center of the Empire, nothing is more rigid than the established practice—namely, that we claim no powers to interfere with the affairs of its self-governing component parts. No supreme court is needed to enforce this rule. We have learned the lessons of the past too well.

And here we must note a dangerous misuse of terminology. "Taking the rigidity out of the American Constitution" means, and is intended to mean, new gigantic accessions of power to the dominating center of government and giving it the means to make new fundamental laws enforceable upon all American citizens.

Such a departure in the British Empire by a chance parliamentary majority or even by aggregate Dominion parliamentary majorities, would shatter it to bits. The so-called "rigidity" of the American Constitution is in fact the guarantee of freedom to its widespread component parts. That a set of persons, however eminent, carried into office upon some populist heave should have the power to make the will of a bare majority effective over the whole of the United States might cause disasters upon the greatest scale from which recovery would not be swift or easy.

I was reading the other day a recent American novel by Sinclair Lewis—*It Can't Happen Here*. Such books render a public service to the English-speaking world. When we see what has happened in Germany, Italy and Russia we cannot neglect their warning. This is an age in which the citizen requires more, and not less, legal protection in the exercise of his rights and liberties.

That is doubtless why, after all the complaints against the rigidity of the United States Constitution and the threats of a presidential election on this issue, none of the suggested constitutional amendments has so far been adopted by the Administration. This may explain why the "Nine Old Men" of the Supreme Court have not been more seriously challenged. But the challenge may come at a later date, though it would perhaps be wiser to dissociate it from any question of the age of the judges, lest it be the liberal element in the court which is weakened.

Now, at the end of these reflections, I must strike a minor and different note. The rigidity of the Constitution of the United States is the shield of the common man. But that rigidity ought not to be interpreted by pedants. In England we continually give new interpretation to the archaic language of our fundamental institutions, and this is no new thing in the United States. The judiciary have obligations which go beyond expounding the mere letter of the law. The Constitution must be made to work.

A true interpretation, however, of the British or the American Constitution is certainly not a chop-logic or pedantic interpretation. So august a body as the Supreme Court in dealing with law must also deal with the life of the United States, and words, however solemn, are only true when they preserve their vital relationship to facts. It would certainly be a great disaster, not only to the American Republic but to the whole world, if a violent collision should take place between the large majority of the American people and the great instrument of government which has so long presided over their expanding fortunes.

APPENDIX III

The Sinews of Peace

*Speech delivered at Westminster College in Fulton, MO, on March 5, 1946

I am glad to come to Westminster College this afternoon, and am complimented that you should give me a degree. The name "Westminster" is somehow familiar to me. I seem to have heard of it before. Indeed, it was at Westminster that I received a very large part of my education in politics, dialectic, rhetoric, and one or two other things. In fact we have both been educated at the same, or similar, or, at any rate, kindred establishments.

It is also an honor, perhaps almost unique, for a private visitor to be introduced to an academic audience by the President of the United States. Amid his heavy burdens, duties, and responsibilities—unsought but not recoiled from—the President has travelled a thousand miles to dignify and magnify our meeting here today and to give me an opportunity of addressing this kindred nation, as well as my own countrymen across the ocean, and perhaps some other countries too. The President has told you that it is his wish, as I am sure it is yours, that I should have full liberty to give my true and faithful counsel in these anxious and baffling times. I shall certainly avail myself of this freedom, and feel the more right to do so because any private ambitions I may have cherished in my younger days have been satisfied beyond my wildest dreams. Let me, however, make it clear that I have no official mission or status of any kind, and that I speak only for myself. There is nothing here but what you see.

I can therefore allow my mind, with the experience of a lifetime, to play over the problems which beset us on the morrow of our absolute victory in arms, and to try to make sure with what strength I have that what has been gained with so much sacrifice and suffering shall be preserved for the future glory and safety of mankind.

The United States stands at this time at the pinnacle of world power. It is a solemn moment for the American Democracy. For with primacy in power is also joined an awe-inspiring accountability to the future. If you look around you, you must feel not only the sense of duty done but also you must feel anxiety lest you fall below the level of achievement. Opportunity is here now, clear and shining for both our countries. To reject it or ignore it or fritter it away will bring upon us all the long reproaches of the after-time. It is necessary that constancy of mind, persistency of purpose, and the grand simplicity of decision shall guide and rule the conduct of the English-speaking peoples in peace as they did in war. We must, and I believe we shall, prove ourselves equal to this severe requirement.

When American military men approach some serious situation they are wont to write at the head of their directive the words "over-all strategic concept." There is wisdom in this, as it leads to clarity of thought. What then is the over-all strategic concept which we should inscribe today? It is nothing less than the safety and welfare, the freedom and progress, of all the homes and families of all the men and women in all the lands. And here I speak particularly of the myriad cottage or apartment homes where the wage-earner strives amid the accidents and difficulties of life to guard his wife and children from privation and bring the family up in the fear of the Lord, or upon ethical conceptions which often play their potent part.

To give security to these countless homes, they must be shielded from the two giant marauders, war and tyranny. We all know the frightful disturbances in which the ordinary family is plunged when the curse of war swoops down upon the breadwinner and those for whom he works and contrives. The awful ruin of Europe, with all its vanished glories, and of large parts of Asia glares us in the eyes. When the designs of wicked men or the aggressive urge of mighty States dissolve over large areas the frame of civilized society, humble folk are confronted with difficulties with which they cannot cope. For them all is distorted, all is broken, even ground to pulp.

When I stand here this quiet afternoon I shudder to visualize what is actually happening to millions now and what is going to happen in this period when famine stalks the earth. None can compute what has been called "the unestimated sum of human pain." Our supreme task and duty is to guard the homes of the common people from the horrors and miseries of another war. We are all agreed on that.

Our American military colleagues, after having proclaimed their "over-all strategic concept" and computed available resources, always proceed to the next step—namely, the method.

Here again there is widespread agreement. A world organization has already been erected for the prime purpose of preventing war, UNO, the successor of the League of Nations, with the decisive addition of the United States and all that that means, is already at work. We must make sure that its work is fruitful, that it is a reality and not a sham, that it is a force for action, and not merely a frothing of words, that it is a true temple of peace in which the shields of many nations can some day be hung up, and not merely a cockpit in a Tower of Babel. Before we cast away the solid assurances of national armaments for self-preservation we must be certain that our temple is built, not upon shifting sands or quagmires, but upon the rock. Anyone can see with his eyes open that our path will be difficult and also long, but if we persevere together as we did in the two world wars—though not, alas, in the interval between them—I cannot doubt that we shall achieve our common purpose in the end.

I have, however, a definite and practical proposal to make for action. Courts and magistrates may be set up but they cannot function without sheriffs and constables. The United Nations Organization must immediately begin to be equipped with an international armed force. In such a matter we can only go step by step, but we must begin now. I propose that each of the Powers and States should be invited to delegate a certain number of air squadrons to the service of the world organization. These squadrons would be trained and prepared in their own countries, but would move around in rotation from one country to another. They would wear the uniform of their own countries but with different badges. They would not be required to act against their own nation, but in other respects they would be directed by the world organization. This might be started on a modest scale and would grow as confidence grew. I wished to see this done after the first world war, and I devoutly trust it may be done forthwith.

It would nevertheless be wrong and imprudent to entrust the secret knowledge or experience of the atomic bomb, which the United States, Great Britain, and Canada now share, to the world organization, while it is still in its infancy. It would be criminal madness to cast it adrift in this still agitated and un-united world. No one in any country has slept less well in their beds because this knowledge and the method and the raw materials to apply it, are at present largely retained in American hands. I do not believe we should all have slept so soundly had the positions been reversed and if some Communist or neo-Fascist State monopolized for the time being these dread agencies. The fear of them alone might easily have been used to enforce totalitarian systems upon the free democratic world, with consequences appalling to human imagination. God has willed that this shall not be and we have at least a breathing space to set our house in order before this peril has to be encountered: and even then, if no effort is spared, we should still possess so formidable a superiority as to impose effective deterrents upon its employment, or threat of employment, by others. Ultimately, when the essential brotherhood of man is truly embodied and expressed in a world organization with all the necessary practical safeguards to make it effective, these powers would naturally be confided to that world organization.

Now I come to the second danger of these two marauders which threatens the cottage, the home, and the ordinary people—namely, tyranny. We cannot be blind to the fact that the liberties enjoyed by individual citizens throughout the British Empire are not valid in a considerable number of countries, some of which are very powerful. In these States control is enforced upon the common people by various kinds of all-embracing police governments. The power of the State is exercised without restraint, either by dictators or by compact oligarchies operating through a privileged party and a political police. It is not our duty at this time when difficulties are so numerous to interfere forcibly in the internal affairs of countries which we have not conquered in war. But we must never cease to proclaim in fearless tones the great principles of freedom and the rights of man which are the joint inheritance of the English-speaking world and which through Magna Carta, the Bill of Rights, the Habeas Corpus, trial by jury, and the English common law find their most famous expression in the American Declaration of Independence.

All this means that the people of any country have the right, and should have the power by constitutional action, by free unfettered elections, with secret ballot, to choose or change the character or form of government under which they dwell; that freedom of speech and thought should reign; that courts of justice, independent of the executive, unbiased by any party, should administer laws which have received the broad assent of large majorities or are consecrated by time and custom. Here are the title deeds of freedom which should lie in every cottage home. Here is the message of the British and American peoples to mankind. Let us preach what we practice—let us practice what we preach.

I have now stated the two great dangers which menace the homes of the people: War and Tyranny. I have not yet spoken of poverty and privation which are in many cases the prevailing anxiety. But if the dangers of war and tyranny are removed, there is no doubt that science and co-operation can bring in the next few years to the world, certainly in the next few decades newly taught in the sharpening school of war, an expansion of material well-being beyond anything that has yet occurred in human experience. Now, at this sad and breathless moment, we are plunged in the hunger and distress which are the aftermath of our stupendous struggle; but this will pass and may pass quickly, and there is no reason except human folly or sub-human crime which should deny to all the nations the inauguration and enjoyment of an age of plenty. I have often used words which I learned fifty years ago from a great Irish-American orator, a friend of mine, Mr. Bourke Cockran. "There is enough for all. The earth is a generous mother; she will provide in plentiful abundance food for all her children if they will but cultivate her soil in justice and peace." So far I feel that we are in full agreement.

Now, while still pursuing the method of realizing our overall strategic concept, I come to the crux of what I have travelled here to say. Neither the sure prevention of war, nor the continuous rise of world organization will be gained without what I have called the fraternal association of the English-speaking peoples. This means a special relationship between the British Commonwealth and Empire and the United States. This is no time for generalities, and I will venture to be precise. Fraternal association requires not only the growing friendship and mutual understanding between our two vast but kindred systems of society, but the continuance of the intimate relationship between our military advisers, leading to common study of potential dangers, the similarity of weapons and manuals of instructions, and to the interchange of officers and cadets at technical colleges. It should carry with it the continuance of the present facilities for mutual security by the joint use of all Naval and Air Force bases in the possession of either country all over the world. This would perhaps double the mobility of the American Navy and Air Force. It would greatly expand that of the British Empire Forces and it might well lead, if and as the world calms down, to important financial savings. Already we use together a large number of islands; more may well be entrusted to our joint care in the near future.

The United States has already a Permanent Defense Agreement with the Dominion of Canada, which is so devotedly attached to the British Commonwealth and Empire. This Agreement is more effective than many of those which have often been made under formal alliances. This principle should be extended to all British Commonwealths with full reciprocity. Thus, whatever happens, and thus only, shall we be secure ourselves and able to work together for the high and simple causes that are dear to us and bode no ill to any. Eventually there may come—I feel eventually there will come—the principle of common citizenship, but that we may be content to leave to destiny, whose outstretched arm many of us can already clearly see.

There is however an important question which we must ask ourselves. Would a special relationship between the United States and the British Commonwealth be inconsistent with our over-riding loyalties to the World Organization? I reply that, on the contrary, it is probably the only means by which that organization will achieve its full stature and strength. There are already the special United States relations with Canada which I have just mentioned, and there are the special relations between the United States and the South American Republics. We British have our twenty years Treaty of Collaboration and Mutual Assistance with Soviet Russia. I agree with Mr. Bevin, the Foreign Secretary of Great Britain, that it might well be a fifty years Treaty so far as we are concerned. We aim at nothing but mutual assistance and collaboration. The British have an alliance with Portugal unbroken since 1384, and which produced fruitful results at critical moments in the late war. None of these clash with the general interest of a world agreement, or a world organization; on the contrary they help it. "In my father's house are many mansions." Special associations between members of the United Nations which have no aggressive point against any other country, which harbor no design incompatible with the Charter of the United Nations, far from being harmful, are beneficial and, as I believe, indispensable.

I spoke earlier of the Temple of Peace. Workmen from all countries must build that temple. If two of the workmen know each other particularly well and are old friends, if their families are inter-mingled, and if they have "faith in each other's purpose, hope in each other's future and charity towards each other's shortcomings"—to quote some good words I read here the other day—why cannot they work together at the common task as friends and partners? Why cannot they share their tools and thus increase each other's working powers? Indeed they must do so or else the temple may not be built, or, being built, it may collapse, and we shall all be proved again unteachable and have to go and try to learn again for a third time in a school of war, incomparably more rigorous than that from which we have just been released. The dark ages may return, the Stone Age may return on the gleaming wings of science, and what might now shower immeasurable material blessings upon mankind, may even bring about its total destruction. Beware, I say; time may be short. Do not let us take the course of allowing events to drift along until it is too late. If there is to be a fraternal association of the kind I have described, with all the extra strength and security which both our countries can derive from it, let us make sure that that great fact is known to the world, and that it plays its part in steadying and stabilizing the foundations of peace. There is the path of wisdom. Prevention is better than cure.

A shadow has fallen upon the scenes so lately lighted by the Allied victory. Nobody knows what Soviet Russia and its Communist international organization intends to do in the immediate future, or what are the limits, if any, to their expansive and proselytizing tendencies. I have a strong admiration and regard for the valiant Russian people and for my wartime comrade, Marshal Stalin. There is deep sympathy and goodwill in Britain—and I doubt not here also—towards the peoples of all the Russias and a resolve to persevere through many differences and rebuffs in establishing lasting friendships. We understand the Russian need to be secure on her western frontiers by the removal of all possibility of German aggression. We welcome Russia to her rightful place among the leading nations of the world. We welcome her flag upon the seas. Above all, we welcome constant, frequent and growing contacts between the Russian people and our own people on both sides of the Atlantic. It is my duty however, for I am sure you would wish me to state the facts as I see them to you, to place before you certain facts about the present position in Europe.

From Stettin in the Baltic to Trieste in the Adriatic, an iron curtain has descended across the Continent. Behind that line lie all the capitals of the ancient states of Central and Eastern Europe. Warsaw, Berlin, Prague, Vienna, Budapest, Belgrade,

Bucharest and Sofia, all these famous cities and the populations around them lie in what I must call the Soviet sphere, and all are subject in one form or another, not only to Soviet influence but to a very high and, in many cases, increasing measure of control from Moscow. Athens alone—Greece with its immortal glories—is free to decide its future at an election under British, American and French observation. The Russian-dominated Polish Government has been encouraged to make enormous and wrongful inroads upon Germany, and mass expulsions of millions of Germans on a scale grievous and undreamed-of are now taking place. The Communist parties, which were very small in all these Eastern States of Europe, have been raised to pre-eminence and power far beyond their numbers and are seeking everywhere to obtain totalitarian control. Police governments are prevailing in nearly every case, and so far, except in Czechoslovakia, there is no true democracy.

Turkey and Persia are both profoundly alarmed and disturbed at the claims which are being made upon them and at the pressure exerted by the Moscow Government. An attempt is being made by the Russians in Berlin to build up a quasi-Communist party in their zone of Occupied Germany by showing special favors to groups of left-wing German leaders. At the end of the fighting last June, the American and British Armies withdrew westwards, in accordance with an earlier agreement, to a depth at some points of 150 miles upon a front of nearly four hundred miles, in order to allow our Russian allies to occupy this vast expanse of territory which the Western Democracies had conquered.

If now the Soviet Government tries, by separate action, to build up a pro-Communist Germany in their areas, this will cause new serious difficulties in the British and American zones, and will give the defeated Germans the power of putting themselves up to auction between the Soviets and the Western Democracies. Whatever conclusions may be drawn from these facts—and facts they are—this is certainly not the Liberated Europe we fought to build up. Nor is it one which contains the essentials of permanent peace.

The safety of the world requires a new unity in Europe, from which no nation should be permanently outcast. It is from the quarrels of the strong parent races in Europe that the world wars we have witnessed, or which occurred in former times, have sprung. Twice in our own lifetime we have seen the United States, against their wishes and their traditions, against arguments, the force of which it is impossible not to comprehend, drawn by irresistible forces, into these wars in time to secure the victory of the good cause, but only after frightful slaughter and devastation had occurred. Twice the United States has had to send several millions of its young men across the Atlantic to find the war; but now war can find any nation, wherever it may dwell between dusk and dawn. Surely we should work with conscious purpose for a grand pacification of Europe, within the structure of the United Nations and in accordance with its Charter. That I feel is an open cause of policy of very great importance.

In front of the iron curtain which lies across Europe are other causes for anxiety. In Italy the Communist Party is seriously hampered by having to support the Communist-trained Marshal Tito's claims to former Italian territory at the head of the Adriatic. Nevertheless the future of Italy hangs in the balance. Again one cannot imagine a regenerated Europe without a strong France. All my public life I have worked for a strong France and I never lost faith in her destiny, even in the darkest hours. I will not lose faith now. However, in a great number of countries, far from the Russian frontiers and throughout the world, Communist fifth columns are established and work in complete unity and absolute obedience to the directions they receive from the Communist center. Except in the British Commonwealth and in the United States where Communism is in its infancy, the Communist parties or fifth columns constitute a growing challenge and peril to Christian civilization. These are somber facts for anyone to have to recite on the morrow of a victory gained by so much splendid comradeship in arms and in the cause of freedom and democracy; but we should be most unwise not to face them squarely while time remains.

The outlook is also anxious in the Far East and especially in Manchuria. The Agreement which was made at Yalta, to which I was a party, was extremely favorable to Soviet Russia, but it was made at a time when no one could say that the German war might not extend all through the summer and autumn of 1945 and when the Japanese war was expected to last for a further 18 months from the end of the German war. In this country you are all so well-informed about the Far East, and such devoted friends of China, that I do not need to expatiate on the situation there.

I have felt bound to portray the shadow which, alike in the west and in the east, falls upon the world. I was a high minister at the time of the Versailles Treaty and a close friend of Mr. Lloyd-George, who was the head of the British delegation at Versailles. I did not myself agree with many things that were done, but I have a very strong impression in my mind of that situation, and I find it painful to contrast it with that which prevails now. In those days there were high hopes and unbounded confidence that the wars were over, and that the League of Nations would become all-powerful. I do not see or feel that same confidence or even the same hopes in the haggard world at the present time.

On the other hand I repulse the idea that a new war is inevitable; still more that it is imminent. It is because I am sure that our fortunes are still in our own hands and that we hold the power to save the future, that I feel the duty to speak out now that I have the occasion and the opportunity to do so. I do not believe that Soviet Russia desires war. What they desire is the fruits of war and the indefinite expansion of their power and doctrines. But what we have to consider here today while time remains, is the permanent prevention of war and the establishment of conditions of freedom and democracy as rapidly as possible in all countries. Our difficulties and dangers will not be removed by closing our eyes to them. They will not be removed by mere waiting to see what happens; nor will they be removed by a policy of appeasement. What is needed is a settlement, and the longer this is delayed, the more difficult it will be and the greater our dangers will become.

From what I have seen of our Russian friends and Allies during the war, I am convinced that there is nothing they admire so much as strength, and there is nothing for which they have less respect than for weakness, especially military weakness. For that reason the old doctrine of a balance of power is unsound. We cannot afford, if we can help it, to work on narrow margins, offering temptations to a trial of strength. If the Western Democracies stand together in strict adherence to the principles of the United Nations Charter, their influence for furthering those principles will be immense and no one is likely to molest them. If however they become divided or falter in their duty and if these all-important years are allowed to slip away then indeed catastrophe may overwhelm us all.

Last time I saw it all coming and cried aloud to my own fellow-countrymen and to the world, but no one paid any attention. Up till the year 1933 or even 1935, Germany might have been saved from the awful fate which has overtaken her and we might all have been spared the miseries Hitler let loose upon mankind. There never was a war in all history easier to prevent by timely action than the one which has just desolated such great areas of the globe. It could have been prevented in my belief without the firing of a single shot, and Germany might be powerful, prosperous and honored today; but no one would listen and one by one we were all sucked into the awful whirlpool. We surely must not let that happen again. This can only be achieved by reaching now, in 1946, a good understanding on all points with Russia under the general authority of the United Nations Organization and by the maintenance of that good understanding through many peaceful years, by the world instrument, supported by the whole strength of the English-speaking world and all its connections. There is the solution which I respectfully offer to you in this Address to which I have given the title "The Sinews of Peace."

Let no man underrate the abiding power of the British Empire and the Commonwealth. Because you see the 46 millions in our island harassed about their food supply, of which they only grow one half, even in war-time, or because we have difficulty in restarting our industries and export trade after six years of passionate war effort, do not suppose that we shall not come through these dark years of privation as we have come through the glorious years of agony, or that half a century from now, you will not see 70 or 80 millions of Britons spread about the world and united in defense of our traditions, our way of life, and of the world causes which you and we espouse. If the population of the English-speaking Commonwealths be added to that of the United States with all that such co-operation implies in the air, on the sea, all over the globe and in science and in industry, and in moral force, there will be no quivering, precarious balance of power to offer its temptation to ambition or adventure. On the contrary, there will be an overwhelming assurance of security. If we adhere faithfully to the Charter of the United Nations and walk forward in sedate and sober strength seeking no one's land or treasure, seeking to lay no arbitrary control upon the thoughts of men; if all British moral and material forces and convictions are joined with your own in fraternal association, the high-roads of the future will be clear, not only for us but for all, not only for our time, but for a century to come.

NOTES

Preface

1. Aristotle, *Nicomachean Ethics*, 1141b9–21.
2. Ibid., 1140a24–25.
3. Robert Rhodes James, *Churchill: A Study in Failure, 1900–1939* (New York: World Publishing, 1970), ix–x.
4. "For my part, I consider that it will be found much better by all Parties to leave the past to history, especially as I propose to write that history myself." Winston Churchill, "Foreign Affairs," January 23, 1948, in *Winston S. Churchill: His Complete Speeches*, vol. 7, *1943–1949*, ed. Robert Rhodes James (New York: Chelsea House, 1974), 7587.

Introduction

1. He said, for example, "Do not, whatever be the torrent of abuse which may obstruct the necessary action, think too poorly of the greatness of our fellow countrymen. Let the House do its duty. Let the Government give the lead, and the nation will not fail in the hour of need." Winston S. Churchill, "The German Air Menace," November 28, 1934, in *Winston S. Churchill: His Complete Speeches*, vol. 5, *1928–1935*, ed. Robert Rhodes James (New York: Chelsea House, 1974), 5449.
2. Winston S. Churchill, *Marlborough: His Life and Times, Book One* (Chicago: University of Chicago Press, 2002), 569.

3. See, for example, Thucydides, who wrote of the Peloponnesian War that it was the greatest movement among the Greeks, "I had almost said of mankind." A work of the right kind about this movement is fit to be a "possession for all-time." Thucydides, *The Landmark Thucydides,* ed. Robert B. Strassler (New York: Free Press, 1996), chapter 1.1; 1.22.

4. For excellent accounts of the life of Adolf Hitler, see Ian Kershaw, *Hitler, 1889–1936: Hubris* (New York: W.W. Norton, 1999); and *Hitler, 1936–1945: Nemesis* (New York: W.W. Norton, 2000).

5. The Treaty of London in 1839. Martin Gilbert wrote: "On August 3 Germany declared war on France. As a first step to victory, her troops crossed into Belgium. That day [German Chancellor] Bethmann-Hollweg told the Reichstag: 'The wrong—I speak openly—that we are committing we will endeavour to make good as soon as our military goal is reached.'" In *The First World War: A Complete History* (New York: Henry Holt, 1994), 32.

6. Winston S. Churchill, "The Third Great Title-Deed of Anglo-American Liberties," July 14, 1918, in *Winston S. Churchill: His Complete Speeches,* vol. 3, *1914–1922,* ed. Robert Rhodes James (New York: Chelsea House, 1974), 2615.

7. Churchill explained his understanding of Germany and its kaiser before the Great War in "The Ex-Kaiser," in *Great Contemporaries,* ed. James W. Muller (Wilmington: ISI Books, 2012), 17–25; and in "The German Splendor," in *Thoughts and Adventures: Churchill Reflects on Spies, Cartoons, Flying and the Future,* ed. James W. Muller (Wilmington: ISI Books, 2009), 75–85.

8. *The Dictionary of the First World War,* eds. Stephen Pope and Elizabeth Anne-Wheal (New York: St. Martin's Press, 1995), s.v. "US Army."

9. Kershaw, *Hitler, 1889–1936: Hubris,* 52.

10. Alan Bullock, *Hitler: A Study in Tyranny* (Harmondsworth, England: Penguin Books, 1962), especially the chapter "Months of Opportunity," 222–37. See also Kershaw, *Hitler, 1889–1936: Hubris*, chapters 9 and 10, 313–78, especially 374–78.

11. As Churchill said, "I am reminded of the North Pole and South Pole. They are at opposite ends of the earth, but if you woke up at either Pole tomorrow morning you could not tell which one it was." *The Churchill Documents*, vol. 13, *The Coming of War, 1936–1939*, ed. Martin Gilbert (Hillsdale, MI: Hillsdale College Press, 2009), 681 n. 2.

12. Winston S. Churchill, *The World Crisis*, vol. 4, *The Aftermath* (Norwalk, CT: Easton Press, 1991), 73. See also Dmitri Volkogonov, *Lenin: A New Biography* (New York: Free Press, 2013), 110–11.

13. Simon Sebag Montefiore wrote: "Contemptuous of the workers and peasants, Lenin was nonetheless surprised to discover that neither of these classes supported them. Lenin thus proposed a single organ to rule and oversee the creation of socialism: the Party. It was this embarrassing gap between reality and aspiration that made the Party's quasi-religious fidelity to ideological purity so important, its military discipline so obligatory." *Stalin: The Court of the Red Tsar* (New York: Vintage, 2003), 34.

14. Robert Conquest, *The Great Terror: A Reassessment* (Oxford: Oxford University Press, 2007), 6. Radek, born in what is now the Ukraine, was a longtime associate of Lenin. He traveled on the "sealed train" in 1917 with Lenin and others to begin the Communist Revolution in Russia.

15. Vladimir Lenin, *V. I. Lenin: Collected Works*, vol. 36, *1900–1923*, ed. Yuri Sdobnikov (Moscow: Progress Publishers, 1971), 593–611.

16. John V. Fleming, *The Anti-Communist Manifestos: Four Books That Shaped the Cold War* (New York: W. W. Norton & Company, 2009), 28–29, 34–36.

17. Arthur Koestler, *Darkness at Noon*, trans. Daphne Hardy (New York: Macmillan, 1987), 38–44.

18. Ibid., 43–44.

19. Montefiore, *Stalin*, 86–89.

20. See David Pryce-Jones, *Treason of the Heart: From Thomas Paine to Kim Philby* (New York and London: Encounter Books, 2011); and Ian Kershaw, *Making Friends with Hitler: Lord Londonderry, the Nazis and the Road to World War II* (New York: Penguin Group, 2004).

21. Martin Gilbert wrote, "During the course of his speech Churchill praised 'the Roman genius' of Mussolini, whom he described as 'the greatest lawgiver among living men.' . . . [B]ut he rejected Fascism as a model for Britain. 'It is not a sign-post which would direct us here.'" In *Winston S. Churchill*, vol. 5, *Prophet of Truth: 1922–1929* (Hillsdale, MI: Hillsdale College Press, 2009), 457.

22. Winston S. Churchill, "What Good's a Constitution?" in *The U.S. Constitution: A Reader* (Hillsdale, MI: Hillsdale College Press, 2012), 739.

23. Kenneth Harris, *Attlee* (New York: W. W. Norton & Company, 1982), 244.

24. Churchill, "President Roosevelt," April 17, 1945, in *His Complete Speeches*, vol. 7, *1943–1949*, ed. Robert Rhodes James, 7141.

25. Ibid., 7139.

Chapter 1: The Fighter

1. Abraham Lincoln, "To Cuthbert Bullitt," July 28, 1862, in *The Collected Works of Abraham Lincoln*, vol. 5, *1861–1862*, ed. Roy P. Basler (New Brunswick, NJ: Rutgers University Press, 1953), 346.

2. "Winston S. Churchill: speech," January 27, 1942, in *The Churchill Documents*, vol. 17, *Testing Times, 1942*, ed. Martin Gilbert (Hillsdale, MI: Hillsdale College Press, 2014), 158.

3. Winston S. Churchill, "Westward Look, the Land Is Bright," April 27, 1941, in *Winston S. Churchill: His Complete Speeches*, vol. 6, *1935–1942*, ed. Robert Rhodes James (New York: Chelsea House, 1974), 6384.

4. This story of the armored train and Churchill's escape from the Boer prison is adapted from my article, "Thoughts and Adventures," published in the *Claremont Review of Books* 8, no. 2 (2008), 61–65.

5. "To the Editor, Army and Navy Gazette," December 17, 1898, in *The Churchill Documents*, vol. 2, *Young Soldier, 1896–1901*, ed. Randolph S. Churchill (Hillsdale, MI: Hillsdale College Press, 2006), 999.

6. "WSC to the Editor, Army and Navy Gazette," January 8, 1899, in *The Churchill Documents*, vol. 2, 1001.

7. "Captain Aylmer Haldane to the Chief of Staff, Natal Field Force," November 30, 1899, in *The Churchill Documents*, vol. 2, 1065.

8. Randolph Churchill, *Winston S. Churchill*, vol. 1, *Youth: 1874–1900* (Hillsdale, MI: Hillsdale College Press, 2006), 467.

9. Winston S. Churchill, *My Early Life: 1874–1904* (New York: Simon & Schuster, 1996), 246.

10. As stated in the text, Churchill's self-possession under fire went beyond his exploits in South Africa. One of his officers offers this illuminating description of his conduct in trench warfare:

> He would often go into no-man's-land. It was a nerve-racking experience to go with him. He would call out in his loud, gruff voice—far too loud it seemed to us—"you go that way, I will go this. . . . Come here, I have found a gap in the German wire. Come over here at once!" He was like a baby elephant out in no-man's-land at night. He never fell when a shell went off; he never ducked when a bullet went past with its loud crack. He used to say, after watching me duck: "It's no damn use ducking; the bullet has gone a long way past you by now."

See Martin Gilbert, *Winston S. Churchill*, vol. 3 *The Challenge of War: 1914–1916* (Hillsdale, MI: Hillsdale College Press, 2008), 658.

11. "Captain Aylmer Haldane to the Chief of Staff, Natal Field Force," November 30, 1899, in *The Churchill Documents*, vol. 2, 1066.

12. "*Natal Witness*, November 17, 1899," in *The Churchill Documents*, vol. 2, 1063.

13. From a letter by Thomas Walden to Lady Randolph, November 17, 1899. Thomas Walden served as Lord Randolph's servant and accompanied Churchill to South Africa. See Randolph Churchill, *Winston S. Churchill*, vol. 1, *Youth: 1874–1900*, 467.
14. "Lizzie B. Walls to Lady Randolph," December 18, 1899, in *The Churchill Documents*, vol. 2, 1069.
15. "P. J. Joubert to F. W. Reitz," November 19, 1899, in *The Churchill Documents*, vol. 2, 1075.
16. "WSC to Lady Randolph," December 22, 1897, in *The Churchill Documents*, vol. 2, 839.
17. Winston S. Churchill, *The Story of Malakand Field Force: An Episode of Frontier War* (London: Longmans, Green, 1901), 172. This is reminiscent of the young George Washington: "I can with trust assure you, I heard Bullets whistle and believe me there was something charming in the sound." George Washington, "To John Augustine Washington," May 31, 1754, in *George Washington: Writings*, ed. John Rhodehamel (New York: Literary Classics of the United States, 1997), 48.
18. "WSC to Bourke Cockran," November 30, 1899, in *The Churchill Documents*, vol. 2, 1083.
19. Randolph Churchill, *Winston S. Churchill*, vol. 1, *Youth: 1874–1900*, 474.
20. Churchill, *My Early Life*, 259.
21. "Clementine Churchill to H. H. Asquith," May 20, 1915, in *The Churchill Documents*, vol. 7, *"The Escaped Scapegoat," May 1915–December 1916*, ed. Martin Gilbert (Hillsdale, MI: Hillsdale College Press, 2008), 921, emphasis in original.
22. See Martin Gilbert, *Churchill: A Life* (New York: Henry Holt, 1992), 285.
23. See Gilbert, *Winston S. Churchill*, vol. 3, 125.
24. Churchill, "A Second Choice," in *Thoughts and Adventures*, 11–12.
25. Churchill, "Mass Effects in Modern Life," in *Thoughts and Adventures*, 276.

26. For the account of the king's successful appeal to keep Churchill from viewing D-Day aboard the HMS *Belfast,* see Winston Churchill, *The Second World War,* vol. 5, *Closing the Ring* (Boston: Houghton Mifflin, 1951), 619–24.

27. Carlos D'Este, *Warlord: A Life of Winston Churchill at War, 1874–1945* (New York: HarperCollins, 2008).

28. Martin Gilbert, *Winston S. Churchill,* vol. 6, *Finest Hour: 1939–1941* (Hillsdale, MI: Hillsdale College Press, 2011), 277.

29. "Winston S. Churchill to Lord Halifax," March 14, 1940, in *The Churchill Documents,* vol. 14, *At the Admiralty: September 1939–May 1940,* ed. Martin Gilbert (Hillsdale, MI: Hillsdale College Press, 2011), 883.

30. Ibid.

31. Churchill, "Blood, Toil, Tears and Sweat," May 13, 1940, in *His Complete Speeches,* vol. 6, *1935–1942,* 6220.

32. Gilbert, *Winston S. Churchill,* vol. 6, 332.

33. Ibid., 418.

34. Ibid.

35. Ibid.

36. Ibid.

37. These discussions between Churchill and the cabinet occurred from May 26 to 28. For an account of the meetings, see Gilbert, *Winston S. Churchill,* vol. 6, 402–21. Also see John Lukacs, *Five Days in London: May 1940* (New Haven: Yale University Press, 1999).

38. "Early on the morning of May 11 I sent a message to Mr. Chamberlain: 'No one changes houses for a month.' This avoided petty inconveniences during the crisis of the battle. I continued to live at Admiralty House and made its map room and the fine rooms downstairs my temporary headquarters." Winston S. Churchill, *The Second World War,* vol. 2, *Their Finest Hour* (Boston: Houghton Mifflin, 1949), 10.

39. Chamberlain died November 9, 1940. Churchill gave a beautiful eulogy to him in the House of Commons on November 12, which includes the passage:

> It fell to Neville Chamberlain in one of the supreme crises of the world to be contradicted by events, to be disappointed in his hopes, and to be deceived and cheated by a wicked man. But what were these hopes in which he was disappointed? What were these wishes in which he was frustrated? What was that faith that was abused? They were surely among the most noble and benevolent instincts of the human heart—the love of peace, the toil for peace, the strife for peace, the pursuit of peace, even at great peril, and certainly to the utter disdain of popularity or clamor. Whatever else history may or may not say about these terrible, tremendous years, we can be sure that Neville Chamberlain acted with perfect sincerity according to his lights and strove to the utmost of his capacity and authority, which were powerful, to save the world from the awful, devastating struggle in which we are now engaged. This alone will stand him in good stead as far as what is called the verdict of history is concerned.

Churchill, "Neville Chamberlain," November 12, 1940, in *His Complete Speeches,* vol. 6, 6307.
40. "WSC to Clementine," in *The Churchill Documents,* vol. 12, *The Wilderness Years: 1929–1935,* ed. Martin Gilbert (Hillsdale, MI: Hillsdale College Press, 2009), 983.
41. Churchill, "The Scaffolding of Rhetoric," in *The Churchill Documents,* vol. 2, 816–21.
42. Gilbert, *Winston S. Churchill,* vol. 6, 419.
43. Ibid.
44. Ibid., 419–20.
45. Ibid., 420.
46. Churchill, *The Second World War,* vol. 2, *Their Finest Hour,* 100.
47. Gilbert, *Winston S. Churchill,* vol. 6, *Finest Hour: 1939–1941,* 421.
48. Ibid., 406.

49. From a conversation Richard Langworth observed between Lady Soames and a Belgian woman named Ria Wiggers DeVries on May 31, 1983.
50. Churchill, "Wars Are Not Won by Evacuations," June 4, 1940, in *His Complete Speeches*, vol. 6, 6231.
51. Churchill, "The Few," August 20, 1940, in *His Complete Speeches*, vol. 6, 6266.
52. Churchill, "Their Finest Hour," June 18, 1940, in *His Complete Speeches*, vol. 6, 6238.
53. Churchill, *The Second World War*, vol. 2, *Their Finest Hour*, 279.

Chapter 2: A More Terrible Kind of War

1. After the war in the Sudan, Kitchener served as commander in chief of the British army in India (1902–9), consul general in Egypt (1909–14), then secretary of state for war at the outset of the Great War. He served in that post until his death in 1916, when a warship upon which he was sailing was sunk by a German mine. After the Battle of Omdurman, Churchill angered Kitchener with his criticisms of executing surrendered prisoners and desecrating the tomb of the Mahdi (who had died of typhus in 1885, six months after the beheading of General Gordon). In 1911, Churchill and Kitchener dined in London and talked about the defense of the Mediterranean; their relations improved somewhat at that time. In 1915, while Kitchener was the cabinet minister responsible for the army and Churchill for the navy, a joint effort was made by the two services to force the Straits of the Dardanelles. The army landed on the Gallipoli Peninsula inside the Straits, and the navy attacked Turkish forts on the eastern side of the Straits. At the outset, Kitchener advocated some kind of demonstration at the Dardanelles to distract German forces from the main front in France and Flanders. The Dardanelles assaults by land and sea were unsuccessful. Churchill believed that Kitchener was both inconstant and tardy in his support for the assault.

2. Michael Asher, *Khartoum: The Ultimate Imperial Adventure* (London: Penguin Books, 2005), 1–4.

3. Ibid., 406–7.

4. Winston S. Churchill, *The River War: An Historical Account of the Reconquest of the Soudan,* vol. 2, ed. Col. F. Rhodes (London: Longmans, Green, and Co., 1899), 248–49. I am grateful to James Muller, who is editing a new version of the book, for this and other references to the first edition.

5. Ibid., 250.

6. Ibid., 119.

7. Ibid., 221.

8. Ibid., 127–28.

9. Ibid., 119.

10. Ibid., 114–15.

11. Churchill, "Shall We All Commit Suicide?," September 1924, in *Thoughts and Adventures,* 261.

12. Churchill, *The River War,* vol. 2, 116.

13. Churchill, *The River War: An Historical Account of the Reconquest of the Soudan,* vol. 1, ed. Col. F. Rhodes (London: Longmans, Green, and Co., 1899), 284.

14. Churchill, *The River War,* vol. 2, 131.

15. Ibid., 138.

16. See the conversation between Karl Kreutze and another revolutionary in Winston S. Churchill, *Savrola: A Tale of the Revolution in Laurania* (London: Longmans, Green, 1900), 154–55.

17. Young Churchill at this age courted ladies by the memorization of noble poetry and the discussion of grand themes. He eventually got better at courtship and landed Clementine.

18. Churchill, *Savrola,* 115–16.

19. Ibid., 116.

20. Churchill, *The River War,* vol. 2, 250.

21. Churchill, "Shall We All Commit Suicide?" in *Thoughts and Adventures,* 265, emphasis in the original.

22. See Randolph Churchill, *Winston S. Churchill*, vol. 1, *Youth: 1874–1900*, chapters 11–16.
23. Winston S. Churchill, "The Maiden Speech," February 18, 1901, in *Winston S. Churchill: His Complete Speeches*, vol. 1, *1897–1908* (New York: Chelsea House, 1974), 65–66.
24. Churchill, "Army Reform," May 13, 1901, in *His Complete Speeches*, vol. 1, 82.
25. Ibid.
26. Ibid., 82–83.
27. Winston S. Churchill, *The World Crisis*, vol. 1, *1911–1914* (Norwalk, CT: The Easton Press, 1991), 10–11.
28. Ibid.
29. Ibid., 11–12.
30. See John Maurer, "Churchill's 'Naval Holiday': His Plan to Avert the Great War," *Finest Hour* 163 (Summer 2014): 10–19.
31. Churchill, *Marlborough: His Life and Times, Book One*, 555.
32. Ibid., 556.
33. Ibid.
34. Churchill, "'The Third Great Title-Deed' of Anglo-American Liberties," July 4, 1918, in *His Complete Speeches*, vol. 3, *1914–1922*, 2615.
35. Churchill, "Shall We All Commit Suicide?" in *Thoughts and Adventures*, 259.
36. Ibid., 259–60.
37. Ibid., 260.
38. Ibid., 262.
39. Churchill, "Fifty Years Hence," in *Thoughts and Adventures*, 284.
40. Churchill, "Shall We All Commit Suicide?" in *Thoughts and Adventures*, 265.

NOTES

41. In 1924, during the writing of "Shall We All Commit Suicide?" Professor Frederick Lindemann advised Churchill on the topic of future developments in warfare. In his essay Churchill predicted, "Might not a bomb no bigger than an orange be found to possess a secret power to destroy a whole block of buildings—nay to concentrate the force of a thousand tons of cordite and blast a township at a stroke?" This article was written seven years after Ernest Rutherford split the atom. For an account of Lindemann's help with this article, see Martin Gilbert, *Winston S. Churchill*, vol. 5, 49–52.

42. Martin Gilbert, *Winston S. Churchill*, vol. 8, *Never Despair: 1945-1965* (Hillsdale, MI: Hillsdale College Press, 2013), 157. Gilbert wrote,

> With reference to the Anglo-American aspect of atom bomb research since 1941, Churchill told Attlee: "Moreover we have a special relationship with them [the Americans] in this matter as defined in my agreement with President Roosevelt. This almost amounts to a military understanding between us and the mightiest power in the world. I should greatly regret if we seemed not to value this and pressed them to melt our dual agreement down into a general international arrangement consisting, I fear, of pious empty phrases and undertakings which will not be carried out. (See what happened about the submarines.)" Churchill then turned to the question of the bomb as a deterrent, and the control of any international agreement: "Nothing will give a foundation except the supreme resolve of all nations who possess or may possess the weapon to use it at once unitedly against any nation that uses it in war. For this purpose the greater the power of the US and GB in the next few years the better are the hopes. The US therefore should not share their knowledge and advantage except in return for a system of inspection of this and all other weapon preparations in every country, which they are satisfied after trial is genuine. Evidently we all have to hasten."

43. Winston S. Churchill, "The Deterrent—Nuclear Warfare," March 1, 1955, in *Winston S. Churchill: His Complete Speeches,* vol. 8, *1950–1963,* ed. Robert Rhodes James (New York: Chelsea House, 1974), 8626.

44. Ibid., 8631.

45. "Mass Effects in Modern Life" was first published in *Strand Magazine* in May 1931.

46. Churchill, "Mass Effects in Modern Life," in *Thoughts and Adventures,* 275–76.

47. Ibid.

48. "Edward Marsh to R. C. Sherriff," February 1, 1929, and "R.C. Sherriff to Winston S. Churchill," February 15, 1929, in *The Churchill Documents,* vol. 11, *The Exchequer Years, 1922–1929,* ed. Martin Gilbert (Hillsdale, MI: Hillsdale College Press, 2009), 1420, 1425. Sherriff also wrote the screenplay for one of Churchill's favorite films, *That Hamilton Woman.*

49. Churchill, *The World Crisis,* vol. 1, *1911–1914,* 11.

50. A phrase introduced by H. G. Wells in articles and a book at the outset of the Great War.

51. F. L. Carsten, *The Reichswehr and Politics: 1918–1933* (Oxford: Oxford University Press, 1966), 148, 150, 155, 220–32, 265, 273.

52. Churchill, "A Disarmament Fable," October 24, 1928, in *His Complete Speeches,* vol. 5, *1928–1935,* 4521.

53. Churchill, "The Deterrent—Nuclear Warfare," 8627–28.

54. Ibid., 8625.

Chapter 3: The Statesman's Virtue

1. See Gilbert, *Winston S. Churchill,* vol. 6, 419.

2. Churchill, *Marlborough: His Life and Times, Book One,* 17.

3. Ibid., 464.

4. Ibid., 494.

5. Churchill, "What Good's a Constitution?," in *The U.S. Constitution: A Reader,* 737–38.

6. Alexander Hamilton, "No. 1: General Introduction," in *Federalist Papers,* ed. Clinton Rossiter (New York: Signet Classics, 2003), 27.

7. Churchill, *The World Crisis*, vol. 1, *1911–1914*, 13.

8. Churchill, "Mass Effects in Modern Life," in *Thoughts and Adventures*, 269, emphasis added.

9. See Harry V. Jaffa, "Can There Ever Be Another Winston Churchill?" in *Statesmanship: Essays in Honor of Sir Winston S. Churchill*, ed. Harry V. Jaffa (Durham, NC: Carolina Academic Press, 1981), 25–40. His explanation of this point and other significant points is compact and beautiful.

10. Churchill, "Mass Effects in Modern Life," in *Thoughts and Adventures*, 269–70.

11. Churchill, *Marlborough: His Life and Times, Book One*, 15.

12. Churchill, "Plugstreet," in *Thoughts and Adventures*, 119–26. For an excellent discussion of Churchill's understanding of chance by editor James Muller, see the introduction, xxviii–xxix.

13. Churchill, *The World Crisis*, vol. 1, *1911–1914*, 13.

14. Churchill, *Marlborough: His Life and Times, Book One*, 569.

15. Churchill, *My Early Life*, 113.

16. Churchill, *Marlborough: His Life and Times, Book One*, 569.

17. Plato, *The Republic*, 473c–d, 487d–489c.

18. Churchill, "Painting as a Pastime," in *Thoughts and Adventures*, 323.

19. Ibid., 327.

20. Ibid., 327–28.

21. Joseph Mallord William Turner, 1775–1851. Known as "the painter of light." British artist particularly well known for his watercolors and often seen as a Romantic precursor to Impressionism. Born in Covent Garden, London; son of a wig-maker. Studied under the architect Thomas Malton, Jr. Educated at the Royal Academy, London, 1789. Exhibited at the Royal Academy Exhibition for the first time, 1790. Awarded the Great Silver Pallet for landscape drawing, 1793. Elected Associate of the Royal Academy, 1799; elected Academician, 1802; elected Professor of Perspective, 1807. Acting President of the Royal Academy, 1845. By the time of his death, had completed nearly

NOTES

two thousand paintings and watercolors, and more than nineteen thousand drawings and sketches. Some of his works include *Snow Storm: Hannibal and His Army Crossing the Alps* (1812), *Dido Building Carthage* (1815), *The Battle of Trafalgar* (1824), *Ulysses Deriding Polyphemus* (1829), *The Burning of the House of Lords and Commons* (1835), and *The Fighting Temeraire* (1839).

22. Churchill, "Painting as a Pastime," in *Thoughts and Adventures*, 328.
23. Churchill, "Consistency in Politics," in *Thoughts and Adventures*, 38–42.
24. Churchill, "Westward, Look, The Land is Bright," April 27, 1941, in *His Complete Speeches*, vol. 6, 6380.
25. Churchill, "Painting as a Pastime," in *Thoughts and Adventures*, 325.
26. Ibid.
27. Winston S. Churchill, "The Effect of Modern Amusements on Life and Character: Our Democratic Parliament is an Example to the World," September 18, 1938, in *The Collected Essays of Sir Winston Churchill*, vol. 4, *Churchill at Large*, ed. Michael Wolff (London: Library of Imperial History, 1976), 468.
28. Churchill, "Defence of Freedom and Peace," October 16, 1938, in *His Complete Speeches*, vol. 6, 6017.
29. Churchill, "Fifty Years Hence," in *Thoughts and Adventures*, 292, 295. Churchill writes that this was suggested to him by a play entitled *Rossum's Universal Robots*. Of course the idea is most famous in Huxley's *Brave New World*, which was written in 1931 ("Fifty Years Hence" was published first in December of that year). There is no record of Churchill reading *Brave New World* until he wrote to his wife about it in 1957. Gilbert, *Winston S. Churchill*, vol. 8, 1228.
30. Churchill, "Fifty Years Hence," in *Thoughts and Adventures*, 295.
31. Churchill, "Painting as a Pastime," in *Thoughts and Adventures*, 329–30.
32. Ibid.

33. Churchill, "Civilization," July 2, 1938, in *His Complete Speeches*, vol. 6, 5990–91.
34. Ibid., 5991.

Chapter 4: The Strategist

1. Winston S. Churchill, *The World Crisis*, vol. 2, *1915* (Norwalk, CT: The Easton Press, 1991), 20.
2. Ibid., 21.
3. Churchill, *Marlborough: His Life and Times, Book One*, 17.
4. Winston S. Churchill, *Marlborough: His Life and Times, Book Two* (Chicago: University of Chicago Press, 2002), 629.
5. Ibid., 632.
6. Churchill, *The World Crisis*, vol. 2, *1915*, 21.
7. Ibid., 11.
8. Churchill, "A Second Choice," in *Thoughts and Adventures*, 12.
9. Winston S. Churchill, *The Second World War*, vol. 4, *The Hinge of Fate* (Boston: Houghton Mifflin, 1950), 391–409.
10. Churchill, "To The U.S. Congress," May 19, 1943, in *His Complete Speeches*, vol. 7, 6779.
11. Churchill, *The World Crisis*, vol. 2, *1915*, 17–18.
12. "Winston S. Churchill: memorandum," October 15, 1915, in *The Churchill Documents*, vol. 7, 1221.
13. "Winston S. Churchill to Archibald Sinclair," December 16, 1916, in *The Churchill Documents*, vol. 8, *War and Aftermath, December 1916–June 1919*, ed. Martin Gilbert (Hillsdale, MI: Hillsdale College Press, 2008), 36.
14. Churchill, *The World Crisis*, vol. 2, *1915*, 21.
15. Gilbert, *Winston S. Churchill*, vol. 3, 534–38. Churchill turned to Captain Eustace Tennyson D'Eyncourt, one of the foremost designers at the admiralty, to develop the tank.
16. Gilbert, *Winston S. Churchill*, vol. 8, 196.
17. The Long Telegram argued that conflict with the Soviet Union was inevitable and would likely be protracted. It also argued that military confrontation could likely be avoided through a policy of strength in support of strategic objectives clearly defined. See

George F. Kennan, Memoirs: 1925–1950 (Boston: Little, Brown, 1967), 547–59.

18. See Gilbert, *Winston S. Churchill*, vol. 8, 32.

19. Ibid., 197.

20. Churchill was sufficiently disturbed by the attack in the *Chicago Sun* that he wrote to its proprietor, Marshall Field, to withdraw from an arrangement he had with the newspaper to publish his "Secret Session Speeches." See Gilbert, *Winston S. Churchill*, vol. 8, 204.

21. Churchill, "The Sinews of Peace," March 5, 1946, in *His Complete Speeches*, vol. 7, 7286.

22. Ibid., 7286–87.

23. Churchill, "Shall We All Commit Suicide?" in *Thoughts and Adventures*, 265–66.

24. Churchill, "The Sinews of Peace," March 5, 1946, in *His Complete Speeches*, vol. 7, 7287.

25. Ibid.

26. Ibid.

27. Ibid., 7288.

28. Ibid., 7287–88.

29. "Winston S. Churchill: memorandum," October 25, 1919, in *The Churchill Documents*, vol. 9, *Disruption and Chaos, July 1919–March 21*, ed. Martin Gilbert (Hillsdale, MI: Hillsdale College Press, 2008), 947. For Churchill's Middle East policies as colonial secretary see David Fromkin, *A Peace to End all Peace: The Fall of the Ottoman Empire and the Creation of the Modern Middle East* (New York: Henry Holt, 2001), 493–529.

30. See Martin Gilbert, *Winston S. Churchill*, vol. 4, *World in Torment: 1916–1922* (Hillsdale, MI: Hillsdale College Press, 2008), 638.

31. See Randolph Churchill, *Winston S. Churchill*, vol. 2, *Young Statesman: 1901–1914* (Hillsdale, MI: Hillsdale College Press, 2007), 596.

32. See Gilbert, *Winston S. Churchill*, vol. 5, 121.

33. Record of a dinner conversation at Chequers, the British prime minister's country retreat, Monday, April 26, 1954. Public Record Office, *Premier papers, 11/645/68710.*

34. In the debate over the Munich agreement in 1938, Churchill said, "What I find unendurable is the sense of our country falling into the power, into the orbit and influence of Nazi Germany, and of our existence becoming dependent upon their good will or pleasure." Churchill, "A Total and Unmitigated Defeat," October 5, 1938, in *His Complete Speeches*, vol. 6, 6011.

35. Winston S. Churchill, *The Second World War*, vol. 1, *The Gathering Storm* (Boston: Houghton Mifflin Company, 1948), iv.

36. Churchill, "The Sinews of Peace," March 5, 1946, in *His Complete Speeches*, vol. 7, 7288.

37. Ibid.

38. Ibid.

39. See Michael McMenamin and Curt J. Zoller, *Becoming Winston Churchill: The Untold Story of Young Winston and His American Mentor* (New York: Enigma Books, 2009); and James McGurrin, *Bourke Cockran: A Free Lance in American Politics* (New York: Charles Scribner's Sons, 1948).

40. Churchill, "The Sinews of Peace," March 5, 1946, in *His Complete Speeches*, vol. 7, 7288.

41. George Bernard Shaw, "The Basis of Socialism: Economic," in *Fabian Essays in Socialism,* ed. George Bernard Shaw (New York: Humboldt Publishing, 1891), 129.

42. See Martin Gilbert, *Winston S. Churchill*, vol. 7, *Road to Victory: 1941–1945* (Hillsdale, MI: Hillsdale College Press, 2013), 1320.

43. Churchill, "The Sinews of Peace," March 5, 1946, in *His Complete Speeches*, vol. 7, 7289.

44. Churchill, "Education," February 26, 1946, in *His Complete Speeches,* vol. 7, 7285.

45. Churchill, "The Sinews of Peace," March 5, 1946, in *His Complete Speeches*, vol. 7, 7290.

46. Ibid., 7289.

47. Ibid.
48. Ibid.
49. In October 1944 Churchill traveled to Moscow to make the famous—or infamous—"percentages agreement." This was an agreement between Stalin and Churchill that the three Allied powers would share authority, pending free elections after the war, over the countries liberated from Nazi Germany. The agreement gave Britain 90 percent influence in Greece. This, along with Russia's 90 percent influence in Romania, was the highest percentage allotted and was helpful in attracting Greece to democracy, and ultimately, to NATO. See Gilbert, *Winston S. Churchill*, vol. 7, 989–1005. Churchill also argued for Operation Manna, a British military operation to stop a communist attack on Athens. See Ibid., 1020–21.
50. Churchill, "The Sinews of Peace," March 5, 1946, in *His Complete Speeches*, vol. 7, 7292.
51. Ibid., 7291.
52. Ibid., 7292.

Chapter 5: Strategy and Empire

1. Churchill, "Sinews of Peace," March 5, 1946, in *His Complete Speeches*, vol. 7, 7292.
2. Ibid., 7293.
3. Churchill, "Finance Bill," June 22, 1903, in *His Complete Speeches*, vol. 1, 197–98.
4. Churchill, "Constituency Address," September 24, 1921, in *His Complete Speeches*, vol. 3, 3138.
5. Winston S. Churchill, "The Political Scene from a Distance," May 4, 1923, in *Winston S. Churchill: His Complete Speeches*, vol. 4, *1922–1928*, ed. Robert Rhodes James (New York: Chelsea House, 1974), 3387.
6. Churchill, "Army Reform," May 13, 1901, in *His Complete Speeches*, vol. 1, 83.
7. Churchill, "Air Estimates," March 21, 1922, in *His Complete Speeches*, vol. 3, 3268.

8. Churchill, "Election Address," February 14, 1950, in *His Complete Speeches*, vol. 8, 7937.

9. Churchill, "Four Years at the Exchequer," July 19, 1928, in *His Complete Speeches*, vol. 5, 4499.

10. For example, see Churchill, "Free Speech and Free Trade," November 11, 1903, in *His Complete Speeches*, vol. 1, 224, where Churchill says, "I have seen enough in peace and war of the frontiers of our Empire to know that the British dominion all over the world could not endure for a year, perhaps not for a month, if it was founded upon a material basis." See also "Imperial Unity," November 2, 1921, in *His Complete Speeches*, vol. 3, 3144.

11. Winston S. Churchill, *A History of the English-Speaking Peoples*, vol. 1, *The Birth of Britain* (New York: Dodd, Mead, 1956), viii–ix.

12. Churchill, *Marlborough: His Life and Times, Book One*, 65.

13. Winston S. Churchill, *A History of the English-Speaking Peoples*, vol. 3, *The Age of Revolution* (New York: Dodd, Mead, 1957), 223.

14. Churchill, "The Future of the Empire," April 21, 1944, in *His Complete Speeches*, vol. 7, 6920.

15. "Harold Nicolson: diary," June 14, 1939, in *The Churchill Documents*, vol. 13, *The Coming War, 1936–1939*, ed. Martin Gilbert (Hillsdale, MI: Hillsdale College Press, 2009), 1519. The conversation was recorded in the diaries of Harold Nicolson, who attended the dinner where Churchill said this.

16. *Statistics of the Military Effort of the British Empire During the Great War 1914–1920* (London: H. M. Stationery Office, 1922). See *Commonwealth War Graves Commission Annual Report 2013–2014* (Maidenhead, Berkshire: Commonwealth War Graves Commission, 2014). See "Military Casualties-World War-Estimated" (Statistics Branch, GS, War Department, February 25, 1924), cited in *World War I: People, Politics, and Power* (New York: Britannica Educational Publishing, 2010). See Chris Baker, "Some British Army Statistics of the Great War," in *The Long, Long Trail: The British Army in the Great War*, http://www.1914–1918.net/faq.htm.

17. John Ellis, *World War II: A Statistical Survey* (New York: Facts on File, 1993). See *Commonwealth War Graves Commission Annual Report 2013–2014*, and "By the Numbers: World-Wide Deaths," National WWII Museum, http://www.nationalww2museum. org/learn/education/for-students/ww2-history/ww2-by-the-numbers/world-wide-deaths.html.

18. The number of Soviet troops in World War II was, by the by, about twice as high as the number of British Empire and Commonwealth troops, and more than twice as high as the number of American troops. Soviets killed and wounded exceeded the total casualties of the Western Allies by a factor of nearly ten. The Soviets had 34.5 million men and women in uniform; they suffered an estimated 8.8 to 10.7 million killed and almost 15 million wounded. Chinese killed are estimated at 3 to 4 million. From, "By the Numbers: World-Wide Deaths," National WWII Museum. For additional figures on the Soviet war effort, see G. F. Krivosheev, *Soviet Casualties and Combat Losses* (London: Greenhill Books, 1997), 85–87.

19. Rita J. Simon and Mohamed Alaa Abdel-Moneim, *A Handbook of Military Conscription and Composition the World Over* (Lanham, MD: Lexington Books, 2011), 174.

20. Churchill, "The Sinews of Peace," March 5, 1946, in *His Complete Speeches*, vol. 7, 7293.

21. Chris Baker, "Some British Army Statistics of the Great War," in *The Long, Long Trail: The British Army in the Great War*, http:// www.19141918.net/faq.htm. Cf. "Fact File: Commonwealth and Allied Forces," BBC, http://www.bbc.co.uk/history/ ww2peopleswar/timeline/factfiles/nonflash/a6651218. shtml?sectionId=0&articleId=6651218 (Accessed January 19, 2015).

22. Gilbert, *Winston S. Churchill*, vol. 7, 342–44.

23. "Winston S. Churchill to Attlee and Amery," May 23, 1943, in *The Churchill Documents*, vol. 18, 1390. See also Roosevelt's letter to Churchill from March 11, 1942, in *The Churchill Documents*, vol. 17, 379–81.

24. Lawrence James, *Churchill and Empire: A Portrait of an Imperialist* (New York: Pegasus Books, 2014), 22.
25. See Richard Toye, *Churchill's Empire: The World that Made Him and the World He Made* (New York: Henry Holt, 2010), 121.
26. Ibid., 315. The famine was significantly the result of Japanese military action in Burma and other points east, which had cut off supplies of rice and other grains to Bengal. Churchill, Britain, and the Allied countries all expressed sympathy for the famine but took insufficient steps to relieve it. They claimed that they did not have shipping to get food to Bengal, or at least not given the time allowed amidst other wartime priorities. See "The Bengali Famine," Churchill Centre, www.winstonchurchill.org/learn/in-the-media/churchill-in-the-new/575-the-bengali-famine. Richard Langworth writes, "Without Churchill, the 1943 Bengal famine would have been *worse.*" See "Reflections on Churchill's Funeral," *Weekly Standard,* January 23, 2015, http://www.weeklystandard.com/blogs/reflections-churchill-s-funeral_824348.html?page=2.
27. Geoffrey Best—whose book, *Churchill: A Study in Greatness*, I have reviewed and praised, and reaffirm the praise here—wrote, "I stick by what I wrote about Churchill's general ignorance about the cultures of the Empire's non-white populations. He was ignorant and prejudiced about them, and positively avoided meeting members of them, on the rare occasions when he might have done so." Letter from Best cited in "Churchill's Imperialism," *The Claremont Review of Books* 4, no. 2 (Fall 2002). There are many instances, however, of Churchill meeting with and admiring non-white people. For example, G. D. Birla, Gandhi's associate and representative in London, wrote to Gandhi on August 25, 1935: "Curiously enough one of my most pleasant experiences was meeting Mr. Winston Churchill, the strongest opponent of the Bill, who had the advantage of delivering his attacks from the Government side of the House. Yet I found him no fire-eater. He asked me to lunch at Chartwell, his country home." From *The Churchill Documents*, vol. 12, 1243.

28. Winston S. Churchill, *My African Journey* (Toronto: William Briggs, 1909), 37–38.
29. Churchill, "South Africa (Native Races)," February 28, 1906, in *His Complete Speeches*, vol. 1, 574.
30. "Winston S. Churchill to Edwin Montagu," October 8, 1921, in *The Churchill Documents*, vol. 10, *Conciliation and Reconstruction, April 1921–November 1922*, ed. Martin Gilbert (Hillsdale, MI: Hillsdale College Press, 2008), 1644.
31. Winston S. Churchill, "A General View," January 30, 1931, in *India: Defending the Jewel in the Crown* (Hopkinton, NH: Dragonwyck Publishing, 1990), 80.
32. Ibid., 77.
33. Churchill, "Our Duty in India," March 18, 1931, in *His Complete Speeches*, vol. 5, 5007.
34. In a letter to Gandhi recounting his visit with Churchill, Birla wrote, "He [Churchill] asked what Mr. Gandhi was doing. I explained. He was immensely interested and said 'Mr. Gandhi has gone very high in my esteem since he stood up for the untouchables.' He wanted to know in detail about the untouchability work. I explained. He was glad that I was the President of the Anti-Untouchability League." In *The Churchill Documents*, vol. 12, 1244.
35. Churchill, "Our Duty in India," January 30, 1931, in *India: Defending the Jewel in the Crown*, 5007.
36. Ibid.
37. Churchill, "India (Government Policy)," December 3, 1931, in *His Complete Speeches*, vol. 5, 5111.
38. Churchill, "India (The Round Table Conference)," December 11, 1930, in *His Complete Speeches,* vol. 5, 4935–37.
39. "WSC to Lord Elgin," March 15, 1906, in *The Churchill Documents*, vol. 3, 529. Churchill wrote in this letter that 20,000 Boer women and children died in British concentration camps during the Boer War.

40. For example, see Winston S. Churchill, *London to Ladysmith Via Pretoria* (London: Longmans, Green, 1900), 134–35. Churchill wrote: "What is the true and original root of Dutch aversion to British rule? It is not Slagters Nek, nor Broomplatz, nor Majuba, nor the Jameson Raid. Those incidents only fostered its growth. It is the abiding fear and the hatred of the movement that seeks to place the native on a level with the white man. British government is associated in the Boer farmer's mind with violent social revolution. Black is to be proclaimed the same as white. The servant is to be raised against the master; the Kaffir is to be declared the brother of the European, to be constituted his legal equal, to be armed with political rights."

41. Churchill, "South Africa (Native Races)," February 28, 1906, in *His Complete Speeches*, vol. 1, 577.

42. James Madison, "Speech in the Virginia Constitutional Convention," December 2, 1829, in *James Madison: Writings,* ed. Jack N. Rakove (New York: Literary Classics of the United States, 1999), 824.

43. Thomas Jefferson, "First Inaugural Address," March 4, 1801, in *The Inaugural Addresses of President Thomas Jefferson, 1801 and 1805,* ed. Noble E. Cunningham Jr. (Columbia: University of Missouri Press, 2001), 4.

44. Abraham Lincoln, "Speech on the Kansas Nebraska Act," October 16, 1854, in *The U.S. Constitution: A Reader,* 468.

45. Abraham Lincoln, "First Joint Debate (Ottawa)," August 21, 1858, in *The Lincoln-Douglas Debates of 1858,* ed. Robert W. Johannsen (New York: Oxford University Press, 1965), 64–65.

46. Churchill, "South Africa (Native Races)," February 28, 1906, in *His Complete Speeches*, vol. 1, 577–78.

47. Abraham Lincoln, "First Joint Debate (Ottawa)," August 21, 1858, in *The Lincoln-Douglas Debates of 1858,* 65.

48. "Winston S. Churchill to Herbert Morrison," January 7, 1943, in *The Churchill Documents*, vol. 18, 59–60.

49. Winston S. Churchill, "A General View," January 30, 1931, in *India: Defending the Jewel in the Crown*, 79.

50. Ibid., 77–78.

51. "G. D. Birla: report to M.K. Gandhi," August 25, 1935, in *The Churchill Documents*, vol. 12, 1245.

52. Churchill, *London to Ladysmith via Pretoria*, 134.

53. "Winston S. Churchill to Herbert Morrison," January 7, 1943, in *The Churchill Documents*, vol. 18, 59.

54. Churchill, "The Third Great Title-Deed of Anglo-American Liberties," July 4, 1918, in *His Complete Speeches*, vol. 3, 2614.

55. Churchill, "Hyderabad and Kashmir," July 30, 1948, in *His Complete Speeches*, vol. 7, 7704.

56. Nick Lloyd, *The Amritsar Massacre: The Untold Story of One Fateful Day* (London: I. B. Tauris, 2011), xxvi. Lloyd cites evidence that Dyer's actions had helped to stop the rebellion, and that worse actions, less justified, happened under martial law in the following days. See p. 106, and chapter 13, "The Introduction of Martial Law."

57. Ibid., xix.

58. Churchill, "The Punjab Disturbances," July 8, 1920, in *His Complete Speeches*, vol. 3, 3009–10.

59. Ibid., 3011.

60. Churchill, "Civilization," July 2, 1938, in *His Complete Speeches*, vol. 6, 5990–91.

61. Churchill, "Our Duty in India," March 18, 1931, in *His Complete Speeches*, vol. 5, 5006.

62. Churchill, "India (Government Policy)," December 3, 1931, in *His Complete Speeches*, vol. 5, 5110–11.

63. See Hillsdale College, *The U.S. Constitution: A Reader*, Section VII: "The Founders on Slavery, the Rise of the Positive Good School, and the Roots of the Secession Crisis" for original source material on this question.

64. Abraham Lincoln, "Second Inaugural Address," in *The U.S. Constitution: A Reader*, 614.

65. Churchill, "A General View," January 30, 1931, in *India: Defending the Jewel in the Crown*, 75–76.

66. Ramachandra Guha, *India After Gandhi: The History of the World's Largest Democracy* (New York: Harper, 2007), xi–xiii.

67. Gilbert, *Winston S. Churchill*, vol. 5, 618.

68. Barbara D. Metcalf and Thomas R. Metcalf, *A Concise History of Modern India* (Cambridge: Cambridge University Press, 2006), 203–30.

69. Guha, *India After Gandhi*, 605–7.

70. Churchill, "The age of control in Imperial relationships has ended. . . . The Age of Control is gone, the Age of Comprehension has begun." From "Canada," January 3, 1927, in *His Complete Speeches*, vol. 4, 4124.

Chapter 6: "Lo! A New England"

1. Churchill, "Mass Effects in Modern Life," in *Thoughts and Adventures*, 269–80.

2. Gilbert described the following story from Churchill's farewell to the Cabinet in 1955, "Churchill's final words to those Ministers not in the Cabinet made a strong impact on those who heard them. 'He wished to make two points,' Lord De L'Isle and Dudley later recalled: 'Man is spirit,' and 'Never be separated from the Americans.'" In *Winston S. Churchill*, vol. 8, 1123.

3. Churchill, "Mass Effects in Modern Life," in *Thoughts and Adventures*, 271.

4. Ibid., 272.

5. Mark Bevir, *The Making of British Socialism* (Princeton: Princeton University Press, 2011), 18. Bevir calls Shaw and Webb "the two leading Fabian socialists."

6. Churchill wrote that the Fabians owed "little to dogmatic theory and nothing to Marx." Surely they did not share Marx's view that dictatorship was necessary or that the class struggle had to be violent. They prided themselves on their practicality and patience, not the traits for which Marx made his fame. See Winston S. Churchill, *History of the English-Speaking Peoples*,

vol. 4, *The Great Democracies* (New York: Dodd, Mead, & Company), 364.

7. Churchill, *Great Contemporaries*, 34.

8. George Bernard Shaw, ed. *Fabian Essays in Socialism*. The Online Library of Liberty, Indianapolis. Liberty Fund edits and reprints the 1891 American Edition by Humboldt Publishing. It is available at http://oll.libertyfund.org.

9. Sydney Olivier, "The Basis of Socialism: Moral," in *Fabian Essays in Socialism*, 109–11.

10. George Douglas Howard Cole, *The Simple Case for Socialism* (London: Victor Gollancz, 1935), 10.

11. Hubert Bland, "Transition to Social Democracy: The Outlook," in *Fabian Essays in Socialism*, 249.

12. Sidney Webb, "The Basis of Socialism: Historic," in *Fabian Essays in Socialism*, 6.

13. Bevir, *The Making Of British Socialism*, 177–78.

14. Sidney Webb, "Twentieth Century Politics," November 8, 1901, in *The Basis and Policy of Socialism* (London: A. C. Fifield, 1908), 77.

15. Olivier, "The Basis of Socialism: Moral," in *Fabian Essays in Socialism*, 125.

16. Bevir, *The Making of British Socialism*, 213. Bevir wrote: "The Fabians looked on political reform not as a way to solve social ills but as administrative measures to facilitate good government. Although they did not share [John Stuart] Mill's fear that democracy might erode individual liberty, they rarely promoted greater popular participation in government. Generally, they welcomed the rise of a professional civil service and policy experts."

17. Webb, "Twentieth Century Politics," in *The Basis and Policy of Socialism*, 82.

18. Ibid., 92–95 and throughout.

19. Labour Party Executive Committee, *Labour and the New Social Order: A Report on Reconstruction* (London: Labour Party, 1918), 4–5.

20. John Bellers (1654–1725); Quaker and philanthropist. At the age of thirty, he married Frances Fettiplace. He developed an educational scheme for poor children, supported the establishment of hospitals for the sick in London, advocated for the better management and welfare of prisons, and wrote extensively on religious discourse and philanthropic schemes. His *Proposals for Raising a College of Industry of All Useful Trades and Husbandry* (1695) advocated the establishment of cooperative communities and was quoted by Karl Marx in *Das Kapital*.

21. François-Noël Babeuf (1760–97); French political journalist. Called "Gracchus" for his proposed agrarian reforms because of their similarity to those of the ancient Roman statesman Gracchus. He advocated tax and land reform, was arrested and imprisoned on multiple occasions for his protests, founded the journals *Le Correspondant picard* and *Le Journal de la liberté de la presse*, and was guillotined with Augustin Darthé for participating in insurrectionary committees planning to overthrow the Directory and restore the Constitution of 1793.

22. Robert Owen (1771–1858); second youngest of seven sons of the postmaster in Newtown, Wales. Businessman, cotton-mill owner, and philanthropist. He sought to improve living conditions and education in New Lanark; and advocated for factory reform; founded self-contained, utopian communities in America and Great Britain. A founder of the Grand National Consolidated Trades Union (1834), he is considered one of the seminal figures in British socialism.

23. Sidney Webb, *Socialism in England* (London: Swan Sonnenschein & Co., 1890), 119.

24. J. Ramsay MacDonald, *Socialism and Government: Volume 1* (London: Independent Labour Party, 1909), 72–74. MacDonald wrote that women are the creators and protectors of the family and men of the tribe and the nation. He saw these matters in an older sense, and he objected to the feeding of schoolchildren at

government expense as a taking of "one of the functions essential to family life." He objected to the planning for a "community of wives," arguing that the Socialist state must not be masculine only. MacDonald was not the most radical Socialist.

25. Austen Albu, "The Organization of Industry," in *New Fabian Essays* (London: J. M. Dent & Sons, 1970), 141.

26. C. A. R. Crosland, "The Transition from Capitalism," in *New Fabian Essays*, 43.

27. Labour Party Executive Committee, *Labour and the New Social Order: A Report on Reconstruction* (London: Labour Party, 1918), 3–4.

28. Bevir, *The Making of British Socialism*, 227.

29. Shaw, "The Basis of Socialism: Economic," in *Fabian Essays in Socialism,* 133–34.

30. Olivier, "The Basis of Socialism: Moral," in *Fabian Essays in Socialism*, 123.

31. Webb, "The Basis of Socialism: Historic," in *Fabian Essays in Socialism*, 7.

32. Olivier, "The Basis of Socialism: Moral," in *Fabian Essays in Socialism*, 100.

33. Ibid., 108.

34. Ibid., 117.

35. Annie Besant, "The Organization of Society: Industry under Socialism," in *Fabian Essays in Socialism*, 209.

36. Olivier, "The Basis of Socialism: Moral," in *Fabian Essays in Socialism*, 125.

37. Shaw, "The Basis of Socialism: Economic," in *Fabian Essays in Socialism*, 158.

38. Karl Marx and Friedrich Engels, *The Communist Manifesto* (New York: Simon and Schuster, 2013), 86–88.

39. Olivier, "The Basis of Socialism: Moral," in *Fabian Essays in Socialism*, 95.

40. Graham Wallas, "The Organization of Society: Property Under Socialism," in *Fabian Essays in Socialism*, 167.

41. George Bernard Shaw, *The Intelligent Woman's Guide to Socialism and Capitalism* (New York: Brentano's, 1928), 408–9.

42. Wallas, "The Organization of Society: Property Under Socialism," in *Fabian Essays in Socialism*, 177.

43. Ibid., 182.

44. George Douglas Howard Cole (1889–1959); born in Cambridge. A lecturer, writer, and advocate of Guild Socialism, he served as reader in Economics at Oxford, 1925–44; and of Social and Political Theory, 1944–57. An active member of the Labour Party and of the Fabian Research Department, he founded the National Guilds League; helped to lead the New Fabian Research Bureau as secretary (1931–35) and chairman (1937–39); chaired the Fabian Society (1939–46, 1948–50) and served as its president (1952–59); and was a contributor to and director of the *New Statesman* from 1947.

45. R. H. S. Crossman, "Towards a Philosophy of Socialism," in *New Fabian Essays*, 1–32.

46. Ibid., 10–12.

47. Ibid., 27.

48. Churchill, "Parliamentary Government and the Economic Problem," June 19, 1930, in *Thoughts and Adventures*, 248.

49. Crossman, "Towards a Philosophy of Socialism," in *Fabian Essays in Socialism*, 14–15.

50. Churchill, "Conservative Party Annual Conference Address," October 4, 1947, in *His Complete Speeches*, vol. 7, 7531.

51. Bevir, *The Making of British Socialism*, especially chapters 11 and 14.

Chapter 7: *"Some Form of Gestapo"*

1. Churchill, "Party Politics Again," June 4, 1945, in *His Complete Speeches*, vol. 7, 7172.

2. Churchill, "Palestine," January 26, 1949, in *His Complete Speeches*, vol. 7, 7773–74.

3. See Gilbert, *Winston S. Churchill*, vol. 8, 19–22.

4. William Manchester and Paul Reid, *The Last Lion, Winston Spencer Churchill: Defender of the Realm, 1940–1965* (New York: Little, Brown, 2012), 950.
5. Laurence Thompson, *1940* (New York: William Morrow, 1966), 146.
6. Manchester and Reid, *The Last Lion*, 950.
7. According to Mary Churchill, Clementine "begged" her husband "to delete the odious and invidious reference to the Gestapo." His daughter Sarah warned,

> . . . I am not quite sure they will understand how what you say would really be so. Because Socialism as practiced in the war, did no one any harm, and quite a lot of people good. The children of this country have never been so well fed or healthy, what milk there was, was shared equally, the rich didn't die because their meat ration was no larger than the poor; and there is no doubt that this common sharing and feeling of sacrifice was one of the strongest bonds that unified us. So why, they say, cannot this common feeling of sacrifice be made to work as effectively in peace? Don't think I am a rebel! But I thought that as this morning there is not very much to do, I would try and put down what I hear and see, of what the people I live and work with feel.

In Gilbert, *Winston S. Churchill*, vol. 8, 32–36.
8. Roy Jenkins, a politician whose career overlapped with Churchill's, wrote,

> The trouble was that his idea of "giving it to them" ran directly counter to his strenuously earned position as leader of the whole nation, which should have been his greatest electoral asset. The sound of the familiar voice, which had so often united and elevated the country, indulging in the exaggerated abuse of party politics made the shock the greater.

In *Churchill: A Biography* (New York: Farrar, Straus, and Giroux, 2001), 792.

9. Richard Toye, "Winston Churchill's 'Crazy Broadcast': Party, Nation, and the 1945 Gestapo Speech," *The Journal of British Studies* 49, no. 3 (July 2010): 655–80.

10. "WSC to Bourke Cockran," November 30, 1899, in *The Churchill Documents*, vol. 2, 1083.

11. Ibid.

12. Churchill, "Mass Effects in Modern Life," in *Thoughts and Adventures*, 269–71. This phrase is from Kipling's poem, "The Old Issue."

13. Ibid.

14. Churchill, "Demobilisation," October 22, 1945, in *His Complete Speeches*, vol. 7, 7235.

15. Churchill, "Roosevelt from Afar," December 29, 1934, in *Great Contemporaries*, 244.

16. Churchill, "The Town and Country Planning Bill and Parliamentary Democracy," March 3, 1947, in *His Complete Speeches*, vol. 7, 7437.

17. Churchill, "Election Address," February 15, 1950, in *His Complete Speeches*, vol. 8, 7945.

18. Churchill, "Painting as a Pastime," in *Thoughts and Adventures*, 333.

19. Churchill, *Savrola*, 154–55.

20. Aristophanes, *Ecclesiazusae* (Assembly of Women), 615–29.

21. Valerie Strauss, "French President Pushing Homework Ban as Part of Ed Reforms," *Washington Post*, October 15, 2012.

22. Churchill, "Election Address," May 2, 1908, in *His Complete Speeches*, vol. 1, 1029.

23. Niccolò Machiavelli, *The Prince*, trans. Harvey Mansfield (Chicago: The University of Chicago Press, 1998), 61.

24. Churchill, "Mass Effects in Modern Life," in *Thoughts and Adventures*, 271.

25. Churchill said this repeatedly throughout his career. See, for example, his speech "The Political Scene from a Distance," May 4, 1923, in *His Complete Speeches*, vol. 4, 3387–88.

26. Churchill, *The Second World War*, vol. 1, *The Gathering Storm*, 187.

27. Churchill, "Minissters and Public Servants (Lynskey Tribunal)," February 3, 1949, in *His Complete Speeches*, vol. 7, 7788. Whether consciously or no, Churchill followed John Adams in using this quotation. Adams quoted Horace in his *Defence of the Constitutions of Government of the United States of America*, vol. 2: "Naturam expellas furca, tamen usque recurret." [You may expel nature with a pitchfork, but it will always return.] In Charles Francis Adams, *The Works of John Adams*, vol. 5 (Boston: Little, Brown, 1851), 151.

28. Churchill, "Finance Bill," June 1, 1937, in *His Complete Speeches*, vol. 6, 5860.

29. Churchill, "Election Address," February 9, 1950, in *His Complete Speeches*, vol. 8, 7930.

30. Winston S. Churchill, "The Creed of Failure," 1929, Churchill papers: CHAR 8/266.

31. *Finance Act 1924, Chapter 21*. Available at: http://www.legislation.gov.uk/ukpga/1924/21/pdfs/ukpga_19240021_en.pdf (Accessed June 11, 2015); *Finance Act 1928, Chapter 17*. Available at: http://www.legislation.gov.uk/ukpga/1928/17/pdfs/ukpga_19280017_en.pdf (Accessed June 11, 2015).

32. *Finance Act 1951, Chapter 43*. Available at: http://www.legislation.gov.uk/ukpga/1951/43/pdfs/ukpga_19510043_en.pdf; *Finance Act 2012, Part 1, Chapter 1*. Available at: http://www.legislation.gov.uk/ukpga/2012/14/pdfs/ukpga_20120014_en.pdf (Accessed June 11, 2015).

33. Gilbert, *Winston S. Churchill*, vol. 5, Chapter 4, "A Reforming Chancellor: 'Great Issues in the Social Sphere.'"

34. Office for Budget Responsibility for the United Kingdom, "Public Finances Databank," 2014, http://budgetresponsibility.independent.gov.uk/data/(Accessed January 15, 2015).

NOTES

35. Churchill, "Army Reform," May 13, 1901, in *His Complete Speeches,* vol. 1, 76–86; and Churchill, "What Good's a Constitution?," August 22, 1936, in *The U.S. Constitution: A Reader,* 737–44.
36. Bourke Cockran and Winston Churchill, quoted in McMenamin and Zoller, *Becoming Winston Churchill,* 14.
37. Paul Addison, *Churchill on the Home Front: 1900–1955* (London: Pimlico, 1993), 25.
38. Churchill, "Election Address," February 14, 1950, in *His Complete Speeches,* vol. 8, 7940.
39. Ibid.
40. Harold Macmillan, "Housing," *Hansard,* vol. 494 (December 4, 1951): 2252, http://hansard.millbanksystems.com/commons/1951/dec/04/housing#S5CV0494P0_19511204_HOC_287 (Accessed February 9, 2015).
41. Alistair Horne, *Harold Macmillan,* vol. 1, *1894–1956* (New York: Viking, 1989), 338–39.
42. Churchill, "Socialism," January 22, 1908, in *His Complete Speeches,* vol. 1, 874.
43. Churchill, "Why Must We Always Fight?" May 13, 1948, in *His Complete Speeches,* vol. 7, 7647.
44. Churchill, "Election Address," October 15, 1951, in *His Complete Speeches,* vol. 8, 8268.
45. Winston S. Churchill, "Election Address," December 17, 1909, in *Winston S. Churchill: His Complete Speeches,* vol. 2, *1908–1913,* ed. Robert Rhodes James (New York: Chelsea House, 1974), 1424.
46. Churchill, "Party Politics Again," June 4, 1945, in *His Complete Speeches,* vol. 7, 7172.
47. Churchill, "Roosevelt from Afar," December 29, 1934, in *Great Contemporaries,* 244.
48. Churchill, "Mass Effects in Modern Life," in *Thoughts and Adventures,* 273.
49. Ibid., 295.
50. Ibid.

51. Churchill, "The Government's Work," October 17, 1906, in *His Complete Speeches*, vol. 1, 679.

52. Churchill, "Chancellor's Address," April 12, 1941, in *His Complete Speeches*, vol. 5, 6377.

53. Churchill, "Postwar Planning," March 21, 1943, in *His Complete Speeches,* vol. 7, 6761.

54. Churchill, "Education," February 26, 1946, in *His Complete Speeches,* vol. 7, 7283–85.

55. Addison, *Churchill on the Home Front,* 414–15. Addison notes that the cuts to adult education were made but less deeply.

56. Bevir, *The Making of British Socialism,* 189.

Chapter 8: Bureaucracy

1. Churchill, "Party Politics Again," June 4, 1945, in *His Complete Speeches*, vol. 7, 7172.

2. Churchill, "Election Address," October 9, 1924, in *His Complete Speeches*, vol. 4, 3484.

3. Churchill, "England," April 24, 1933, in *His Complete Speeches,* vol. 5, 5268.

4. Churchill, "Parliamentary Government and the Economic Problem," June 19, 1930, in *Thoughts and Adventures,* 255.

5. Ibid., 245.

6. On February 22, 1925, Churchill wrote: "I would rather see Finance less proud and Industry more content." In other words, he saw the possibility of deflation as a drag on economic growth. In Gilbert, *Winston S. Churchill,* vol. 5, 98.

7. Churchill, "Parliamentary Government and the Economic Problem," June 19, 1930, in *Thoughts and Adventures,* 254.

8. Ibid., 247.

9. Ibid., 255.

10. Ibid., 256.

11. Churchill, "Army (Annual Bill)," April 2, 1919, in *His Complete Speeches*, vol. 3, 2762.

12. Churchill, "Education," February 26, 1946, in *His Complete Speeches,* vol. 7, 7285.

13. Churchill, "Report of the Dardanelles Commission," March 20, 1917, in *His Complete Speeches*, vol. 3, 2535.

14. Churchill, "Army Estimates," March 21, 1902, in *His Complete Speeches*, vol. 1, 140.

15. Churchill, "British Policy at Home and Abroad," April 8, 1922, in *His Complete Speeches*, vol. 4, 3306.

16. "WSC to Lady Randolph," September 18, 1896, in *The Churchill Documents*, vol. 2, 680.

17. "WSC to Jack," December 2, 1897, in *The Churchill Documents*, vol. 2, 836.

18. Churchill, "The British Case," August 29, 1914, in *His Complete Speeches*, vol. 3, 2327.

19. Churchill, "Winston S. Churchill: Cabinet Memorandum," November 16, 1920, in *The Churchill Documents*, vol. 9, 1239.

20. Churchill, "British Policy at Home and Abroad," April 8, 1922, in *His Complete Speeches*, vol. 4, 3306.

21. Churchill, "What Good's a Constitution?" in *The U.S. Constitution: A Reader*, 742.

22. Churchill, "Trade Disputes Bill," June 22, 1927, in *His Complete Speeches*, vol. 4, 4243–44.

23. Churchill, "Roosevelt from Afar," December 29, 1934, in *Great Contemporaries*, 243.

24. Churchill, "National Service Bill," March 31, 1947, in *His Complete Speeches*, vol. 7, 7466.

25. Churchill, "Ministers and Public Servants (Lynskey Tribunal)," February 3, 1949, in *His Complete Speeches*, vol. 7, 7788.

26. Churchill, "Fuel and Power Crisis," February 10, 1947, in *His Complete Speeches*, vol. 7, 7432; and "Trust the People," May 16, 1947, ibid., 7490.

27. Churchill, "Every Dog Has His Day," October 5, 1946, in *His Complete Speeches*, vol. 7, 7382.

28. Churchill, "Election Address," February 14, 1950, in *His Complete Speeches*, vol. 8, 7939–40.

29. Churchill, "The Government's Record," October 21, 1904, in *His Complete Speeches*, vol. 1, 377.

30. Gilbert, *Winston S. Churchill*, vol. 5, 414.

31. Churchill, "Preferential Tariffs," May 28, 1903, in *His Complete Speeches,* vol. 1, 192.

32. Churchill, "The Government's Record," October 21, 1904, in *His Complete Speeches*, vol. 1, 379.

33. Churchill, "Woodford Adoption Meeting," January 28, 1950, in *His Complete Speeches,* vol. 8, 7912.

34. Churchill, "Election Address," February 9, 1950, in *His Complete Speeches*, vol. 8, 7931. Douglas Jay wrote this in his book *The Socialist Case* (1937). Richard Toye wrote an article, "'The Gentleman in Whitehall' Reconsidered: The Evolution of Douglas Jay's Views on Economic Planning and Consumer Choice, 1937–1947," which argued that Jay, influenced by Hayek, Mises, and others, was skeptical of state planning in this 1937 edition of his book—that Jay was, in the very book that includes the phrase "gentleman in Whitehall," actually an advocate of consumer choice, at least relative to many on the Left. Toye did allow that Jay and others felt some "paternalism" toward the working class. In the 1947 edition of the book, Toye argued, Jay was friendlier to planning, based on its success during World War II. In this he reflected better the mainstream of the Labour Party. Toye characterized these later views as "sensible and pragmatic." In *Labour History Review,* vol. 67, no. 2 (2002), 187–204.

35. Winston S. Churchill, plan for a book entitled *The Creed of Failure,* Churchill papers: CHAR 8/266.

36. Churchill, "A Threat to Freedom," June 21, 1945, in *His Complete Speeches*, vol. 7, 7193.

37. Stafford Cripps, *The Choice for Britain* (London: The Socialist League, 1934), 5–8.

38. Churchill, "The Summer Adjournment," August 2, 1939:

> I would not press this argument so far as to suggest that if the
> House goes on sitting night and day there will be no crisis. That
> would, indeed, be exaggerating the argument, but I have the feeling
> that things are in a great balance, and that even minor matters of a
> favorable character cannot be neglected if they can be thrown in on
> the right side of the scale. Therefore, I should regret it very much if
> we were now to pass a Resolution scattering ourselves to the winds
> till October. This is an odd moment for the House to declare that
> it will go on a two months' holiday. It is only an accident that our
> summer holidays coincide with the danger months in Europe,
> when the harvests have been gathered, and when the powers of
> evil are at their strongest. The situation in Europe is graver than it
> was at this time last year. The German Government have already
> 2,000,000 men under arms actually incorporated in their Army.
> When the new class joins before the end of August more than
> 500,000 will be added to this number automatically.

In *His Complete Speeches*, vol. 6, 6146.

39. Churchill, "The Perils of Socialist Control," November 28, 1945, in *His Complete Speeches*, vol. 7, 7260.

40. Churchill, "Every Dog Has His Day," October 5, 1946, in *His Complete Speeches*, vol. 7, 7389.

41. Churchill, "Parliament Bill," November 11, 1947, in *His Complete Speeches*, vol. 7, 7565.

42. Churchill, "Every Dog Has His Day," October 5, 1946, in *His Complete Speeches*, vol. 7, 7384.

43. Churchill, "Woodford Adoption Meeting," January 28, 1950, in *His Complete Speeches*, vol. 8, 7911.

44. Churchill, "A Threat to Freedom," June 21, 1945, in *His Complete Speeches*, vol. 7, 7193.

45. Churchill, "Election Address," February 15, 1950, in *His Complete Speeches*, vol. 8, 7945.

46. Churchill, "Winston S. Churchill to a correspondent," January 17, 1924, in *The Churchill Documents*, vol. 11, 94.

47. Gilbert, *Churchill: A Life*, 188–89. From Churchill's letter to the journalist J. A. Spender on December 22, 1907.
48. Churchill, "Mass Effects in Modern Life," in *Thoughts and Adventures*, 271–80.
49. Manchester and Reid, *The Last Lion*, 951.
50. See Gilbert, *Winston S. Churchill*, vol. 8, 148.
51. Ibid., 108.

Chapter 9: The Social Reformer

1. Churchill, "The Twentieth Century—Its Promise and Its Realization," March 31, 1949, in *His Complete Speeches*, vol. 7, 7803.
2. Asa Briggs, *Social Thought and Action: A Study of the Work of Seebohm Rowntree* (London: Longmans, 1961).
3. B. Seebohm Rowntree, *Poverty: A Study of Town Life* (New York: Howard Fertig, 1971). Previously published in 1901.
4. Winston S. Churchill, "[Unpublished] Review by WSC of Seebohm Rowntree's *Poverty: A Study of Town Life*," in *The Churchill Documents*, vol. 3, *Early Years in Politics, 1901–1907*, ed. Randolph Churchill (Hillsdale, MI: Hillsdale College Press, 2007), 105–7.
5. Ibid., 111.
6. Churchill, "Election Address," June 27, 1899, in *His Complete Speeches*, vol. 1, 40–41.
7. "WSC to J. Moore Bayley," December 23, 1901, in *The Churchill Documents*, vol. 3, 104.
8. Ibid.
9. That is, a Conservative or a Tory who favored the extension of the franchise and free trade, among other liberal reforms.
10. Winston S. Churchill, *Lord Randolph Churchill*, vol. 1 (London: Macmillan, 1906), 293.
11. Addison, *Churchill on the Home Front: 1900–1955*, 11, citing a Churchill speech of June 26, 1899.
12. Churchill, "The Budget," June 28, 1909, in *His Complete Speeches*, vol. 2, 1274.

13. Addison, *Churchill on the Home Front: 1900–1955*, 226. Churchill was busy having an appendectomy during the campaign, and he wrote of it that "in the twinkling of an eye . . . I found myself without an office, without a seat, without a party and without an appendix." In Gilbert, *Churchill: A Life*, 454.
14. See Gilbert, *Winston S. Churchill*, vol. 6, 405–6.
15. The *Glasgow Herald* reported the death of Nicholson, then a German POW, on July 12, 1943, on page 4. The article mentioned his family. He married the Hon. Ursula Hanbury-Tracey, sister of the sixth Lord Sudeley, in 1935. His brother was Captain Godfrey Nicholson, MP for Farnham, Surrey.
16. Paul Addison, *The Road to 1945* (London: Cape, 1975), 217–19.
17. Churchill, "The Dundee Election," May 14, 1908, in *Liberalism and the Social Problem* (London: Hodder and Stoughton, 1909), 164–65. Churchill said, "In the long war which humanity wages with the elements of nature the main body of the army has won its victory . . . It is to the rearguard of the army that attention should be directed. There is the place for bravest soldiers and the most trusted generals. It is there that all the resources of military science and its heaviest artillery should be employed to extricate the rearguard . . ."
18. Churchill, *Lord Randolph Churchill*, vol. 1, 269.
19. Churchill, "National Finance," January 20, 1926, in *His Complete Speeches*, vol. 4, 3812.
20. Randolph Churchill, *Winston S. Churchill*, vol. 2, 278. The full essay, hard to find, was recovered by Churchill bibliographer Ronald Cohen and published in *Finest Hour*, 137 (Winter 2007–08): 58–60.
21. Robert Eden, "On the Origins of the Regime of Pragmatic Liberalism: John Dewey, Adolf A. Berle, and FDR's Commonwealth Club Address of 1932," *Studies In American Political Development*, 7 (Spring 1993): 74–150.

22. James Madison, "On Property," March 29, 1792, in *The U.S. Constitution: A Reader*, 155.
23. Churchill, "Preferential Tariffs," May 28, 1903, in *His Complete Speeches*, vol. 1, 192.
24. Churchill, "Election Address," December 12, 1910, in *His Complete Speeches*, vol. 2, 1662–63.
25. Churchill, "Great Events in our Time: Chief Factors in our Social Revolution," July 4, 1937, in *The Collected Essays of Sir Winston Churchill*, vol. 4, *Churchill at Large*, 392.
26. See Gilbert, *Churchill: A Life*, 189.
27. Churchill, "Election Address," December 17, 1909, in *His Complete Speeches*, vol. 2, 1424.
28. Churchill, "The Chicago Scandals," in *The Collected Essays of Sir Winston Churchill*, vol. 4, *Churchill at Large*, 16.
29. Ibid., 24.
30. Ibid.
31. James Madison, "No. 51: The Structure of the Government Must Furnish the Proper Checks and Balances Between the Different Departments," in *Federalist Papers*, 319.
32. Churchill, "Finance Bill," May 12, 1902, in *His Complete Speeches*, vol. 1, 152.
33. Addison, *Churchill on the Home Front: 1900–1955*, 11, citing a speech from June 26, 1899. In his excellent book, Addison refers to the statement as Churchill trailing off "into clouds of evasion." I think he means by this that Churchill is not specific about what he will do. In any case it is a principle that Churchill supported consistently, as Addison writes.
34. "Winston S. Churchill: Remarks to a Deputation," March 24, 1925, in *The Churchill Documents*, vol. 11, 448–49.
35. Churchill, "Postwar Planning," March 21, 1943, in *His Complete Speeches*, vol. 7, 6760.
36. Churchill, "Unemployment—the Way Out," April 2, 1933, in *The Collected Essays of Sir Winston Churchill*, vol. 2, *Churchill and Politics*, 285–86.

37. Churchill, "National Insurance Bill," May 25, 1911, in *His Complete Speeches*, vol. 2, 1810.

38. Randolph Churchill, *Winston S. Churchill*, vol. 2, *Young Statesman: 1901–1914*, 305.

39. *National Insurance Act 1911, Chapter 55*. Available at: http://www.sochealth.co.uk/resources/national-health-service/health-law/national-insurance-act-1911/

40. Churchill, "The Abuse of the Dole: Fallacies of the Live Register," March 26, 1930, in *The Collected Essays of Sir Winston Churchill*, vol. 2, *Churchill and Politics*, 193–94.

41. Churchill, "The Budget," September 4, 1909, in *His Complete Speeches*, vol. 2, 1317.

42. "Churchill to Neville Chamberlain," April 3, 1925, in *The Churchill Documents*, vol. 11, 454–55.

43. "Winston S. Churchill to Stanley Baldwin," November 28, 1924, in *The Churchill Documents*, vol. 11, 271.

44. "Winston S. Churchill to King George V," April 23, 1925, in *The Churchill Documents*, vol. 11, 463.

45. Addison, *Churchill on the Home Front*, 240–41.

46. "Winston S. Churchill: remarks to a Deputation," March 4, 1925, in *The Churchill Documents*, vol. 11, 421–22. This is the same document that Addison quotes from the treasury papers immediately above. An extended version of Churchill's remarks, but not the remarks of the deputation, is published in the above volume.

47. Ibid., 422.

48. Ibid.

49. Addison, *Churchill on the Home Front*, 73, 242–43.

50. See Paul Addison: "But here was a landmark nevertheless: the first contributory scheme of state pensions, covering more than 15 million people. In conjunction with other sources of income the new benefits freed thousands of unfortunate people from dependence on the poor law. Churchill's involvement

underlined his commitment to the idea of the state as the provider of a safety net." Ibid., 243.

51. See Paul Addison: "In the case of the unemployment insurance fund, which was already heavily in debt, the effect was to perpetuate the debt. As Churchill had planned, uncovenanted benefit was withdrawn from certain classes of men and women, thus throwing them back on the poor law." Ibid., 255–56.

52. See Gilbert, *Winston S. Churchill*, vol. 5, 242.

53. "Winston S. Churchill: Cabinet memorandum," March 1, 1928, in *The Churchill Documents*, vol. 11, 1217.

54. Churchill, "Great Events of our Time: Chief Factors in our Social Revolution," in *The Collected Essays of Sir Winston Churchill*, vol. 4, *Churchill at Large*, 393.

55. Churchill, "Demobilisation," October 22, 1945, in *His Complete Speeches*, vol. 7, 7235.

Chapter 10: The Constitutionalist

1. Churchill published two extended essays before the war concerning Franklin Roosevelt: "What Good's a Constitution?" and "While the World Watches." The second raises some of the same issues as the first alongside fulsome admiration of Roosevelt, which is general in Churchill. It was republished in the extended editions of Churchill's book *Great Contemporaries* in 1938. The essay was omitted from the 1942 edition published by Macmillan. It reappeared after the war and Roosevelt's death. See Tom Hartman, foreword to Churchill, *Great Contemporaries*, ix.

2. Churchill, "What Good's a Constitution?" in *The U.S. Constitution: A Reader*, 737–38.

3. Ibid., 738.

4. Ibid., 739.

5. Ibid.

6. Franklin D. Roosevelt, "Inaugural Address," March 4, 1933, in *The Public Papers and Addresses of Franklin D. Roosevelt*, vol. 2, *The Year of Crisis: 1933*, ed. Samuel I. Rosenman (New York: Russell & Russell, 1969), 14.

7. Franklin D. Roosevelt, "The Second Inaugural Address," January 20, 1937, in *The Public Papers and Addresses of Franklin D. Roosevelt*, vol. 6, *The Constitution Prevails: 1937*, ed. Samuel I. Rosenman (New York: Russell & Russell, 1969), 3.

8. Churchill, "What Good's a Constitution?" in *The U.S. Constitution: A Reader*, 739.

9. Ibid., 740.

10. Winston S. Churchill, *The World Crisis*, vol. 3, *1916–1918: Part One* (Norwalk, CT: The Easton Press, 1991), 228.

11. Churchill, "The Empire," October 18, 1926, in *His Complete Speeches*, vol. 4, 4104.

12. Churchill, *The World Crisis*, vol. 3, *1916–1918: Part One*, 228–30.

13. Churchill, "War Debts and Reparations," December 14, 1932, in *His Complete Speeches*, vol. 5, 5211.

14. Ibid., 741. The *Schechter* case was decided on May 27, 1935. Churchill's article appeared for the first time in the *The Daily Mail* on June 6, 1935. See *The Collected Essays of Sir Winston Churchill*, vol. 2, *Churchill and Politics*, 393.

15. Churchill, "What Good's a Constitution?" in *The U.S. Constitution: A Reader*, 742.

16. Ibid., 739–40.

17. Ibid., 743. The "leading member of the Convention of 1787" was James Wilson.

18. Churchill, "The Political Scene from a Distance," May 4, 1923, in *His Complete Speeches*, vol. 4, 3386.

19. Churchill, "Socialism," February 12, 1929, in *His Complete Speeches*, vol. 5, 4554.

20. Edmund Burke, *The Works of the Right Honourable Edmund Burke*, vol. 3 (London: J. Dodsley, 1792), 136.

21. Winston S. Churchill, *A History of the English-Speaking Peoples*, vol. 2, *The New World* (New York: Dodd, Mead, 1956), 268.

22. Churchill, "Are Parliaments Obsolete?" in *The Collected Essays of Sir Winston Churchill*, vol. 2, *Churchill and Politics*, 342.

23. Churchill, "Punjab Disturbances," July 8, 1920, in *His Complete Speeches,* vol. 3, 3008.

24. Winston Churchill comments to Alexander MacCullum Scott, May 10, 1917, quoted in Will Morrisey, *Churchill and de Gaulle: The Geopolitics of Liberty* (Lanham: Rowman & Littlefield, 2015), 10.

25. Churchill, "A Sense of Crowd and Urgency," October 28, 1943, in *His Complete Speeches,* vol. 7, 6869.

26. Ibid., 6869–70.

27. Churchill, "The Tasks Which Lie Before Us," November 29, 1944, in *His Complete Speeches,* vol. 7, 7037.

28. Winston S. Churchilll, "A Sense of Crowd and Urgency," October 28, 1943, in *His Complete Speeches,* vol. 7, 6870.

29. Ibid., 6870–71.

30. Gilbert, *Winston S. Churchill,* vol. 8, 1123–24.

31. Churchill, "House of Lords (Government Proposals)", March 31, 1910, in *His Complete Speeches,* vol. 2, 1521.

32. Churchill, "House of Lords (General Legislature)," April 13, 1910, in *His Complete Speeches,* vol. 2, 1553.

33. Churchill, "Parliament Bill," April 18, 1911, in *His Complete Speeches,* vol. 2, 1761.

34. Churchill, "Parliament Bill," May 2, 1911, in *His Complete Speeches,* vol. 2, 1788.

35. Churchill, "The Government's Record," October 21, 1904, in *His Complete Speeches,* vol. 1, 377.

36. Churchill, "The Budget," May 22, 1909, in *His Complete Speeches,* vol. 2, 1255.

37. Churchill, "Election Address," January 8, 1910, in *His Complete Speeches,* vol. 2, 1450.

38. Churchill, "House of Lords (Government Proposals)," May 31, 1910, in *His Complete Speeches,* vol. 2, 1521.

39. Churchill, "The Darkening International Scene," March 15, 1946, in *His Complete Speeches,* vol. 7, 7301.

40. Churchill, "Liberty and Law," July 31, 1957, in *His Complete Speeches,* vol. 8, 8683.

41. Churchill, "Prolongation of Parliament," October 31, 1944, in *His Complete Speeches*, vol. 7, 7023.
42. Churchill, "Indictment of the Government," January 17, 1905, in *His Complete Speeches*, vol. 1, 403.
43. Churchill, "Election Address," April 14, 1908, in *His Complete Speeches*, vol. 1, 944.
44. Churchill, "House of Lords (Government Proposals)," May 31, 1910, in *His Complete Speeches*, vol. 2, 1521.
45. Churchill, "Free Trade and Tariff Reform," December 11, 1909, in *His Complete Speeches*, vol. 2, 1416.
46. Churchill, "The Centre Party," July 15, 1919, in *His Complete Speeches*, vol. 3, 2815.
47. Churchill, "Bolshevism and Imperial Sedition," November 4, 1920, in *His Complete Speeches*, vol. 3, 3026.
48. Churchill, "Cartoons and Cartoonists," in *Thoughts and Adventures*, 22.
49. Churchill, *My Early Life*, 33.
50. Churchill, "Are Parliaments Obsolete?" in *The Collected Essays of Sir Winston Churchill*, vol. 2, *Churchill and Politics*, 340.
51. Churchill, "Election Ahead—And the Same Old Voting System," in *The Collected Essays of Sir Winston Churchill*, vol. 2, *Churchill and Politics*, 378.
52. Ibid.
53. Churchill, "The Conciliation of South Africa," April 5, 1906, in *His Complete Speeches*, vol. 1, 611.
54. Addison, *Churchill on the Home Front*, 132–33.
55. Churchill, "Election Address," May 2, 1908, in *His Complete Speeches*, vol. 1, 1034–35.
56. Ibid., 1029.
57. "Winston S. Churchill to Clementine Churchill," March 8, 1925, in *The Churchill Documents*, vol. 11, 424.
58. Churchill, "Home Rule in a Nutshell," in *The Collected Essays of Sir Winston Churchill*, vol. 2, *Churchill and Politics*, 40.

59. Churchill, "Irish Home Rule and Local Government," September 12, 1912, in *His Complete Speeches,* vol. 2, 2021–22.

60. Churchill, "Party Politics Again," June 4, 1945, in *His Complete Speeches*, vol. 7, 7172.

61. Churchill, "Civil List," March 24, 1937, in *His Complete Speeches*, vol. 6, 5849.

62. Ibid.

63. Ronald J. Pestritto, *Woodrow Wilson and the Roots of Modern Liberalism* (Lanham: Rowman & Littlefield, 2005), 126–27.

64. Churchill, "Parliamentary Debate," March 19, 1926, in *His Complete Speeches,* vol. 4, 3890–91.

65. The Speaker of the House holds a venerable office. He is elected by the House at the beginning of each session; the practice is to reelect Speakers until they retire. The Speaker presides over the House with the power to recognize who may speak and to punish infractions of parliamentary rules. He represents a constituency, but severs connection with his party upon taking office and functions outside party politics.

66. Thomas Quinn, *Electing and Ejecting Party Leaders in Britain* (New York: Palgrave Macmillan, 2012), 21, 25.

67. Churchill, "A Sense of Crowd and Urgency," October 28, 1943, in *His Complete Speeches,* vol. 7, 6871.

68. Of this experience Dickens wrote, "I have worn my knees by writing on them on the old back row of the old gallery of the old House of Commons; and I have worn my feet by standing to write in the preposterous pen in the old House of Lords." In John Camden Hotten, *Charles Dickens: The Story of His Life* (New York: Harper & Brothers, 1870), 13.

69. Churchill, "The Government's Record," October 21, 1904, in *His Complete Speeches*, vol. 1, 377.

70. Churchill, "The Budget," November 13, 1909, in *His Complete Speeches*, vol. 2, 1353.

71. Churchill, *The Second World War,* vol. 5, *Closing the Ring,* 385–86.

72. Churchill, "The General Election," January 4, 1910, in *His Complete Speeches*, vol. 2, 1441.

73. Churchill, *A History of the English-Speaking Peoples*, vol. 2, *The New World*, 330.

74. Churchill, "Situation at Home and Abroad," October 14, 1950, in *His Complete Speeches*, vol. 8, 8099, emphasis in original.

75. Churchill, "Cabinet Memorandum," November 17, 1925, in *The Churchill Documents*, vol. 11, 578.

76. This differs from an earlier proposal of Churchill's during the 1910 battles over the Parliament Act. Then, too, he wished to preserve bicameralism. Then he proposed that an Upper House be elected from a panel or slate of candidates made up of distinguished public servants, nominated ex officio. By 1925 Churchill no longer favored direct election of the House of Lords, a form of which he had endorsed in 1910.

77. Ibid., 580.

78. James Madison, "No. 62: The Senate," in *Federalist Papers*, 374–80.

79. "Winston S. Churchill: Cabinet Memorandum," November 17, 1925, in *The Churchill Documents*, vol. 11, 577.

80. This is the resurrection of a nineteenth-century Tory idea about the proper operation of the House of Lords. See Corrine Comstock Weston's book *House of Lords and Ideological Politics: Lord Salisbury's Referendal Theory and the Conservative Party 1846–1922* (Philadelphia: American Philosophical Society, 1995).

81. "Winston S. Churchill: Cabinet Memorandum," November 17, 1925, in *The Churchill Documents*, vol. 11, 582.

82. James Madison, "No. 39: The Conformity of the Plan to Republican Principles," in *The Federalist Papers*, 237.

83. Gilbert, *Winston S. Churchill*, vol. 8, 648. Exact figures were: 13,948,605 votes for Labour; 13,717,538 for Conservatives.

84. Jeffrey M. Jones, "America's Trust in Executive, Legislative Branches Down," *Gallup*, September 15, 2014, http://www.gallup.com/poll/175790/

americans-trust-executive-legislative-branches-down.aspx
(Accessed January 15, 2015). Cf. "Public Trust in Government:
1958–2014," *Pew Research Center,* November 13, 2014, http://
www.people-press.org/2014/11/13/public-trust-in-government/
(Accessed January 15, 2015).

85. The best example I know is not one of the famous war speeches,
which to my reading are wonderful as well as historic. Read the
transcript of his Christmas 1929 broadcast appeal for money
to purchase wirelesses for the blind. Having asked the listeners
to close their eyes for a while and imagine what it is like to live
in darkness, he says: "If you are rich you can easily afford it. If
you were rich enough to send 25 guineas it can be arranged that
a number of blind people in your particular district should be
specially chosen to have the wireless sets purchased with your
money: & if you like—but I expect you wouldn't—your name can
be on every set. If you are not rich—to give something however
little is the best way to feel rich." Martin Gilbert, who published
the transcript of the broadcast in *The Churchill Documents,* vol.
12, 119–24, often spoke fondly of this broadcast.

86. Churchill, "Election Memories," in *Thoughts and Adventures,*
213–29.

87. Martin Gilbert wrote,

> Among those whom he met for the first time that year was the
> Chancellor of the Exchequer's daughter, Violet Asquith. They were
> sitting next to each other at dinner. "For a long time he remained
> sunk in abstraction," she later recalled. "Then he appeared to
> become suddenly aware of my existence. He turned on me a
> lowering gaze and asked me abruptly how old I was. I replied that
> I was nineteen. "And I," he said almost despairingly, "am thirty-
> two already. Younger than anyone else who counts, though." After
> a long oration he suddenly ended with the immortal words, "We
> are all worms, but I do believe I am a glow-worm."
>
> *Churchill: A Life,* 185.

88. Churchill's aides thought that he sounded bored when he broadcast on the radio one of his speeches from the House of Commons, whereas he had been electric in the Commons. Harold Nicolson wrote: "Now, as delivered in the House of Commons, the speech was magnificent, especially the concluding sentences. But it sounded ghastly on the wireless. All the great vigor he put into it seemed to evaporate." From *The War Years: 1939–1945, Diaries and Letters*, ed. Nigel Nicolson (New York: Atheneum, 1967), 97.

89. Churchill, "Mass Effects in Modern Life," in *Thoughts and Adventures*, 272–73.

Conclusion

1. Churchill, "'Blood and Shame' (Palestine)," January 31, 1947, in *His Complete Speeches*, vol. 7, 7424.

2. Figure from the 2012–2013 fiscal year. See Office for Budget Responsibility for the United Kingdom, "Public Finances Databank," 2014, http://budgetresponsibility.independent.gov. uk/data/ (Accessed January 15, 2015).

3. Martin Loughlin, *The British Constitution: A Very Short Introduction* (Oxford: Oxford University Press, 2013), 58.

4. James Madison, "No. 51: The Structure of the Government Must Furnish the Proper Checks and Balances Between the Different Departments," in *Federalist Papers*, 319. He wrote, "What is government but the profoundest of all commentaries on human nature? If men were angels, no government would be needed. If angels were to govern men, neither internal nor external controls on the government would be necessary."

5. Winston S. Churchill, *For Free Trade*, quoted in McMenamin and Zoller, *Becoming Winston Churchill*, 14.

6. "Winston Churchill: notes for First Plenary Meeting at the Bermuda Conference," December 4, 1953 (*Premier papers*, 11/418).

7. Churchill often quoted Bourke Cockran, who said: "There is enough for all. The earth is a generous mother; she will provide in plentiful abundance food for all her children if they will but cultivate her soil in justice and in peace." See "Sinews of Peace," March 5, 1946, in *His Complete Speeches,* vol. 7, 7288.

8. Churchill, *Marlborough: His Life and Times, Book One,* 569.

9. Churchill, "Mass Effects in Modern Life," in *Thoughts and Adventures,* 271.

10. Churchill, "Education," February 26, 1946, in *His Complete Speeches,* vol. 7, 7285.

11. Churchill, *Savrola,* 175.

12. Lewis, *The Abolition of Man,* 71–74.

13. Gilbert, *Winston S. Churchill,* vol. 8, 1123.

14. Churchill, "The Deterrent—Nuclear Warfare," March 1, 1955, in *His Complete Speeches,* vol. 8, 8633.

BIBLIOGRAPHY

Adams, John. *The Works of John Adams.* Vol. 5. Edited by Charles Francis Adams. Boston: Little, Brown, 1851.

Addison, Paul. *Churchill on the Home Front, 1900–1955.* London: Pimlico, 1993.

———. *The Road to 1945: British Politics and the Second World War.* London: Cape, 1975.

Asher, Michael. *Khartoum: The Ultimate Imperial Adventure.* London: Penguin Books, 2005.

Best, Geoffrey. "Churchill's Imperialism." *The Claremont Review of Books* 4, no. 2 (Fall 2002).

Bevir, Mark. *The Making of British Socialism.* Princeton: Princeton University Press, 2011.

Briggs, Asa. *Social Thought and Action: A Study of the Work of Seebohm Rowntree.* London: Longmans, 1961.

Bullock, Alan. *Hitler: A Study in Tyranny.* Harmondsworth, England: Penguin Books, 1962.

Burke, Edmund. *The Works of the Right Honourable Edmund Burke.* Vol. 3. London: J. Dodsley, 1792.

Carsten, F. L. *The Reichswehr and Politics: 1918–1933.* Oxford: Oxford University Press, 1966.

Churchill, Randolph, and Martin Gilbert. *Winston S. Churchill.* 8 vols. Hillsdale, MI: Hillsdale College Press, 2013.

Churchill, Winston. *Great Contemporaries*. Edited by James W. Muller. New York: W.W. Norton & Company, 1990.

———. *India: Defending the Jewel in the Crown*. Hopkinton, NH: Dragonwyck Publishing, Inc., 1990.

———. *Liberalism and the Social Problem*. London: Hodder and Stoughton, 1909.

———. *London to Ladysmith via Pretoria*. London: Longmans, Green, 1900.

———. *Lord Randolph Churchill*. 2 vols. New York: The Macmillan Company, 1906.

———. *Marlborough: His Life and Times*. 2 vols. Chicago: The University of Chicago Press, 2002.

———. *My African Journey*. Toronto: William Briggs, 1909.

———. *My Early Life: 1874–1904*. New York: Simon & Schuster, 1996.

———. *Savrola: A Tale of the Revolution in Laurania*. London: Longmans, Green, 1900.

———. *The Churchill Documents*. 18 vols. Edited by Martin Gilbert, Randolph Churchill, and Larry P. Arnn. Hillsdale, MI: Hillsdale College Press, 2015.

———. *The Collected Essays of Sir Winston Churchill*. 4 vols. Edited by Michael Wolff. London: Library of Imperial History, 1976.

———. *The History of the English-Speaking Peoples*. 4 vols. New York: Dodd, Mead, and Company, 1958.

———. *The River War: An Historical Account of the Reconquest of the Sudan*. 2 vols. Edited by Col. F. Rhodes, ed. London: Longmans, Green, and Co., 1899.

———. *The Second World War*. 6 vols. Boston: Houghton Mifflin Company, 1953.

———. *The Story of the Malakand Field Force: An Episode of Frontier War*. London: Longmans, Green, and Co., 1901.

———. *The World Crisis*. 5 vols. Norwalk, CT: Easton Press, 1991.

———. *Thoughts and Adventures: Churchill Reflects on Spies, Cartoons, Flying, and the Future*. Edited by James Muller. Wilmington, DE: ISI Books, 2009.

————. *Winston S. Churchill: His Complete Speeches, 1897–1963*. 8 vols. Edited by Robert Rhodes James. New York: Chelsea House Publishers, 1974.

Cole, George Douglas Howard. *The Simple Case for Socialism*. London: Victor Gollancz, 1935.

Conquest, Robert. *The Great Terror: A Reassessment*. Oxford: Oxford University Press, 2007.

Cripps, Stafford. *The Choice for Britain*. London: The Socialist League, 1934.

Crossman, Richard Howard Stafford, ed. *New Fabian Essays*. London: J. M. Dent & Son, 1970.

D'Este, Carlo. *Warlord: A Life of Winston Churchill at War, 1874–1945*. New York: HarperCollins, 2008.

Eden, Robert. "On the Origins of the Regime of Pragmatic Liberalism: John Dewey, Adolf A. Berle, and FDR's Commonwealth Club Address of 1932." *Studies in American Political Development* 7, (Spring 1993): 74–150.

Fleming, John V. *The Anti-Communist Manifestos: Four Books That Shaped the Cold War*. New York: W. W. Norton & Company, 2009.

Fromkin, David. *A Peace to End all Peace: The Fall of the Ottoman Empire and the Creation of the Modern Middle East*. New York: Henry Holt and Company, 2001.

Gilbert, Martin. *Churchill: A Life*. New York: Henry Holt and Company, 1991.

————. *The First World War: A Complete History*. New York: Henry Holt and Company, 1994.

Guha, Ramachandra. *India After Gandhi: The History of the World's Largest Democracy*. New York: Harper, 2007.

Hamilton, Alexander, James Madison, and John Jay. *The Federalist Papers*. Edited by Clinton Rossiter. New York: Signet Classics, 2003.

Harris, Kenneth. *Attlee*. New York: W. W. Norton & Company, 1982.

Hillsdale College Politics Department. *The US Constitution: A Reader*. Hillsdale, MI: Hillsdale College Press, 2012.

Horne, Alistair. *Harold Macmillan.* 2 vols. New York: Viking, 1989.

Hotten, John Camden. *Charles Dickens: The Story of His Life.* New York: Harper & Brothers, 1870.

Jaffa, Harry, ed. *Statesmanship: Essays in Honor of Sir Winston Spencer Churchill.* Durham, NC: Carolina Academic Press, 1981.

James, Lawrence. *Churchill and Empire: A Portrait of an Imperialist.* New York: Pegasus Books, 2014.

James, Robert Rhodes. *Churchill: A Study in Failure, 1900–1939.* New York: World Publishing, 1970.

Jefferson, Thomas. *The Inaugural Addresses of President Thomas Jefferson, 1801 and 1805.* Edited by Noble E. Cunningham Jr. Columbia: University of Missouri Press, 2001.

Jenkins, Roy. *Churchill: A Biography.* New York: Farrar, Straus, and Giroux, 2001.

Johannsen, Robert W., ed. *The Lincoln–Douglas Debates of 1858.* New York: Oxford University Press, 1965.

Kennan, George F. *George F. Kennan, Memoirs: 1925–1950.* Boston: Little, Brown, 1967.

Kershaw, Ian. *Hitler, 1889–1936: Hubris.* New York: Norton, 1999.

———. *Hitler, 1936–1945: Nemesis.* New York: W.W. Norton, 2000.

———. *Making Friends with Hitler: Lord Londonderry, the Nazis and the Road to World War II.* New York: Penguin Group, 2004.

Koestler, Arthur. *Darkness at Noon.* Translated by Daphne Hardy. New York: Macmillan, 1987.

Labour Party Executive Committee. *Labour and the New Social Order: A Report on Reconstruction.* London: Labour Party, 1938.

Lenin, Vladimir. *V. I. Lenin: Collected Works.* Vol. 36, *1900–1923.* Edited by Yuri Sdobnikov. Moscow: Progress Publishers, 1971.

Lewis, C. S. *The Abolition of Man.* New York: HarperCollins, 1944.

Lincoln, Abraham. *The Collected Works of Abraham Lincoln.* Vol. 5, *1861–1862.* Edited by Roy P. Basler. New Brunswick, NJ: Rutgers University Press, 1953.

Lloyd, Nick. *The Amristar Massacre: The Untold Story of One Fateful Day.* London: I. B. Tauris, 2011.

Loughlin, Martin. *The British Constitution: A Very Short Introduction*. Oxford: Oxford University Press, 2013.

Lukacs, John. *Five Days in London: May 1940*. New Haven: Yale University Press, 1999.

MacDonald, J. Ramsay. *Socialism and Government*. London: Independent Labour Party, 1909.

Machiavelli, Niccolò. *The Prince*. Translated by Harvey Mansfield. Chicago: The University of Chicago Press, 1998.

Madison, James. *James Madison: Writings*. Edited by Jack N. Rakove. New York: Literary Classics of the United States, 1999.

Manchester, William, and Paul Reid. *The Last Lion, Winston Spencer Churchill: Defender of the Realm, 1940–1965*. Boston: Little, Brown, 2012.

Marx, Karl, and Friedrich Engels. *The Communist Manifesto*. New York: Simon and Schuster, 2013.

Maurer, John. "Churchill's 'Naval holiday': His Plan to Avert the Great War." *Finest Hour* 163 (Summer 2014): 10–19.

McMenamin, Michael, and Curt J. Zoller. *Becoming Winston Churchill: The Untold Story of Young Winston and His American Mentor*. New York: Enigma Books, 2009.

McGurrin, James. *Bourke Cockran: A Free Lance in American Politics*. New York: Charles Scribner's Sons, 1948.

Metcalf, Barbara D., and Thomas R. Metcalf. *A Concise History of Modern India*. Cambridge: Cambridge Unviersity Press, 2006.

Montefiore, Simon Sebag. *Stalin: The Court of the Red Tsar*. New York: Vintage, 2003.

Morrisey, Will. *Churchill and de Gaulle: The Geopolitics of Liberty*. Lanham: Rowman & Littlefield, 2015.

Nicolson, Harold. *The War Years: 1939–1945, Diaries and Letters*. Edited by Nigel Nicolson. New York: Atheneum, 1967.

Pestritto, Ronald J. *Woodrow Wilson and the Roots of Modern Liberalism*. Lanham: Rowman & Littlefield, 2005.

Pope, Stephen, and Elizabeth Anne-Wheal, eds. *The Dictionary of the First World War*. New York: St. Martin's Press, 1995.

Pryce-Jones, David. *Treason of the Heart: From Thomas Paine to Kim Philby*. New York and London: Encounter Books, 2011.

Quinn, Thomas. *Electing and Ejecting Party Leaders in Britain*. New York: Palgrave Macmillan, 2012.

Roosevelt, Franklin D. *The Public Papers and Addresses of Franklin D. Roosevelt*. Vol. 2. Edited by Samuel I. Rosenman. New York: Russell & Russell, 1969.

———. *The Public Papers and Addresses of Franklin D. Roosevelt*. Vol. 6. Edited by Samuel I. Rosenman. New York: Russell & Russell, 1969.

Rowntree, B. Seebohm. *Poverty: A Study of Town Life*. New York: Howard Fertig, 1971.

Shaw, George Bernard, ed. *Fabian Essays in Socialism*. New York: The Humboldt Publishing Company, 1891.

———. *The Intelligent Woman's Guide to Socialism and Capitalism*. New York: Brentano's, 1928.

Simon, Rita J., and Mohamed Alaa Abdel-Moneim. *A Handbook of Military Conscription and Composition the World Over*. Lanham, MD: Lexington Books, 2011.

Thompson, Laurence. *1940*. New York: William Morrow & Company, 1966.

Toye, Richard. *Churchill's Empire: The World That Made Him and the World He Made*. New York: Henry Holt and Company, 2010.

———. "'The Gentlemen in Whitehall' Reconsidered: The Evolution of Douglas Jay's Views on Economic Planning and Consumer Choice, 1937–1947." *Labour History Review* 67, no. 2 (2002): 187–204.

———. "Winston Churchill's 'Crazy Broadcast': Party, Nation, and the 1945 Gestapo Speech." *The Journal of British Studies* 49, no. 3 (2010): 655–80.

Volkogoov, Dimitri. *Lenin: A New Biography*. New York: Free Press, 2013.

Washington, George. *George Washington: Writings*. Edited by John Rhodehamel. New York: Literary Classics of the United States, 1997.

Webb, Sidney. *The Basis and Policy of Socialism*. London: A. C. Fifield, 1908.

———. *Socialism in England*. London: Swan Sonnenschein & Co., 1890.

Weston, Corrine Comstock. *House of Lords and Ideological Politics: Lord Salisbury's Referendal Theory and the Conservative Party 1846–1922*. Philadelphia: American Philosophical Society, 1995.

SUGGESTED FURTHER READING

Best, Geoffrey. *Churchill: A Study in Greatness*. London: Hambledon and London, 2001.

———. *Churchill and War*. London: Hambledon and London, 2005.

Cannadine, David. *In Churchill's Shadow: Confronting the Past in Modern Britain*. Oxford: Oxford University Press, 2003.

Emmert, Kirk. *Winston S. Churchill on Empire*. Durham: Carolina Academic Press, 1989.

Gilbert, Martin. *Churchill and America*. New York: Free Press, 2005.

———. *In Search of Churchill*. London: HarperCollins, 1994.

———. *The Second World War: A Complete History*. New York: Henry Holt and Company, 1989.

Hayward, Stephen. *Churchill on Leadership: Executive Success in the Face of Adversity*. Rocklin, CA: Forum, 1997.

Herman, Arthur. *Gandhi and Churchill*. New York: Bantam, 2009.

Kimball, Warren F. *Churchill & Roosevelt: The Complete Correspondence*. 3 Vols. Princeton: Princeton University Press, 1984.

Langworth, Richard M., ed. *Churchill in His Own Words*. London: Ebury Press, 2012.

Larres, Klaus. *Churchill's Cold War: The Politics of Personal Diplomacy*. New Haven: Yale University Press, 2002.

Muller, James W. *Churchill as Peacemaker*. Cambridge: Cambridge University Press, 1997.

———. *Churchill's "Iron Curtain" Speech Fifty Years Later*. Columbia: University of Missouri Press, 1999.

Roberts, Andrew. *Hitler and Churchill: Secrets of Leadership*. London: Phoenix, 2003.

Stafford, David. *Churchill and the Secret Service*. Woodstock, NY: Overlook Press, 1998.

Wood, Frederick. *A Bibliography of the Works of Sir Winston Churchill*. Godalming, Surrey: St. Paul's Bibliographies, 1979.

INDEX

"The Abuse of the Dole" (Churchill), 198
action, 67
Adams, John, 335*n*27
adult education, 160
Afghanistan, 30
Agadir Crisis, 37
Ahmad, Muhammad, 24
Albert (King of Belgium), 12
Alexander, Harold, 75
Alexander III of Macedon, 36
All Quiet on the Western Front
  (Remarque), 45
Anne (Queen of Great Britain), 37
Antwerp, defense in 1914, 12
aristocracy
  British, cost of upkeep, 192–193
  bureaucratic, and expertise, 170–173
  socialist, 155–157
Aristophanes, 144–145
Aristotle, xiii
army, 69–70
art works, 54
Asquith, Violet, 351*n*87
atomic weapons. *See* nuclear weapons
Attlee, Clement, xxxii, 15, 138
Austria-Hungary, xxi–xxii
authority
  constitutions and, xix
  from the people, 168

Babeuf, François-Noël, 330*n*21
balance of power, 98
Baldwin, Stanley, 199, 228
beauty, 68
Beef Trust, vs. Municipal Trust, 194–195,
  207
Belgium, in Great War, xxii
Bellers, John, 330*n*20
Beria, Lavrentiy, xxix
bicameralism, 350*n*76
  Churchill's efforts to restore, 236
Bill of Rights, 219
Birla, G.D., 109
Bismarck, Otto von, xxi, 90
Boer War, 105, 110
  assault on armored train, 4–7
  Churchill as war correspondent,
    4–5
  Churchill's capture, 6, 8–9
Bolshevik Communists, xxvi–xxvii
  Churchill on, 242
  extreme conceptions, 120
  vs. Nazism, xxvii
  party as absolute, xxviii–xxix
Borrow, George, prayer, 19
boundaries, xix
Brahmins in India, 104–105, 107
Brave New World (Huxley), 317*n*29
Briand, Aristide, 46, 47

Britain
    conditions after WW II, 98–99
    difficulties and risks, 218
    economic conditions in, 180–181
    German bombing of, 19
    Great War and, xxiii
    as island, 99
    potential landing of German troops, 20
    reimbursement for bombed houses,
        188–189
    socialism in, xxx–xxxi
British cabinet, meeting on offer of peace
  conference, 17–19
British Constitution, xix, 210, 282
    Churchill on, 243
    evolutionary and historical, 219
    flexibility, 214
    and House of Commons, 239
    reputation, xx
British East India Company, 100
British empire, 100–101
    Churchill's efforts to preserve, 97
    power of, 301–302
British government
    administrative agencies, 246
    coalition in 1940s, 138
    cost of, 246
    executive and legislature, 282
    expenditures, 152
    as protector of freedom, 224
    war cabinet, 15–16, 18–19
British military
    Churchill's opposition to increase,
        32–33
    from dominion nations, 101
    general prohibition on frightfulness, 111
British Parliament. *See also* House of
  Commons; House of Lords
    change and, 247
    election of members, 224–225
    Socialist members, 121
    supremacy of, 216–217
British people, Churchill's views on, 249
Bryce Report of 1918, 236
bureaucracy, 151, 163–183, 247
bureaucratic rule, 229
    aristocrats and expertise, 170–173
    Churchill opposition to, 242

Burke, Edmund, 172, 218
business, state competition with, 180

Canada, U.S. Permanent Defense
  Agreement with, 294
capitalism, 122, 151
    vice of, 142, 205
Carter, Violet Bonham, 241
caste system in India, 104–105, 107, 115
casualty rates, for British forces, 101
Catholic Church, 127
Chamber of Elder Statesmen, 237–238
Chamberlain, Austen, 46
Chamberlain, Neville, 15, 16, 19, 177, 199
    Churchill's eulogy, 310n39
chance, failure of, 53–57
change, 122, 228, 261
    speed of, 262–264
charm, 17
children, socialist views on, 130–131
choice
    failure of, 53–57
    public vs. private, 196–203
Christianity, Churchill on, 29–30
church and state, 247
Churchill, Clementine, 11, 333n7
Churchill, John (first Duke of
  Marlborough), 53, 55
    Churchill on genius of, 70–71
Churchill, Sarah, 333n7
Churchill, Winston, 15
    admiration of, 254–255
    appeal to Stalin, 88–89
    on boyhood, 225–226
    capture in Boer War, 6, 8–9
    as chancellor of University of Bristol,
        67–68
    commitment to principle, 143
    historical record, xiv–xv
    imperial principles of, 103–116
    knowledge of war, 64
    lessons of, 248–253
    as national hero, 139–140
    photograph after capture, 9–11
    reasons for study of, xv
    social reform of, vs. socialism,
        204–206
    statue, 223

strategic thinking examples, 77
travels, 1899 to 1900, 31–32
trench warfare, 307n10
trial of peace, 246
trial of war, 245–255
as war correspondent, 4–5
Churchill, Winston: government roles
1945 election loss, 182–183
chair as Military Coordination
Committee, 13
as chancellor of the exchequer,
152–153, 236
farewell to Cabinet (1955), 328n2
as first lord of the admiralty, 13
as prime minister and minister of
defence, 75
resignation as prime minister, 255
Churchill, Winston: speeches, 253
1908 election address, 146
"Blood, Toil, Tears and Sweat," 75
"Civilization" (speech), 67–68
"Disarmament Fable" speech, 47–48
eulogy of Chamberlain, 310n39
eulogy of F. Roosevelt, xxxii
first as prime minister, 14–15
Gestapo speech, 143
"Iron Curtain" speech, 78–93, 98, 101
June 1945 election campaign, 137,
140, 164
as orator, 240–242
Romanes Lecture in Oxford, 165,
167–168
speech at University of Bristol, 111
Churchill, Winston: views and opinions
on Boer train assault, 7
defense of British rule of India, 114
on military fighting, 31
and non-white populations, 103–105,
324n27
opposition to British army increase,
32–33
opposition to socialism, 137, 144–151
opposition to Vietnam intervention,
84–85
resistance to Socialist change, 129
on socialism, 133, 135
switch to Liberal party, 140
on WW II as preventable, 85, 91–92

Churchill, Winston: writings, xviii, 21,
32, 253
"The Abuse of the Dole," 198
"Consistency in Politics," 62
The Creed of Failure, 151–152,
175–176
"Fifty Years Hence," 41, 65–66, 147,
158, 261–274
London to Ladysmith, 110
Lord Randolph Churchill, 190
Marlborough, 57, 63
"Mass Effect in Modern Life," 43, 54,
141–142, 147, 148, 181–182, 211,
242–243
My Early Life, 159
"Painting as a Pastime," 60, 64,
66–67, 144
The River War, 4–5, 22, 23–24, 55
Savrola (fiction), 28–30, 144, 145
The Second World War, 18
"Shall We All Commit Suicide?," 39,
49–50, 248
"The Sinews of Peace," 287–302
"The Untrodden Field in Politics," 190
"What Good's a Constitution?," 211,
215, 275–286
The World Crisis, 35–37, 45–46, 57, 72,
213, 214
citizen, vs. state, 211
civic spirit, in British decline, 226
civil liberties, secure property and, 191
civil servants, 250
and stability, 283
transformation, Churchill on, 164
civilization, 97–98, 208, 252
along Nile and Euphrates, 263–264
aristocracies and, 156
and officials as servants, 279
rule of law and, 112
tests of, 279
class struggle, 227–228
Cockran, Bourke, 7, 87–88, 141, 153, 293
Coke, Edward, 234–235
Cole, G.D.H., 131, 332n44
common law, 234
common sense, 174
Commonwealth Club Address, by F.
Roosevelt (1932), 190–191

commonwealth countries, cooperation with imperial, 100
communication, 268
Communist fifth columns, 299
Communist parties, in Eastern Europe, 297
community, Fabians' understanding of, 124
compromise, 58
conception, unity of, 60–68
conflict, cost of, 89
Congress Party, 114
consent of the governed, 112–113
Conservative Party
    government of 1924–29, 239
    members of Parliament, 232
Conservative Party conference, 172
"Consistency in Politics" (Churchill), 62
constitution, 207–208, 209. *See also* British Constitution; U.S. Constitution
    fixed, 280
constitutionalism, xviii–xix, 251–252
    Hitler's abnegation of, xxv
    and statesmanship, xix
containment policy, 79
coolies, 104
Cooper, Alfred Duff, 182
cooperation in war, 52
corporations, 142
    regulation of, 141
cost, of conflict, 89
cost of war, 189
The Creed of Failure (Churchill), 151–152, 175–176
Cripps, Stafford, 176
Cromwell, Oliver, 234
Crossman, R.H.S., 255
    "Towards a Philosophy of Socialism," 131–132
Curzon, Lord, 156
Czechoslovakia, 297

Dalit (untouchable) class in India, 104, 115
Dalton, Hugh, 17–18
danger, Churchill on, 7–8
Dardanelles campaign, 72–75
Darkness at Noon (Koestler), xxviii–xxix

deadlock, in WW II, 76–77
debate, 220, 228–229, 231, 251
    government ministers participation in, 233
Declaration of Independence, 103, 110, 113, 217, 280
deglutition, 132
dehumanizing, socialism as, 150
democracy, 156, 168, 176, 272
    evolution of, 228
    in India, 114
    and wars, 34–35
    Western, leftward turn in, xxx–xxxiii
democrat, Churchill as, xvii
depression
    in Germany, xxiv, xxv
    Great, 166–167
dervishes, 23, 24–25
    fate of, 44
    and Omdurman battle, 27
despotism, 119, 248–249, 253
    in future, 271
    resistance to, 66
    tendency to universal, 148
    tendency toward, 38
D'Este, Carlo, 13
d'Eyncourt, Eustace Tennyson, 169–170
Dickens, Charles, 232–233, 349n68
dictatorship in Germany, 276–277
disarmament, 48
"Disarmament Fable" speech, 47–48
Disraeli, Benjamin, 159, 230, 261
Downing Street, 16–17
Dyer, Reginald, firing on unarmed demonstration, 110–111

East Africa, Indians in, 104
economic conditions
    in Britain, 180–181
    Parliament inadequacy to deal with problems, 272
economic distribution, politics and, 169
economic justice, Socialist focus on, 133
"Economic sub-Parliament," 165, 167–168
economy, and strategy, 72
Eden, Anthony, 173
education, 157–161
Einstein, Albert, 56

Eisenhower, Dwight, 85
election of Parliamentary members, 223
   campaign in 1945, 137, 140, 164
   Churchill's 1908 address, 146
   Churchill's campaign, 31
   Churchill's proposal for, 226–227
   Labour Party in 1945, 139, 229
Elizabeth (Queen), and British
   sovereignty, 230
empire. *See* British empire
Enabling Act (Germany), xxv
English-speaking peoples, "special
   relationship" of, 89–90, 293
entitlements, vs. savings plans, 201
equal rights of minority, 106
equality, 144
   Churchill argument for, 110
   nature and, 150
evolution, 123
executive government
   Churchill warning against growing
     power of, 233
   dangers of power, 229–233
   power of, 173–175
experimentation, in socialism, 126
expertise, 169
   and bureaucratic aristocrats, 170–173
   Churchill on, 165–170

Fabian Essays on Socialism (Shaw), 88,
   121–122, 212
   on family, 129–131
   on religion and Christianity, 127
Fabian Society, 120–123, 328n6
   passion for extension of freedom and
     love, 128
   view on political reform, 329n16
Fabius Maximus, 121
fairness, 26
family, 129, 210
   meals, 212
   as source of inequality, 145
   war impact on, 289
famine in Bengal, 324n26
The Federalist Papers (Madison), 238
"Fifty Years Hence" (Churchill), 41,
   65–66, 147, 158, 261–274
fight, as nature of human race, 49

"fighting man," importance of, 30
First World War. *See* Great War
food production, 269–270
force, as source of political authority, 82
foreign nationals, treatment of, 37–38
France, Great War and, xxii, xxiii
Franz Ferdinand (archduke), xxii
free market system, 195, 208, 250
   and liberal society, 209
   social and ethical case for, 151–155
free nations, vs. tyrannies, 115
freedom, 86, 217, 248
   and humanity, 158
   threat in U.S., xxxi
Friedman, Milton, 166
frontal assault, 71

Gandhi, Mahatma, 102, 114
Gardner, Brian, 182
generalship
   mass effects complicating, 43–44
   and statesman, 72–78
George V (king), 236
Germany
   army collapse in Great War, xxiii
   in Great War, xxi–xxiii
   modern unified, xxi
   occupation zones, 92
   scientific barbarism of, 38
   signatory of Kellogg-Briand Pact, 47
   Weimar Constitution, 211–212, 276
   withdrawal of American and British
     armies from occupation zones,
     297–298
Gestapo, 137–161, 163
Gilbert, Martin, 17, 306n21, 351n87
global strategy, Churchill's proposal for, 90
Gordon, Charles George, 24
government
   benefit of divided, 234–243
   control, xviii
   expansive, 240
   limited, 208
   power of, 194
   representative, 250
   and servants of citizens, 278
Government of India Act, 109
Grayson, Victor, 155

Great Depression, 166–167
Great Treaty for Renunciation of War as
  an Instrument of National Policy, 47
Great War
  beginning, 35
  British and French military
    authorities' actions, 70
  Churchill's efforts to avoid, 37
  German army collapse in, xxiii
  Germany in, xxi–xxiii
  U.S. demand for repayment of war
    debts, 214
Greece, 91, 321n49
  Churchill statement on sending relief,
    62–64
Greenwood, Arthur, 15
Grey, Edward, 12

Haldane, J.A.L., 4, 5, 8
Halifax, Lord, 13
  in war cabinet, 16
Halifax, Viscount, 75
Hindenburg, Paul von, xxv, 140
Hinduism in India, 104
history, socialism, and nature, 122–131
Hitler, Adolf, xx–xxi, xxiv, 68, 87
  as chancellor of Germany, xxiv
  early German perspective, xxiv
  nonfatal gassing in Great War, 56
  view of Churchill, 11
Hoare, Samuel, 75
home rule for India, 102–103
Hopkins, Harry, 233
hormones, 269–270
Houghton, Denis, 189
House of Commons, 240–241, 282
  authority of, 223
  and British Constitution, 220–223,
    239
  British opinions and, 251
  Churchill on Labour Party as
    disruptive, 176–177
  Churchill's election campaign, 31
  Churchill's last major speech, 42–43
  debates on details, 174
  election of members, 223
  equality, 155–156
  executive government in, 231–232

executive power of, 229–233
  German bombing of chamber, 221
  vitality and authority of, 222
House of Lords, 15, 155, 240
  curtailing of authority, 223
  power reduction, 236
Hughes, Charles E., 215
human beings, and freedom, 158
human nature, 147, 272–273
  Churchill on socialism and, 146
  expression of, 205
humanity
  attributes, 149
  breeding of, 270–271
  potential extermination, 40–41
  speed of change, 262–264
Huxley, Aldous, Brave New World, 317n29
hydrogen bomb, 42

ideologies, 253, 255
imperial principles, of Churchill, 103–116
"Imperialist expansion," 100
independence, property and, 154
India, 100
  caste system, 104–105, 107, 115
  Churchill's defense of British rule, 114
  Churchill's perspective, 104
  home rule for, 102–103
  management, 108–109
  partitioning, 114
  soldiers for Great War and WW II, 101
Indian National Congress Party, British
  struggle with, 102
individual, change in status, 175
industry, 151, 210
inflation in Germany, 1920s, xxiv
institutions of modern liberalism, 134
insurance companies, 196–197
insurance, unemployment, 202–203
intellectualism, Churchill on, 165–170
The Intelligent Woman's Guide to
  Socialism and Capitalism (Shaw), 130
internal affairs of countries, 85
iron curtain, 91, 296–297, 298
"Iron Curtain" speech (Churchill), 78–93,
  98, 101
Italy, xxvi, 15
  Communist Party, 298

Jay, Douglas, 174
Jefferson, Thomas, 106
Jenkins, Roy, 333n8
Jesus, 126, 128
Joubert, Genera (Boer commander), 6
Journey's End (Sherriff), 45
Judicial Reform Bill of 1937, 215–216
judicial review, 216
judiciary, 234
just government, Churchill's list of
    attributes, 148–149
just rule, vs. tyranny, 38
justice, 26

Kellogg, Frank B., 47
Kellogg-Briand Pact, 47
Kennan, George, 79
Keynes, John Maynard, 166
Khartoum, 24
khozyain, xxvii
Kitchener, Herbert, 24, 311n1
    railway in Sudan, 26–27
Koestler, Arthur, *Darkness at Noon*,
    xxviii–xxix

Labour Exchanges, 201
Labour Party (Britain), xxxi, 121, 133
    in 1945 election, 139, 229
    Churchill on, xxxii
    control of the people, 177–178
    declining popularity of 1945
        government, 131
    nationalization campaign, 172
    plan to nationalize steel industry, 178
    rule in 1945–51, 170
leadership in war, 3–4
League of Nations, 46, 81
Lenin, Vladimir, xxvii, 305n13
    Testament, xxvii–xxviii
Lewis, C.S., 255
Lewis, Sinclair, *It Can't Happen Here*, 285
liberal government, challenge of, 31–35,
    209–219
Liberal party, Churchill move to, 188
liberal regime, 210
liberal society, and free market system, 209
liberty, war and, 278–279
limited government, 208

Lincoln, Abraham, 52, 106, 108
Lindemann, Frederick, 169, 313n41
lip service, 87
Lippman, Walter, 100
Lloyd George, David, 197
Lloyd-George, David, 299
"Locksley Hall" (Tennyson), 264–265
London, German threat to, 20
London to Ladysmith (Churchill), 110
Long Telegram, 79, 318n17
Lord Randolph Churchill (Churchill), 190
Loughlin, Martin, 246
love, as *Fabian Essays* theme, 127

Macmillan, Harold, 154–155, 173
Madison, James, 106, 191, 195, 217, 247
    The Federalist Papers, 238
Magna Carta, 219
Mahdi, 23
al-Mahdi, Sadiq, 23
"makeweight," 101
Malplaquet, Marlborough at, 71
managerial society, 132
mankind. *See* humanity
Marlborough (Churchill), 57, 63
Marlborough, first Duke of (John
    Churchill), 53, 55
    Churchill on genius of, 70–71
Marshall Plan, 79
Martin, John, 19
Marx, Karl, 121, 129
"Mass Effect in Modern Life," 211
"Mass Effect in Modern Life" (Churchill),
    43, 54, 141–142, 147, 148, 181–182,
    242–243
mass effects, 56, 119
    causes of, 120
material progress, 274
Maxim, 29–30
Maxim, Hiram Stevens, 30
"merchant princes," 141, 142
Military Coordination Committee,
    Churchill as chair, 13
military leaders, failure of, 70
minority, respect for rights of, 106
modern life, in war and peace, 119
Mohammedanism, Churchill on, 23–24
Monarch of Britain, 230–231

monopoly, prevention of, 153
Montefiore, Simon Sebag, 305*n*13
moral duties, 109–110
moral philosophy, 273
moral problem of war, 26
morality, 127
Morrison, Herbert, 108, 110
Moscow, Churchill travel to, 321*n*49
Munich agreement in 1938, Churchill in debate over, 320*n*34
Municipal Trust, vs. Beef Trust, 194–195, 207
Muslims, in India, 104
Mussolini, Benito, 306*n*21
    offer of peace conference, 15
My Early Life (Churchill), 159

Napoleon Bonaparte, 53
National Confederation of Employers Organizations, 200
National Industrial Recovery Act of 1933, 215
National Insurance Act of 1911, 197–198
National Labor Relations Board v. Jones & Laughlin Steel, 216
National Recovery Administration (NRA), 215
National Socialist German Workers' Party, xxiv
nationalism, and socialism, 211
nationalized industries, in Britain, 121
nations, distinction among, 83
nature, 146
    Churchill on, 150
    of man, 272–273. *See also* human nature
    socialism, history and, 122–131
Nazism, 211
    vs. Bolshevism, xxvii
    Churchill's criticism of, 65
    rise of, xx–xxvi
New Fabian Essays, 131
Nicholson, Claude, 189, 342n15
Nicolson, Harold, 351n88
9/11 terrorists, 31
Nobel Peace Prize, 46
non-white populations, Churchill perspective on, 103–105, 329

nuclear deterrence, 42
nuclear energy, 267
nuclear weapons, 42–43, 78, 82–83, 248, 291
    Churchill on research of, 314*n*42
    Churchill on threat of, 48–49

Olivier, Sydney, 127
Omdurman, Battle of (1898), 22, 24
    British cavalry charge, 28
    dervish assault, 27
opportunism, xiv
optimism, of Fabians, 124
Owen, Robert, 330*n*22

Pact of Locarno, 46
"Painting as a Pastime" (Churchill), 60, 64, 144
painting, Churchill knowledge of, 60–62
Parliament, 282
    inadequacy to deal with economic problems, 272
Parliament Act of 1911, 223–224, 236, 350*n*76
parliamentary government, 220–221
parliamentary rule, enemy of, 175–183
patriotism, 212
peace, 119, 213
    victory serving purposes of, 72
Peel, Robert, 264
people, 252
    Labour Party control of, 177–178
"People's Budget," 1909–11 controversy over, 225
"percentages agreement," 321*n*49
Persia, 297
    Russian pressure on, 92
    Soviet Union in, 79
personal inequalities, 142
    Socialist efforts to overcome, 143
Pétain, Marshal Philippe, 52
Petition of Right, 219
Plato, ideal republic, 59
police governments, 83
policy, Churchill defense of change, 62
political parties, in United States, 214
politics, 168–169, 239
    Churchill's thoughts on, 8

vs. strategy, 73
and war, 8
vs. war, 51–53
poor, case of, 186–189
Poor Law of 1834, 202
poverty, 250
Poverty: A Study of Town Life (Rowntree),
186–187
power, 250
balance of, 98
division of, 235
of executive government, 173–175
of government, 194
new sources of, 267
and principle, 97
of United States, 288
vs. virtue, 30
prime minister, vote of confidence, 232
principle
politicians' fidelity to, 58
and power, 97
prison, Churchill's escape plan, 9
private choice, and public choice, 196–203
private insurance, 196
private property, 153
progress, as problem, 40–41
progressivism, in United States, xxxi
Prometheus, 132
property
private possession of, 191
protection of, 151
property rights, 153–155
prophesies, 264–266
prosperity, 153–154
prudence, xiii
public choice, and private choice, 196–203
public policy, 124
public-sector expenditures, 152
public sentiment, 108

Radek, Karl, xxvii
Radfor, Arthur, 85
reason, 107–108, 148
as source of political authority, 82
redistribution, of resources, 185–186
reforms, need for, 192
religion, 210
in 1930s Germany, 277

Remarque, Erich Maria, All Quiet on the
Western Front, 45
resources, allocation, 88
restraint, Churchill counsel of, 84
Reynaud, Paul, 19
rhetoric, 17
right and might, 98, 102–103
rights, entitlement of all people to, 112
The River War (Churchill), 4–5, 22,
23–24, 55
Robots, 271
Romanes Lecture in Oxford, 165, 167–168
Romania, 321n49
Roosevelt, Franklin, xxxi, 190–191, 211, 233
Churchill's eulogy, xxxii
criticism of Supreme Court, 215–216
first inaugural address, 1933, 212–213
Roosevelt, Theodore, xxxi
Rossum's Universal Robots, 317n29
Rowntree, Benjamin Seebohm, 186
Poverty: A Study of Town Life,
186–187
Royal Academy of the Arts, 60
rule of law, 208
Russia, xxii, 91–93, 271, 277, 296. *See also*
Soviet Union
admiration of strength, 300
Communist principles of equal
distribution, 87
pressure on Turkey and Persia, 92
Treaty of Collaboration and Mutual
Assistance, 294–295
troops in World War II, 323n18

savings plans, vs. entitlements, 201
Savrola (fiction by Churchill), 28–30,
144, 145
Schechter Poultry Corp. v. United States
(1935), 215
science, 292–293
attitude to, and moral outlook, 38
change from, 146–147
destruction from, 273
impact of, 30, 41
technical education to permit
application to public affairs,
124–125
and war, 262–263

scientific method, 167
The Second World War (Churchill), 18
secret police, 163
secrets, 273
self-government
  capacity of undeveloped world for, 104
  India movement for, 102
  in South Africa, 107
selfishness, Socialist state and, 133
separation of powers, 234, 252
September 11 terrorists, 31
Serbia, xxii
"Shall We All Commit Suicide?"
  (Churchill), 39, 49–50, 248
sharia law in Sudan, 23
Shaw, George Bernard, 120
  Fabian Essays on Socialism, 88,
    121–122, 212
  The Intelligent Woman's Guide to
    Socialism and Capitalism, 130
  on slavery, 175
Sherriff, R.C., *Journey's End*, 45
Sinclair, Upton, *The Jungle*, Churchill's
  review, 193
"The Sinews of Peace" speech, 78–93
slavery, 113, 175
  Crossman on, 132
social insurance, political benefits,
  199–202
social management, politics and, 169
social reform, 185–206
social safety net, 196, 208, 228
  Churchill support for, 189
  and free market, 209
Social Security Act, 215
social welfare state, 247
socialism, 99
  in Britain, xxx–xxxi, 78, 171
  Churchill on, 133, 135, 150
  vs. Churchill's social reform, 204–206
  family and, 145
  history, and nature, 122–131
  and nationalism, 211
  qualities sought, 134
  religious foundations, 126–127
  vulnerability to claims, 181
socialist aristocracy, 155–157
Socialist movement, 276

in Britain, 120–131
  changing opinions, 126
  Churchill opposition to, 242
  early, in Britain, 163–164
society, regulation of, 210
South Africa, 104, 105–108. *See also*
  Boer War
"Soviet sphere," 91
Soviet Union, 148. *See also* Russia
  in Persia, 79
  rise of, xxvi–xxx
Speaker of the House, 349n65
"special relationship," of English-speaking
  peoples, 89–90, 97
Stalin, Josef, xxvii–xxviii, xxvii
  Churchill's appeal to, 88–89
  greatest weapons, xxx
  iron discipline of, xxix
  show trials of former colleagues, xxviii
  "terror-famine" of, xxx
standard of right, xiii
State planning, 151
state, vs. citizen, 211, 275
statesman, xiii
  Churchill views on, 239
  and generals, 72–78
  measure of, 57–60
  war as business for, 76
  weapons of, 15–20
statesmanship, 50, 251
  and constitutionalism, xix
  qualities of, xviii
  success of, 53–54
statue, 207
statute, 207
steel industry, Labour Party plan to
  nationalize, 178
strategist, general as, 71
strategy, 69–70
  and economy, 72
  and politics, 52–53
  vs. politics, 73
strength
  Russian admiration of, 300
  Russia's respect for, 92
Stresemann, Gustav, 46
Sudan, Battle of Omdurman (1898), 22, 24
surrender, 52

Taft, William Howard, xxxi
tanks, invention, 169–170
tariffs, 140–141, 192
    Churchill opposition to, 173–174
taxation, 154, 199
technical achievement, 267
technical education, 159–160
technology, 49
Temple of Peace, 295
Tennyson, Lord Alfred, "Locksley Hall,"
    264–265
"terror-famine," of Stalin, xxx
Testament (Lenin), xxvii–xxviii
Thatcher, Margaret, 152, 155, 233
Tories, 282–283
totalitarian states, 42
"Towards a Philosophy of Socialism"
    (Crossman), 131–132
trade, 250
trade transactions, benefits, 153
Treaty of Collaboration and Mutual
    Assistance, 294–295
Treaty of London (1839), 304n5
trench warfare, 45, 74
trial by jury, 234
Trotsky, Leon, xxvii
Truman, Harry, 78–80
trust, 49
    decline for government, 240, 248
    of nations with nuclear weapons,
        82–83
    in parents to care for family, 174
    in the people, 249
    in United Nations, 83
trusts (business), Beef vs. Municipal,
    194–195, 207
al-Turabi, Hassan, 23
Turkey, 297
    Russian pressure on, 92
Turner, J.M.W., 61–62, 66, 316n21
twentieth century, destruction in, 39–40
tyranny, 83–84, 280–281, 291–292
    Churchill's views on, 82
    vs. free nations, 115
    in future, 271
    in Germany, xxv–xxvi
    help for, 85–86
    vs. just rule, 38

undeveloped world, capacity for self-
    government, 104
unemployment insurance, 202–203
United Nations, 81, 290, 300
    Churchill's plan for, 89
    force and authority, 82
United States, 281
    1900 presidential election, 141
    Congress legislative power, 215
    Convention of 1787, 284
    Declaration of Independence, 103,
        110, 113
    economic crisis, 212, 277–278
    Great War and, xxiii
    Permanent Defense Agreement with
        Canada, 294
    politics, 211
    power of, 288
    presidential powers, 213
    progressivism in, xxxi
    Supreme Court, 215, 281–282, 286
    threat to freedom, xxxi
U. S. Constitution, xix
    advantages, 217–218
    amending, 216
    and attention to national affairs, 214
    Churchill's objections to, 213
    rigidity of, 285
unity of command, 75–76
universal ambitions, 81
University of Bristol, 111, 158
University of Miami, 159
untouchable (Dalit) class in India, 104,
    115
"The Untrodden FIELD in Politics"
    (Churchill), 190
useless things, 65–66

Versailles, Palace of, xxi
victory, 15
    Churchill's thoughts on, 8–9
Vietnam, Churchill's opposition to
    intervention, 84–85
virtue, vs. power, 30
voting age, of British women, 226

wager earners, Churchill warning about,
    178–179

Walden, Thomas, 6
Wallas, Graham, 130
war, 248–249
    Churchill beliefs on danger, 69
    Churchill's views on, 33–34, 82
    cooperation in, 52
    cost of, 189
    devastation of modern, 27
    impact on family, 289
    inevitability, 300
    leadership in, 3–4
    liberty and, 278–279
    mass effects, 43–50
    modern problems, 39
    moral problem of, 26
    perpetual state of, 211
    and politics, 8
    vs. politics, 51–53
    problem of modern, 49
    randomness of death, 45
war atmosphere, 276
war cabinet (Britain), 15–16, 18–19
War of the Spanish Succession, 57
"war to end all wars," 46
warrior-statesmen, 53
Washington, George, 308n17
Watson-Watt, Robert, 56
weapons, xv
Webb, Sidney, 120, 123, 127, 161, 205
Weimar republic, xxiii–xxiv
    constitution, 211–212, 276
Weir, Lord, 200
welfare state, size and scope of, 205
Western democracies, leftward turn in,
    xxx–xxxiii

"What Good's a Constitution?"
    (Churchill), 211, 215, 275–286
Whigs, 282–283
Wilhelm I (Prussian kaiser), xxi
Wilhelm II (German emperor), xxi,
    xxii–xxiii
William III (king), 53
Wilson, Woodrow, xxxi, 214
women, 330n24
    Mohammedan law on property, 23–24
women in Britain
    Churchill support for suffrage, 227
    voting age of, 226
workers, in Soviet Union, xxvii
Works Progress Administration, 215
world conditions, post-WW II, 78
The World Crisis (Churchill), 35–37,
    45–46, 57, 72, 213, 214
World War I. See Great War
World War II
    Churchill's view as preventable, 85,
        91–92
    as preventable, 301
    reimbursement for bombed houses,
        188–189
    world conditions after, 78
world wars, xv
Wylie, Captain, 6

Yalta, 92
Yes Minister (television series), 132
York, poverty in, 186–18